Anonymous

Report of the Commission to improve the Highways of the Commonwealth. February, 1893

Anonymous

Report of the Commission to improve the Highways of the Commonwealth. February, 1893

ISBN/EAN: 9783337157494

Printed in Europe, USA, Canada, Australia, Japan

Cover: Foto ©ninafisch / pixelio.de

Compliments of the

MASSACHUSETTS HIGHWAY COMMISSION.

REPORT OF THE COMMISSION

TO IMPROVE THE

HIGHWAYS OF THE COMMONWEALTH.

FEBRUARY, 1893.

BOSTON:
WRIGHT & POTTER PRINTING CO., STATE PRINTERS,
18 POST OFFICE SQUARE.
1893.

Commonwealth of Massachusetts.

To the Honorable Senate and House of Representatives of the Commonwealth of Massachusetts in General Court Assembled.

We, the undersigned, the commissioners appointed under the provisions of chapter 338 of the Acts of 1892, entitled "An Act to establish a commission to improve the highways of this Commonwealth," hereby submit the following report.

GEO. S. PERKINS.
W. E. McCLINTOCK.
N. S. SHALER.

INTRODUCTION.

Roadways are at once the agents and the index of the culture to which a Commonwealth has attained. All social and economic life above the most primitive conditions rests upon the transportation of human beings or of goods. In the earliest stage of social advance, commerce was effected by footmen, or, if the conditions favored, by boats of a simple kind. A step in advance is marked by the use of pack animals traversing paths worn by the feet of the beasts of burden. Then came the use of wheeled vehicles, at first on rude ways such as the natural surface might afford. Gradually these routes were improved, until even in the earlier civilizations the main channels of communication were more or less cared for. The last stage in the development of land roads is found in the modern railway.

It is a noteworthy fact that each advance in the method of land transportation has tended to destroy the earlier method of carriage. The use of pack animals quickly replaced the plan of carrying burdens on the shoulders of men. The development of ordinary roads lead to the disuse of pack-trains; and, in turn, the railway has induced people more or less completely to neglect their wagon roads. The reason for the last-named change is evident. So long as the commerce of the country depended on these ways in such measure that the great cities could be supplied only by wagons, and the State and national needs met by long and well-constructed routes, the interest in ordinary roads was necessarily maintained. Considerations of public defence, as well as those of commerce, made it necessary that the highways which gave a ready access to different parts of the land should be kept in good order. Now that railways afford a swifter and cheaper communication, the ordinary roads have become matters which appear at first sight to be only of local importance. The public has been accustomed of late to commit their care altogether to the people of the districts in which they lie.

The relegation of our carriage ways to the care of the local authorities has not been the result of a deliberate plan. It has been brought about in an accidental way, and has apparently been due to excessive, and, as experience has shown, quite unfounded, expectations as to the measure of benefit which may be derived from railways. It was long and naturally supposed that transportation routes of this description might in time, and indeed rapidly, be so generally extended over the country that no distant wagon carriage of any kind would be required. It is now, however, clear that railways cannot take the place of wagon roads. The cost of their construction and the expense of operating them is so great that we must turn once again to the care of the old-fashioned routes.

A little consideration will show us that the development of railways in a manner requires the improvement of our common roads. The economic effect of the iron ways is to bring the commercial products of distant regions into free competition in all our great markets. One of the results of the cheap carriage on these modern ways of communication has been to put the farmer of Massachusetts at a singular and often hopeless disadvantage, as compared with the position of his competitors in distant parts of the country; if he lives five miles from a railway town, and has to market the products of his farm by carrying them over a bad road, he may, in a commercial sense, be farther away from that town than he would be if he dwelt on the line of a railway in Illinois or Iowa. Among the several influences which have led to the decay of New England agriculture, this tax imposed by bad roads, which serves to favor the distant producer, deserves a foremost place. Of all the burdens which our farmers bear, this is the one which can be most readily and completely removed. That it ever was imposed is a discredit to our people.

Although the commercial value of good roads is a matter of the utmost importance to a people, their greatest value is to be found in the influence they exercise on the social and moral conditions of the districts which they serve. In all societies the tone of the life to a great extent depends on the ease with which the intercourse between the households can be maintained. The people of this country are, however, particularly dependent on their contacts; a self-governed folk, their communities need a ready access to each other. Common understandings bred of close acquaintance are the basis of their life. The tax which bad roads put upon town meetings, attendance on schools and churches, and their other modes of associated action, is an evil which should not be patiently endured.

The statistics of this country show an ever-increasing tendency on the part of our people to gather into the cities. Although this relative gain in the urban population is doubtless due to a diversity of influences, there can be no question that one of the reasons for it is to be found in the condition of our country roads. In the present state of these ways, country life is made much less agreeable and profitable than it would be if the tax which bad roads imposed were done away with. The evidence goes to show that our people are in many regards better placed in well-conditioned rural districts than in the great towns. All those who are considerate of our future desire to see every hindrance to the development of our rural population removed, in order that the folk may be induced to retain that hold upon the soil which has been for ages the basis of their strength. Clearly the first step to attain this end is to improve the condition of our highways.

CHAPTER I.

Topography of Massachusetts.

In Relation to Highways.

The condition of the roads of this Commonwealth is to a great extent determined by the peculiar shape of its surface. In most countries the form of the land is brought about by the forces which have uplifted the underlying rocks, and by the down-wearing action of the water which has flowed over the earth on its way from the uplands to the sea. In these conditions we generally find that the surface of the earth exhibits continuous declivities extending from the divides between the great streams to the lower levels of the main roads, and thence to the sea. All the slopes, in a word, are such as favor an uninterrupted flow of the surface waters.

Wherever, as in Massachusetts, the country has recently been much affected by glacial action, this normal state of the surface of the earth is to a greater or less extent lost. The rocks become carved into irregular basins and ridges, and the diversity of the earth's outline is still further increased by irregular and often very great mounds of rubbish. The ancient valleys, formed before the glacial epoch, can usually be traced, but the details of the topography given by the ancient streams are profoundly modified. The reason for this change of conditions is simple; the motion of a glacier differs from that of a river in that the stream of ice not only cuts with intense energy but tends to excavate the rocks in the measure of their hardness. In the course of its action it may carve out deep basins, into which the ice in its movement descends and from which it ascends with considerable freedom. If we could strip away the deposits of sand, clay and boulders which cover Massachusetts, we should find the surface of the bed rocks to exhibit a great number of these basins, varying in depth and area, but in some places occupying an extent of many square miles, and descending a hundred feet or more below the general level of the country.

As the glacial sheet moved over the surface which it occupied, large quantities of detritus worn from the bed rocks were mingled with the ice, the fragments working up in many cases to a height of perhaps a hundred feet or more above the base of the glacier. When the glacial sheet melted away, this debris fell in a confused order upon the surface, and forms the sheet of commingled pebbles and clay to which geologists give the name of "till," a deposit which covers nearly all the areas which were occupied by the glacial envelope. Owing to the irregular way in which the waste from the rocks was mingled with the ice, and to other accidents which it is not necessary to consider, this till layer is of irregular thickness, and serves still further to diversify the form of the surface.

At various times during the retreat of the ice sheet, when its wall-like front fell back to the northward, there were pauses in the backward movement, and even temporary readvances, which brought about the accumulation of long, irregular mounds of boulders, pebbles and sands next the ice front, which are termed "moraines." In some parts of Massachusetts, particularly in the south-eastern section of the Commonwealth, these frontal moraines attain a considerable height, and have an important effect on the topography. They are particularly conspicuous in the section between Plymouth and the southern end of Elizabeth Islands. At Manomet Hill one of these moraines rises to the height of about four hundred feet above the sea, and is evidently continued downward for some hundred feet below the ocean level. In the region to the north and west there are numerous less defined frontal moraines, which, though much less conspicuous, have a marked effect on the form of the surface.

While the ice lay on this region, and particularly during the time when it was melting away, considerable streams of fluid water flowed over the surface of the earth beneath ice arches which led to the margin of the glacier. These subglacial rivers flowed with great energy, conveying large quantities of sand and gravel which were accumulated in the open air or beneath the sea, the shore being then lower than at present, in the form of extensive sand plains, such as form the south-eastern portion of Martha's Vineyard, a great part of Cape Cod and much of the area of Bristol and Plymouth counties. Similar though much smaller sand plains, produced in a like manner, are found in other parts of the Commonwealth. The greater portion of the plain which borders the Connecticut River owes its origin to actions of this class.

Towards the close of the glacial epoch, as the subglacial streams became enfeebled, the ice arches in which they had flowed were to a great extent filled in with rock debris, so that when the ice had entirely disappeared the position of the old stream arches was marked by long, low mounds of sand and gravel, shaped in the glacial caverns ; these deposits, even in an early day, attracted the attention of observant people ; their very artificial look led to the supposition that they had been formed by the hand of man, and they received in New England the name of Indian ridges. Certain deposits of this nature remain so well preserved that they may be traced with tolerable distinctness for a distance of thirty miles or more in their general course from north to south. They usually lie in the valleys, but, as the caverns in which they were formed went up hill and down, they sometimes crossed considerable elevations.

Yet another and as yet unexplained group of glacial deposits, known as drumlins or lenticular hills, sometimes termed "hog backs," plentifully occur in various parts of southern New England ; they are well exhibited in the country between the Connecticut valley and the sea. These regularly arched hills often rise to the height of a hundred and fifty feet or more above the general surface of the country on which they lie. They are composed of firmly packed clay, commingled with sand, gravel and boulders ; in this regard they closely resemble the before-mentioned deposits of till. In their regular outline, where this feature is most characteristically exhibited, they differ greatly from the other deposits of glacial waste. Although there are a few instances in which solitary drumlins occur within the limits of this Commonwealth, as a rule they are grouped in fields, in which they lie so crowded together that their bases are almost in contact with each other. The richest field of their development in Massachusetts is in the section just west of Worcester. As the elevations of this group are always steep sides, their effect upon the distribution of the highways of the State is singularly great. They qualify the direction of these ways in a more important manner than any other features in the topography except the high mountain ridges.

Near the sea-shore, where the winds from the quarters between the north and south around by the west blow upon the shore, and even in some cases where the shore is exposed only to easterly winds, there are considerable accumulations of dune sands, i. e., those brought together by wind action. These deposits have a characteristic incoherent structure, — they are always composed of fine sand or very small pebbles; the mass contains little except the silicious fragments, and on this account the grains never adhere to each other. Fortunately in Massachusetts the dune deposits occupy an aggregate area of less than a hundred square miles, for here, as elsewhere, the material of this nature is among the most difficult with which the road architect has to deal.

On a properly constructed geological road map of Massachusetts it would be necessary to add to the foregoing list of deposits two other small groups, namely, the beach sands and the swamp accumulations. Although accumulations belonging to these classes occupy a considerable part of the surface of the Commonwealth, it is rarely the case that any effort is made to carry highways over their areas, it being well known that where possible it is best to make extensive detours rather than to endeavor to construct ways over materials of this nature.

The distribution of the classes of superficial deposits above mentioned is peculiar and striking. The material known as till generally occupies the high-lying ground of the Commonwealth; thus, in the region west of the Connecticut valley deposits of this nature occupy more than nine-tenths of the area within the boundaries of the Commonwealth. In the Connecticut valley, at least in the region near the level of the stream, the washed gravels and sands and their associated clays occupy very nearly the whole of the surface. In the high ground between the Connecticut valley and the sea, which we may well term the Worcester table lands, the till again predominates; indeed, in this part of the Commonwealth it probably constitutes, if we reckon with it the deposits of the drumlins, three-fourths of the surface. On the lowlands next the coast, especially in the counties of Bristol, Plymouth, Barnstable, Dukes and Nantucket, the stratified sands and gravels occupy by far the greater part of the area, being as predominant in that field as are the accumulations of till in the Berkshire district.

Having thus briefly sketched the distribution of the superficial deposits in Massachusetts, we may proceed to consider the effect of the conditions which these groups of deposits impose upon the areas they occupy. Beginning with the Berkshire district, and including in that region all the elevated land west of the great plain of the Connecticut valley, we find a field favorable for the study as to the topographic and road effects of accumulations of till which abound in this field. Those who are acquainted with the state of the roads in that part of the Commonwealth will recognize the fact that the mixture of clay, sand and pebbles which constitutes the till has a very decided effect upon the condition of the roads. In dry seasons, and generally in the summer half of the year, the highways have an excellent character, being fairly smooth in all parts of the hill district, except where the ground is more than usually wet or has been subjected to very heavy wagon travel. On the other hand, when the frost enters the ground, and so long as the effect of freezing is traceable, the condition of the roads, except when their surfaces may be masked by a coating of ice or snow, is commonly very bad. In the beginning of the winter, when the roads are partly frozen, and again in the spring, when they are thawed but not yet dried, a large part of the ways in this section of the State are essentially impassable, being in this regard much like the clay roads of other countries.

An observant person will remark the fact that the resistance to the wheels of the till roads in the Berkshire district and elsewhere may be pretty closely measured by noting the proportion of pebbly and sandy matter to the more finely divided matter which we commonly term clay. Where the coarse material largely predominates, the effect of wetness or of frost becomes lessened; there are indeed forms of till which afford excellent road material for all seasons of the year. In many cases the feature above indicated may serve as a valuable guide in determining the treatment which should be given to roads which lie upon till deposits; in general, the aim should be to increase the amount of small yet visible fragments in the material of the roadway; in fact, the coarser this waste imbedded in the clay may be, so far at least as is consistent with a smooth road, the better for the ways. Where other coarse materials are wanting, experience in

Massachusetts and elsewhere shows that any vegetable matter of a shredded nature and of a tough fibre — such as chopped straw, wood shredded in the manner of material called "excelsior," or even slender twigs and shoots chopped into bits by the axe and mingled with the clay — is likely to improve the roadway.

It is well for those who are interested in roads to recognize the reason why a way resting upon clay is so peculiarly soft at the time when the frost leaves the ground. A clear understanding on this point makes the task of seeking a remedy more simple, though curiously enough it has not yet found a place in our text-books or treatises on the soil. This explanation is as follows: When the winter rains have entered the earth, and there freeze, the water, or rather the crystals of ice formed from it, by the expansion which takes place in the process of freezing, is forced in between the faces of all the grains of the soil, thus pushing them apart and breaking up the old adhesions of the adjacent surfaces which in a dry time give the road its character. When the next thawing takes place, the water returning to its molten state near the surface, while in the deeper parts it remains frozen, the interspaces between the grains just released from the bondage of frost become again filled with water, which is in turn expanded by the next freezing; in this manner the fine fragments which compose the soil are to a certain extent separated from each other in a way which they were not in the dry and warm time. The film of water between these grains is not easily expelled and does not readily drain away, being held in its position by the action known as capillarity, the condition which sucks water into a sponge or oil into a lamp wick.

When the particles of clay have been separated from each other by the action of repeated frost in the manner above described, their condition is substantially that of quicksand; the water is so firmly held that it will not drain away; it must be dried out. The aim of any admixtures which may be made with this clay is to prevent the particles slipping on each other by introducing some material which may serve to bind them together. If there be a great number of fibres introduced into the mass, the pressure of a wheel will be distributed over so large a number of bits that even the imperfect adhesion of the particles on each other will serve to uphold the weight. If the reader would get an idea of how capillary attraction may hold water between two adjacent surfaces, permitting them to move over each other with a certain but not complete freedom, he may find an excellent illustration by putting two sheets of glass together, with a film of water between them.

From the above description it is easily seen that any fibrous substance mixed with clay acts in two ways: —

First, it assists in draining off the water in far less time than it can dry out.

Second, it distributes the load through the fibres over a larger area, thus preventing the wheel from breaking through the surface and settling down to the yet unthawed clay which lies at the lower plane.

While temporary relief may be obtained by such treatment, it cannot give conditions that are permanently satisfactory, and cannot be recommended except in cases where good materials are not obtainable without the outlay of more money than is warranted by the traffic on the road. Even the light wagons settle the surface, until the fibres carry the load; and with heavy wagons the wheels are at all times in a depression, and the horses are constantly wasting power to force down the wave in front of the wheel. Light carriages may easily pass over such a road, but wagons of burden would, during the spring thaws, probably be unable to carry more than a half ton to each horse.

This brings us to the first principle of scientific road building, which can be expressed in three words, viz., a dry foundation. Without a dry foundation, the labor of the roadmaster will be wasted, and the maximum cost with the minimum good will result. A further discussion of methods required to obtain and retain a dry foundation will be found in the chapter on road building.

In the fields occupied by sand and gravel, materials deposited from the water which escaped in the sub-glacial rivers to the open ground beyond the limits of the ice, we find roadway conditions which are sharply contrasted with those last mentioned. Owing to the circumstances of their formation, these stratified beds are composed of materials from which the clay has been washed out, leaving generally only the angular fragments of sand and the small pebbles, all of which being so large that the water is not held in the interspaces by the capillary attraction in such quantities as will permit the particles to slide over each other. The result is that when moistened there are still enough of the surfaces in contact to produce the friction necessary to keep the particles from slipping by each other when pressed by the wheel. The small amount of water which is retained in the mass tends in a way to hold the bits against each other. To these conditions is probably due the fact that sandy roads when damp are usually rather firm; on the other hand, when dry and subject to frequent treading by wheels, the surfaces of the grains, having nothing to bind them together, slip over each other with something like the ease with which shot move when pressed by the hand.

The sand deposits accumulated by the wind and the higher lying sands on the beaches, which have generally been brought into their position in part by wind and in part by wave action, have, when trodden by the wheels, the same quality as have those which have been accumulated by the streams emerging from the glacier. When wet they are tolerably firm, but when dry the fragments move readily under the shearing action of the wheel, and make difficult ways for carriages. The same is the case in those rather exceptional fields where the ground is covered by a layer of pebbles. These smooth fragments are easily shoved about by pressure in the same manner as the smaller bits of sand. These pebble roads are instructive, for they show in a large way, in a manner which is visible to the eye, the effect of pressure on the small fragments of rock, thus enabling us to understand the conditions which the wheel encounters on sand roads. These deposits of pebbles are not affected by moisture, the interspaces being so large that the water is not retained between the adjacent faces.

Where frontal moraines have been formed, we generally find thick accumulations of debris, in part composed of wasted sand and gravel, but to a considerable extent made up of large boulders. In some cases these fragments of great size are so numerous that they completely cover the ground and are piled one on top of the other, looking like the ruins of cyclopean masonry. In all cases these moraines contain so much stony material in the form of large boulders that the construction of roads over them is difficult and sometimes almost impossible. Fortunately almost all the moraines of New England are somewhat discontinuous, their walls being breached at the points where the streams from beneath the glacier maintained gorges for their passage. These openings are generally floored with sand or gravel, and thus provide places for roadways. A conspicuous case of this nature is found in the breach through the Elizabeth Island moraine in the town of Bourne, which affords a pass for the railway and carriage road.

The bouldery fields of Massachusetts are not limited to the moraines. In those places where the glacier passed over areas of rock which, owing to the form of the joints and other fracture lines, afforded large masses to the ice, we often find that the till is to a great extent made up of large fragments of rock which afford very serious obstacles to the construction of highways. These stony belts are, as might be expected, occasionally extended in the direction of the glacial movement for distances of many miles. In some parts of the Commonwealth, notably in the western portion of the Berkshire hills and in the Worcester table lands, these trails of great boulders not infrequently are found to be very inconvenient obstacles, not only to the farmer whose fields they make untillable, but to the road-master who has to build his way past them.

The deposits of stratified sand and gravel, though generally affording tolerably level paths for roadways, occasionally present either of two topographic features which are very inconvenient to those who have to construct highways in such districts. The eskers, or Indian ridges, those accumulations of boulders, sand and gravel which were formed beneath the ancient ice arches, are often continuous embankments, with sides having slopes of thirty degrees or more, and with an altitude of from thirty to a hundred feet. It is sometimes necessary to undertake costly excavations in order to provide a moderately level way by these ridges. In other cases the sand plains which commonly are formed at the end of the eskers are in their northern parts varied by deep pits, which may contain small lakes or bogs which have been formed in them. It sometimes happens that these irregularities are so numerous as to make the construction of ways very difficult.

The swamps of Massachusetts, though occupying perhaps not more than one-twentieth of the surface, have proved exceedingly embarrassing features in a construction of roadways, when as in most cases the area which they occupy does not exceed a square mile; the impediments which they impose in the way of the roads which surround them are not necessarily serious, but many deposits of this description are of great extent, and have an elongate form which makes them serious barriers in the way of our roads. An instance of this sort is found in Great Cedar Swamp, north of Taunton, which from the settlement of the country to the present day has hindered the communication between adjacent towns. Large bogs generally contain deep deposits of peat, and, owing to the yielding nature of this substance, they are as impassable as the lakes in which they were formed would have been had they remained in a state of open water.

Although the lakes of Massachusetts have to a great extent been closed by accumulations of vegetable deposits, they still remain to the number of thousands, though the greater part of them are of relatively small size. Of the hundreds which exceed half a mile in length, nearly all have added something to the cost of our roadways by requiring considerable detours in the line of these constructions. A careful study of the roadways of the Commonwealth would probably show that more than a thousand miles of somewhat costly roads have been made necessary by the detours required by the existing lakes, and perhaps a yet greater amount to escape the bogs which occupy the former sites of such water areas.

Yet another tax in the way of road construction, due to the conditions of the surface of Massachusetts which were imposed by the events of the glacial period, is to be found in the form of the coast lines. This fringe of the shore is characterized by a very great number of originally wide and deep re-entrances, which admit the sea waters far into the land. At many points these basins which are visited by the tide have been in a measure closed by marine marshes, but everywhere they remain formidable difficulties in the way of road construction. The tidal channels have to be bridged, and the surface of the neighboring marshes, which never rise to the level of high tide, has to be crossed on considerable embankments. Roads in these positions are relatively very costly, and the hundred miles or more of such ways which have been constructed within the limits of the Commonwealth have entailed a very large expenditure.

Owing to the imperfectly organized condition of the drainage in Massachusetts, a feature which is due to the perturbations brought about by the glacial period, the number of streams is uncommonly great. The banks and bottoms of even the smaller rivulets are commonly marshy, and need to be crossed by bridges. The result is that for its area this Commonwealth has perhaps a greater number of these structures than any other region in the world. Moreover, the conditions of their foundations are often such as to entail a large first cost. Fortunately this region, owing to the generally porous character of the drift coating, and to the numerous lakes which likewise serve to retain for a time the storm waters, is remarkably exempt from floods which are likely to carry bridges away.

The foregoing statement will show the reader that the surface conditions of this Commonwealth entail great difficulties in the construction and maintenance of good highways. The disturbance of the ancient topography, brought about by the glacial period, has given an exceeding variety of outline to the surface; the result is that level roads, except in parts of the Connecticut valley and on the sand plains in the south-eastern portion of the State, are almost unknown. The average grade of the highways is necessarily great, while the care and skill required of the roadmaster in determining the alignment of the proposed way is such that only the well-trained engineer, conducting his work with all the resources which his science affords, is competent to execute the task in a proper manner.

It is difficult to give the reader an adequate conception of the complexity of the problems which the diversity in form and earth materials imposes upon those who have to do with the construction and maintenance of highways in this Commonwealth. With each change in the slope of the roadway, commonly in less than each mile of its length, there is likely to be an important alteration in the character of the underlying materials which demands some special treatment from those who would build or preserve at the least cost a high-grade road. It is doubtful if there be another equally extensive area in this country or Europe where the considerations by which the roadmaster needs to be guided are so multifarious, or demand such an intimate knowledge of the conditions of the earth with which he deals.

If the conditions of the ground in Massachusetts were perfectly uniform, the topography remaining the same as at present, the matter of alignment of roads would of itself afford questions demanding very careful and extended consideration, in order to avoid the excessive costs in traction, as well as the increased expense of repairs brought about by ill-placed ways. A lack of due skill entails in many cases a grave and permanent tax on the community which the roadway is intended to serve. The annual cost arising from such misadventures in planning roads is now a serious burden upon the people of this Commonwealth.

CHAPTER II.

Road Materials of Massachusetts.

In Relation to the Construction of Highways.

Experience in all countries has shown that the soil covering is in its normal state unfitted to be converted into a roadway. Whether this sheet be formed upon glacial deposits, as is usually the case in this State, or produced by the decay of the immediately underlying rocks, as is characteristic of those regions which have not been affected by glacial ice, the upper layer of the earth is commonly of a very incoherent nature. The dividing action which the roots exercise on a soil layer, aided generally by the work of frost, serves to make the upper foot or so of the section very incoherent. Moreover, the process of decay, which is assisted by the decomposing vegetable matter, softens the fragments of rock in the soil layer so that they commonly grind to powder under the tread of the wheel.

The depth of the soil layer in Massachusetts varies greatly. In the regions which are occupied by till or boulder clay, we commonly find that this incoherent stratum passes at the depth of a foot or so into the more solid material often known as hard pan, a section which has been unaffected by the action of roots and only moderately disturbed by frost. In the districts underlaid by sand, the difference in condition between the superficial deposits and those of greater depth may be so slight as to be unnoticeable. In general, it may be said that the part of the earth which has the characteristics of soil is distinctively unsuited for use on a road bed.

The glacial waste which underlies the soil varies much in its fitness to be used as road material. In general, the till deposits contain such large amounts of clay, that, even when mingled with stone, they afford when wet a pasty mass which insures difficult wheeling. In dry weather, or even when but slightly moistened by summer rains, they may serve fairly well; but in the season of coming and going frost, in the autumn and spring, roads founded on this material are generally unfit for use. In proportion as the pebbly element is more considerable, provided, as is rarely the case, that the contained stones are small and the fine detritus largely composed of sand grains, till may afford material suitable for use upon a road which needs to be cheaply constructed. In general, however, the till deposits in their natural condition may be regarded as unsuited for use on highways. There may be places, where a road leads over a hill with a steep grade, where a proper mixing of till with a fairly large proportion of pebbles or broken stone of medium size would make it possible to prevent a washing out during severe rains, — an end which it would be difficult to attain in any other way.

The gravel beds of Massachusetts vary exceedingly in their fitness for road construction. Where the pebbles are mainly of quartz or other flinty rock, and have been much rounded and smoothed by water action, the material is certain to afford a shifting foundation for ordinary wheels, unless a large amount of binding material is used with the pebbles, in which case the road becomes very muddy in wet weather. Where, however, the pebbly matter has been derived from rocks of varied constitution, especially where, as is often the case, the bits have generally undergone a certain amount of decay, the mass is likely, when well rolled either by steam rollers or even by broad-tired wheels, to become consolidated so as to afford a fairly good road. In general the recommendable gravels of Massachusetts are limited to those districts where the stratified pebbly beds are commingled with the deposits of till. In the eastern and southeastern sections of the State, where we find wide areas composed almost altogether of these gravels and sands which have been washed free of clay, the pebbles are generally of a flinty nature, and, without the addition of some binding material, are unfitted for use on roads. The reason for this peculiarity in distribution is to be found in the fact that the pebbles on this extreme border of the glacial field have generally journeyed far, and only the hardest of the materials have survived the wearing which the distant carriage imposed upon them.

Here and there in Massachusetts, particularly in the eastern section of the State, beds of gravel may be found where the fragments, not much worn by water action, retain an angular character and have a slight admixture of clay which has served to prevent the process of superficial decay, so that the mass has the bluish hue of broken rock which is often noticeable in stone after it has passed through the crusher. Gravel of this nature is always well suited to road making, provided the fragments are properly selected, and are not to too great an extent composed of slate. In general it is the best suited for road material of any deposits which can be used without breaking, and in conditions of moderate use makes a good, enduring and economical roadway.

As yet the distribution of blue gravels in Massachusetts is not well determined; they probably exist in very many places where they have not been found, and this for the reason that the surface of such beds always exhibits a characteristic reddish-yellow hue common to the upper parts of all gravel beds which have been subjected to the action of the weather.

The sands of this and other countries are essentially unsuited for use as road material. If fine grained and well filled with water, they may, in the manner of some of our sand beaches, afford an excellent surface for wheels bearing light loads; but for the greater part of the year, even a few hours after a rain, they become so far dried that the adjacent surface of the grains, deprived of the slight degree of adhesion which the capillary attraction operating on a film of water affords, easily slip by each other when pressed with the weight of a light carriage. Wherever it is possible to commingle a certain amount of clay with the sand, the adhesion of the grain thus brought about is certain greatly to improve the character of the road bed.

In many parts of the Commonwealth, particularly in the south-eastern portion of the State, where the ways are generally founded on the washed sands or gravels, the readiest means of bettering their condition is to be found in the admixture of clays with the sandy or gravelly material, although it is questionable whether this method of treatment is in the long run economical.

The bed rocks of Massachusetts afford a remarkable variety of materials suitable for the construction of roads. There is scarcely a point in the Commonwealth where, from the deposits formed before the glacial period, it is not possible within five miles to find deposits which are tolerably well suited for the construction of smooth and enduring ways. In their character these materials vary from the soft rocks of the tertiary and the cretaceous ages, such as occur in south-eastern Massachusetts, to the hard and tough trap rocks which are so plentifully distributed throughout the greater part of the Common-wealth. Within the limits of this report it will not be possible to give a detailed account as to the quality of these various stones, or the places in which they may be found. It may be well, however, to make some few statements concerning the fitness of these materials for road making, and the circumstances of their occurrence.

In general, it may be said that, for purposes of road construction, a rock should be at once hard, tough, resistant to the ordinary agents of decay, yet easily broken into bits by the road hammer, or its modern equivalent, the crushing engine. When fractured, the fragments of stone must not have smooth faces; they should on the contrary have very rough surfaces, in order that when driven together they may unite in a somewhat solid manner. It is also very advantageous if the powdery material formed by the broken stone have some share of that cementing or "setting" quality which pertains to mortars and cements. Within the limits of Massachusetts only one group of rocks, those known as traps, possess in a high degree the above-mentioned assemblage of qualities. These trappean deposits in all cases consist of materials once molten, which in their fluid state were forced into or through fissures of the more ancient rocks; afterwards these lavas cooled down at the time when what is the present surface was buried beneath a great thickness of formations which have since been worn away. Produced under these conditions, these volcanic deposits in this and other countries are admirably adapted for the needs of the roadmaker; the exceptions in which they are not so fit are but few; in general, it may be said that the traps of Massachusetts afford excellent road metal. In addition to the qualities above mentioned, rocks of this nature generally contain considerable amounts of iron, which, becoming more oxidized in the road bed, add to the cementing value of the material.

The trappean rocks of Massachusetts are altogether limited to the older strata. In the Berkshire hill district masses of this nature are relatively rare, and are generally deposited in rather narrow fissures. In that portion of the Commonwealth rocks of this description cannot therefore be regarded as of value for the purpose we are considering. In the valley of the Connecticut River, from Greenfield southward to the border of the State and beyond that limit to near the sea, trap deposits plentifully occur, intermingled with the red sandstones and conglomerates of that district. Numerous great hills, of which Mountains Tom and Holyoke are the most striking examples, are in the main made up of thick beds of trap. Many of these localities are admirably placed for access by railway and common road; in time the crushed rock from these deposits will doubtless be made an extensive matter of commerce, so that the towns in the valley and in the adjacent hill districts will be able to obtain it at low cost.

From the eastern border of the Connecticut valley as far west as Framingham and Fitchburg trap rocks are again rather rare, and the localities not well known. East of a line drawn between these two towns to the sea border, and south to a line drawn from Attleborough to Hingham, there are many hundreds if not thousands of these trap dikes, many of them known to be sufficiently large and well placed to have a value for road material. In this part of the State, however, the rocks of this general nature are more varied in their quality than elsewhere; a considerable portion of them are not well suited for roadway use.

About two miles south of the southern border of Massachusetts, in the town of Cumberland, R. I, in a position which could be made convenient of access by railway to eastern and southern Massachusetts, there exists in what is known as Iron Hill a very great mass of magnetite of black magnetic oxide of iron, which, owing to certain impurities, is not well suited for the smelter's use. This deposit apparently affords a remarkably good material for use in constructing macadam roads. It is by far the hardest rock known in New England. When broken the fragments are very rough and strong, and, though not as yet tried for road material, may doubtless prove of great value for that use.

In a grade below the trap rock we may rank the numerous and extensive beds of a silicious nature, in their original form sandstones, which in their changed state received the name of quartzites. Beds of this description occur at very many points from the western part of the Berkshire district to the shores of Massachusetts Bay. Although hard, these materials are prevailingly very brittle and smooth; they break up in a rapid manner under heavy wheeling, and form a fine sand much like powdered glass, and their smooth surfaces prevent a good bond; though superior for road use to some of the rocks hereafter described, they must be ranked relatively low in the scale of road materials.

The greater part of the rocks of Massachusetts, particularly those in the region west of Worcester, consist of gneiss and mica-schists. In these rocks we generally have distinct crystals of quartz, felspar, and hornblende or mica, though in the schists one or more of these elements may be wanting, and in the gneiss the minerals are distributed in a banded manner. All these materials usually are either too soft for road making or too brittle to withstand the pressure of the wheel; moreover, the micaceous element causes the fragments to be rather slippery, which quickly leads to the destruction of the road. In general, the gneisses are the least objectionable of these kinds of rock. Some of the deposits of this nature are tolerably well suited for use on macadam roads, where the vehicles which pass over them are relatively light.

The granites and kindred syenites, though not so well suited for use in the ordinary broken state on our roadways as some of the other stones, generally serve well for block pavements. In this form the flat surface of the stones, owing to the hardness of the material, resists the impact of the wheels, while the brittleness, which becomes so evident in the ordinarily broken stone, is not such as to jeopardize the endurance of the masses. This is one of the many cases in which the roadmaster finds that a slight difference in the method in which particular materials are used may bring about very important variation in the service which they may render his art.

In the eastern part of Massachusetts, particularly in the town of Clinton, some of the ancient stratified rocks have been metamorphosed into hornblende schists. Although the experiments in using this group of schists have yet to be made, laboratory tests which have been instituted in connection with the department of highway engineering in the Lawrence Scientific School of Harvard University indicate a probable value for this group of materials. The rock is prevailingly very tough, and, although rather soft and easily ground by tread of wheels, is likely on account of its toughness to have a fair measure of endurance.

The clay slates of Massachusetts occur in the main in the region near Boston. Materials of this description in their original state closely resembled ordinary brick clays. By the changes to which they have been subjected since their formation they have been altered as regards their hardness; they sometimes indeed have a very rigid character, as is shown by hand tests. Practical experience, however, shows that in the road-bed rock of this nature rapidly grinds to the state of fine mud, which washes away with the rains, or is blown about in the form of dust. Some of the towns in the neighborhood of Boston have used these slate rocks in an extensive way with results which are altogether unsatisfactory except where the travel is light.

Although in general the slate rocks are to be condemned as sources of road materials, some of the beds of this nature, where they approach either the quartzites or the hornblende schist, are tolerably well adapted for the construction of highways. These local modifications of the slates so seldom occur that they may be regarded as of no great importance.

Last of all, among the widely distributed bed rocks of Massachusetts we may mention the deposits of crystalline limestone, or marble, which plentifully occur in the western part of the Berkshire range, and sparingly in other parts of the State. These limestones are prevailingly unsuited for use on roads, for, while the material binds well together, its granular or crystalline structure causes it readily to break up under the tread of the wheel, and the white, powdery dust is offensive to the wayfarers. On the whole, these last-mentioned rocks are perhaps less suited for road making than any other of the common materials of Massachusetts, except the mica schists.

In many parts of Massachusetts the drift materials afford better stone for use in the crusher and for application to roads than any of the bed rocks. This is due to the fact that the fragments which have survived the severe strains to which they have been subjected beneath the glacier are generally of a nature to withstand the wearing which the wheels inflict upon them. Thus, where granites, syenites or gneisses are to be taken for use after breaking for road materials, it is well to choose the bits from some pit the pebbles of which afford no evidence of decay. It is generally not advantageous to take the stones from the surface of the ground, for the reason that they have been submitted to a considerable amount of atmospheric decay; at a little depth below the surface they generally remain nearly as firm as they were at the close of the ice time.

The principal inconvenience arising from the use of loose boulders as a source of rock which is to serve as crushed stone, arises from the fact that the road material thus produced is of very diverse hardness, a feature which is mainly due to the difference in the measure in which the decay-bringing forces have operated. It may thus happen that a roadway constructed of fragments of stone gathered from fields will prove incoherent, occasional pits quickly forming on its surface, where the softer stone wears away. Owing to this prevalence of decay in the superficial materials, it has often been found advantageous, where possible, to use ledge rather than surface stone. This is to be regretted, for the reason that many of our farmers whose places are near to crushers find a profit in selling this otherwise worthless stone to the roadmasters, or to proprietors of private crushing establishments. As this use of crushed stone becomes more general on main highways of fairly light travel, there is reason to expect that the revenue of our farmers, which already from this source amounts to several thousand dollars a year, may be considerably increased.

With very little practice an observant person can at a glance tell a poor boulder from one which is fit for use. The decayed fragment is generally rough-surfaced and often fissured, while that which is solid has a smooth and often a polished look.

In general, the pebbles and boulders accumulated in deposits which are without admixture of clay, and which have been deposited by the streams which flowed beneath the ice, are much harder than those which are found in the till or general coating of waste, composed of a mixture of clay, sand and fragments of rock, which is so widely distributed in all countries which were covered by ice in the glacial epoch. These under-ice streams were evidently furious torrents, which drove the pebbles and boulders violently on their way, and thus wore out all the softer material; even the harder masses have been, as we may see, greatly rounded by the rude treatment to which they have been subjected.

In some cases, perhaps we may say generally within the limits of Massachusetts, the eskers or Indian ridges yield the best boulders for use in the crusher, though in some of the gravelly plains excellent material for this purpose may be found. In the south-eastern portion of the State, where road materials of good quality are of relatively rare occurrence, deposits of the above-named class have great value to the highway engineer.

There are a number of materials of less general importance than those above mentioned, which may prove serviceable for particular uses in road making, and which deserve the attention of those who have highways in their charge. Only a few of them need be mentioned in a general report of this nature, though all of them may well receive a careful study in case a thorough-going examination of the road materials of the Commonwealth is undertaken. First among these very local deposits we may note the accumulations of iron ore which have been formed beneath many of the bogs in New England, and which are particularly abundant in Massachusetts. These bog iron ores, varying in thickness from a few inches to several feet, occur at the bottom of a peaty layer in nearly all of the fresh-water swamps of eastern Massachusetts. They are particularly abundant in the southern part of Middlesex and in Bristol and Plymouth counties. They also occur, though less generally, in other parts of the Commonwealth. Here and there, especially in Plymouth County, some small experiments have been made in using this ore as top coating on sand roads. The results attained appear to be valuable, and to give promise that, with proper exploration, important additions to the road materials of the Commonwealth may be won from this source of supply.

It is characteristic of the bog ores that the iron oxide which they contain, together with the manganese which often occurs plentifully mingled with them, tends to bind the sand and pebbles together in the manner of a cement, giving the way a considerable firmness in all seasons. In many cases where bogs are drained for tillage purposes the iron ore is left as an incumbrance on the surface of the ground; at times, indeed, it renders the soil unfit for cultivation, so that it would be a gain to the farmer to have the material removed. Under such conditions the cost of obtaining the ore would be not much greater than that of procuring sand or gravel, though the masses need to be broken by the hammer or crusher before they are fit for use on the road. A careful search for these sources of iron ores should soon be undertaken in all the sandy districts of the State. A few such deposits in Bristol County are known to the people, for the reason that in the last century, and even in a yet earlier time, small amounts of iron were manufactured from these sources of supply.

In the eastern part of Massachusetts, particularly in Middlesex and Bristol counties, there are considerable deposits of "pudding stones," or, as they are termed by geologists, conglomerates, which have a certain amount of value as sources of road material. These deposits are in their general character much like the glacial drift, they are probably in certain cases indeed the product of ancient ice action; but they differ from our superficial gravels in that by the agents of change they have been converted into a firm rock, having the texture which is common in the ancient deposits.

The pudding stones in the Boston basin have their pebbles mostly composed of original hard rocks, and, as far as these fragments are concerned, afford excellent material for the crusher. It is to be noted, however, that the material which lies between the pebbles was originally sand, and though now the grains are rather firmly united, they break up when the rock is reduced to fragments, and form a powder which is not of service in the construction of roads, as it does not bind together under the action of the roller.

The pudding stones of Bristol County and the neighboring portions of Norfolk are on the whole less suited to road making than those which lie near Boston harbor. The pebbles are prevailingly less hard, and the quantity of sand produced in crushing is greater than in the case of the similar rock from Brookline and Roxbury. Many of these deposits, however, are somewhat ferruginous; the iron which they contain helps the material to bind, and the result is that a road-bed of tolerable strength can be made of the crushed stone.

The pebbles and all the conglomerates of Massachusetts, like those from the washed gravels from the glacial beds, are characteristically very smooth; if the crushed action is not carried to the point where these fragments are broken, they are certain under the tread of wheels to become separated from the sandstone which envelops them, and to become mere rolling stones in the roadway. On this account, where conglomerates are used it is desirable to have the crushing process carried to the point where the material is produced in smaller bits than would otherwise be desirable.

At many points in the State certain of the crystalline rocks have been subjected to a considerable amount of decay; they have, in fact, passed into the condition of a coarse sand, which is often so incoherent that it can be excavated with the pick and shovel. Where this decomposition has affected certain traps and granitic rocks, material thus produced is generally well suited for roadways, provided they are to be travelled only by light vehicles. Owing to the considerable amount of iron this decayed rock generally contains, it binds well together, and can be used to advantage on foot ways and private carriage roads.

In the town of Stoughton a decayed rock of a general granitic character occurs in considerable quantities, and has been made the subject of a slight practical test. Experience seems to show that the material binds well together, forming a tolerably firm road-bed, the only disadvantage being that in the spring-time the surface to the depth of an inch or two becomes softened, forming pasty mud.

At Steep Brook station, immediately north of Fall River, there is a similar deposit of decayed granite, which is now extensively quarried for use as coarse fire clay. This material, which belongs to the coal measures of Massachusetts, was in that age of the earth's history a decayed rock, which was swept about by the waves and streams, afterwards consolidated into a firm bed, and yet later subjected to another process of decay, which has again reduced it to a soft state. Although no extended experiment has been made in the use of this Steep Brook fire clay on roads, it may be found serviceable when used in the manner of a cement to bind gravels together.

Along the coast, particularly on the mud flats of the harbors lying to the north of Cape Cod, thick deposits of oyster shells abound. These beds are generally not shown at the surface, for the reason that the species of oyster which plentifully existed in this region down to the settlement of the country by Europeans has ceased to abound in these waters; thus recent accumulations of clay commonly hide the old oyster beds from view. At some points, notably in the Charles River basin, dredging has shown these shell beds to have a depth of several feet. By the dredge it is possible to lift these shells at a very moderate cost; it will probably be found profitable at certain points to use this material on private roads, and other ways which are traversed only by light carriages. The shells thus obtained would not be quite as good for road material as those which are now obtained in the living state, and this for the reason that a portion of the organic matter has been removed, with the result that the limy matter is more fragile than it originally was.

In considering the general conditions of Massachusetts roads, it is necessary to take into account the amount of frost action to which they are subjected. In this portion of New England the injury done by freezing is considerably greater in amount than it is in the more northern and inland portions of the country. Where the winter is enduring, the ground is usually subjected but once to the deep penetration of frost; the surface is then snow-bound, and so remains until the spring-time, and the covering often goes away so slowly that the late frosts do not penetrate to any considerable depth. It is otherwise in south-eastern New England. In this region it is common for the ground to freeze to a depth of six inches or more at least half a dozen times each year, the freezing on each occasion going to a point where the artificial construction of a road-bed is affected to its base.

Where the ground is left bare of snow, and where it is firmly consolidated, as on a roadway, the frost in Massachusetts, at least in the region about Boston, occasionally enters the ground to a depth of four feet or more. In this process the whole of this earth section so far as it contains water is necessarily set in motion, the amount of movement being determined by the quantity of the fluid which it contains. In passing into the frozen state, water expands to the amount of about one-ninth of its volume; in so doing it thrusts the fragments of mineral matter about so as to obtain the additional room. It is evident that this action of the frost makes it very desirable to keep the foundations of a road in the driest possible conditions. To insure its safety it is indeed necessary to prevent the formation of any considerable amount of ice in the foot or so of depth immediately under the pavement of the roadway. If this part of the section is kept dry it will provide a good non-conductive coating for the lower earth in a measure likely to prevent the downward penetration of the frost. If the freezing cold passes through it, the movement of the lower-lying materials will have but little influence on the solid part of the roadway; the effect will be merely to lift it to a level slightly higher than it was before the frost entered the ground.

In all countries it is very important that the section of the road-bed which receives the stress of the wheels and that which lies immediately below the level of the so-called metal should be as dry as possible, but in regions much affected by frost the upper or trodden level should have all the qualities of a roof of sound construction. It should shed the water to the side drains, and these should be so placed that the moisture does not work laterally under the road-bed. In general, such conditions can only be obtained by the use of materials which form a solid pavement.

With the conveniently located trap dikes of eastern Massachusetts and the Connecticut River valley, it will be easy to supply any part of the State with good road materials at a reasonable price. The railways can be used to advantage, and by their aid stone can be delivered easily to points a hundred or more miles distant from the crusher. Private capital will furnish the plants necessary to prepare the stone on a large scale, and at a price which will probably be less than the same work can be done by the towns.

The Need of a Careful Survey of Road Materials.

The foregoing account of the road materials of Massachusetts will give the reader but an imperfect notion of the exceeding variety of their character, conditions of occurrence and distribution. In no other equal area in this country is the diversity of the bed-rock conditions so far as they pertain to road making so great as in this Commonwealth. The original deposits were exceedingly diverse; their beds have been in most cases greatly altered, the changes having taken place in a varied way in different localities, and having been accompanied by the formation of many thousand trap dikes. The glacial deposits, though more uniform, exhibit considerable diversities which have also to be taken into account by the careful road builder.

To put the roadmasters of the State in possession of the knowledge required in their difficult tasks, it will be necessary to make a somewhat careful study of the bed rocks, from the point of view of their fitness for the construction of highways, and to delineate the results on appropriate maps, to be accompanied by the necessary descriptions. The information thus obtained should be so presented that the supervisors of highways in each town may know the relative value of all the resources in the way of construction materials which they can command. The cost of such an examination and description would probably not exceed the expense now incurred in constructing ten miles of ordinary good highway, and the saving which would be effected in any one year would probably repay many fold the expense of the inquiry.

CHAPTER III.

Condition of Massachusetts Roads.

The time allowed for the preparation of this report has not been sufficient to enable the commissioners to do all which should have been done in the way of obtaining information as to the condition of the highways in the Commonwealth. In their effort to attain the end in view they proceeded in the manner described below.

Immediately after their appointment, the commissioners sent tabulated questions to the selectmen and road commissioners of the several towns. The results thus obtained, though valuable, were evidently insufficient to serve the needs of the inquiry.

As soon as it became evident that no thoroughly satisfactory information could be obtained by correspondence, the commissioners undertook a system of hearings, which were held after due advertisements in the shire towns and at other points designated by the county commissioners. Twelve such hearings were held, which were attended by representatives of thirty-six per cent. of the towns. The record of information thus obtained through the services of a stenographer, and which is herewith submitted, covers many hundred pages of manuscript, and contains a very valuable body of evidence concerning the condition of our roadways and the state of mind of the citizens of the Commonwealth; it also sets forth in a clear way the methods by which the highways of the State are now controlled.

In addition to the methods of inquiry above set forth, your commissioners deemed it important to obtain a photographic record which should present in a most unquestionable way the actual state of the principal thoroughfares in various parts of the Commonwealth. To obtain this end, Mr. C. L. Weeks, an agent of the Board, traversed six hundred miles of highways, including portions of every county of the Commonwealth, except Nantucket. The general results thus obtained are set forth in the report which is submitted for publication. The photographs themselves are held in two large folios which accompany this report; these folios contain in all four hundred photographs.

The system of local government which has proved in so many ways advantageous to the interests of the Commonwealth apparently makes it necessary that the actual work of constructing the highways shall be in the hands of municipal officers, the agents of the cities and towns. These officers who have charge of the highways have at present no other sources of information as to their art save that which may be traditional in the locality. It seems impossible to make any adequate provision whereby they may be enabled to study the better methods which are followed in certain districts; they are thus unable to make use of the great and valuable body of experience gained in this Commonwealth, in other parts of the United States, or in foreign countries.

The yet further difficulty with our system arises from the fact that in most of our towns and cities the tenure of office of the roadmasters is short. It is rare indeed that a man is able to look forward to a career in this employment, and can therefore properly take the pains or have the opportunities to train himself in the work he has to do. In a greater number of cases he knows that the customs of the locality will prevent his holding the place for any number of years. If this method had been devised to secure the perpetuation of bad roads, it could not have been more effectively adapted to the end.

It is difficult, except through the general manuscript matter which gives the records of the hearings and the reports of the town officers, to set before the Legislature in an adequate way the actual state of the highways of the Commonwealth. In this report, which is intended for printing, it will be necessary to give an account of the matter in very general terms, referring to the manuscript statements for the more detailed evidence.

Excepting in a few of the cities and in a small number of the wealthier towns, the highways of the Commonwealth may properly be said to be in bad condition.

In part, this unsatisfactory state of the public roads in the Commonwealth needs to be attributed to the defective ways of construction, and a lack of knowledge as to the proper means of administering the appropriation for that work and for repairs. In a larger share, however, the evils arise from the relatively small amount of money which is devoted or perhaps can properly be given by the municipalities to the use of the highways.

The appended Table K shows the amount of money spent on highways by the towns of the Commonwealth. The statistics given in Tables O and P afford further information on this point. From these tables it will be seen that 73 towns, or 19.7 per cent. of the whole number in the State, expend $1,000 or less, with a total expenditure of $41,493. The total mileage of roads in these poorer towns above referred to is 2,552 miles. It will thus be seen that the average amount appropriable to their roads is only $16.20 per mile, a sum which experience shows is quite inadequate for the work.

Next above the group of towns just mentioned we have a somewhat richer association, including 85 towns, or 26.6 per cent. of the total, where the amount expended on the roads ranges from one to two thousand dollars annually, and the total sum spent $118,748, the amount per mile being on the average $28.80.

Yet higher in the series we have the municipalities, amounting in all to 56, where the amount of money expended ranges from two to three thousand dollars, and the total sum amounts to $133,027, an average per mile of road of $38.20.

In the three grades just mentioned it is perfectly clear that the conditions are such as to make it impossible for the towns to better their condition; that is, the best which they can do is to struggle against further depreciation in the condition of the highways, and to make them safe under a liberal interpretation of the law.

Next higher in the scale of expenditure comes the group of towns, 38 in number, where the annual outlay is from three to four thousand dollars, with a total expenditure of $94,838. In the case of some of these towns it may be possible to make a little progress in the direction of substantial improvements, but it seems safest to include all these in the group of municipalities the roads of which cannot be improved from within.

The list above given includes 232 towns, or 72.5 per cent. out of the total number in the Commonwealth, and 81.1 per cent. of the total areas occupied by them.

There are 21 towns in the Commonwealth which spend between

four and five thousand dollars per annum, or a total of $96,344, an average of $101.20 per mile of roadway. On this grade of expenditure, and of course for all the groups where the appropriation is on a larger scale, it seems clear that we may fairly expect under a proper system of management to secure a progressive improvement in the condition of the highways. In other words, at this point we may in general reckon that we pass from the group of towns needing aid to those which may be expected to improve their condition from their own revenues. It should be understood that this is a general statement, which is open to a certain amount of qualification. Owing to peculiarities in their conditions, some of the towns in the lower group as above described may be in condition to help themselves; and, on the other hand, certain of the municipalities included in the upper group may need assistance.

The first question which arises is whether it is possible that the towns in general, particularly of the lower group, can reasonably be expected to increase the burden of taxation for the purpose of bettering the roads, or devote a larger share of that now levied to the improvement of their highways. The first of these questions is one of exceeding complication, and cannot be to any extent discussed by the commission. It may, however, be noted that the percentage of money annually appropriated to highways, as compared with the total valuation, varies very greatly. The proportion of expenditure in the ratio of valuation is given for the several counties in Table L. The details for each town are given in Table K. From the statistics it may readily be seen that the variation is very wide, ranging from zero in Gay Head and Gosnold to six-tenths of one per cent. in Becket. It may be said that these differences are, to a great extent, determined by the particular conditions of the towns, the amount of debt and the relative improvement of the highways to the population. Thus, in case of Gay Head, the people are but little dependent upon the roads, and their main highway was recently constructed for them by the Commonwealth; while in the town of Becket the local conditions are such as to demand passable roads, and require much expenditure for their maintenance.

Another point of interest in this connection is the per cent. of the tax receipts spent upon the highways. The average of 13.7 per cent.

in the towns is approximately the same as that expended by the cities (11.2). This would seem to indicate that there is a general consensus of opinion to the effect that about a tithe of municipal revenues should be devoted to roadways. The facts seem also to indicate that it is likely to be difficult to change this proportion except by some gradual alteration of public opinion.

It seems out of the question to expect by the progress of public opinion to induce the towns of the Commonwealth to effect any great change in their road conditions through a material increase in taxes. Any such change, if it is to be brought about, must be attained by general enactments, or, in other words, by some method of State aid, in which the richer parts of the Commonwealth will contribute to the needs of the poorer.

The unhappy conditions of our public ways in the greater part of the Commonwealth are not due to any lack of interest or of zeal on the part of the roadmasters, but are to be accounted for in part by the want of expert knowledge concerning road construction, and in the larger part by the insufficiency of money which is at their disposal for the execution of their tasks. If these masters had been called upon for many years past to construct good roads, their native ingenuity would doubtless, though perhaps by way of many blunders, have led them to good results.

Physical Conditions of Massachusetts Highways.

The most important defects in the physical conditions of the Massachusetts roads arise from an inadequate expenditure of money in the first construction of the way. In most cases the paths followed by vehicles are not now, and never have been, in a condition to meet the tax of travel. This statement is true not only of the by-ways of the towns where no effective work whatever has been done upon the road, but also of many of the more costly ways in the State. Thus, in the case of the Salem Turnpike, which was built with a view to bring profit to a corporation, and constructed at considerable expense, the work was never done in a workmanlike manner, with the result that the enterprise which might have been fairly remunerative proved entirely unprofitable to the shareholders.

In general, it may be said that the rural highways of Massachusetts are fairly passable in the part of the year beginning with the 15th of May and closing with the 1st of January, with the exception of the relatively small amount of the mileage where the ways are traversed by very heavy wagons. Such roads, many of them of the greatest economic importance to the Commonwealth, are often bad during every day in the year. This fact is shown by many of the photographs, all of which were taken in the most favorable period of the year, — the early autumn. It is safe to say that at least four-fifths, probably nine-tenths, of the highways of the Commonwealth which are intimately related to its manufacturing industries are in permanently bad condition.

Of the six hundred miles of the roadway on which the photographs were taken, at approximately regular intervals of about one mile, at least five hundred and sixty miles were clearly in bad condition in the most favorable part of the year. It should be noted, however, that the roads photographed are, from their position, among the better of those in the Commonwealth, and include a certain amount of city streets. The greater part of those which were photographed, more than nine-tenths of the whole, consist of old stage routes, which represent, in a way, the result of the road-building energy of our population for two centuries or more of their history.

The tax inflicted upon our people by the condition of the roads cannot be estimated with any accuracy. There are, however, certain indications which give a basis for a general reckoning, not without its value to the public.

One of the methods of approaching the question may be set forth as follows: the total movement of freight by railroads in the Commonwealth amounts annually, according to the report of the Railroad Commissioners for the year 1890, to 27,900,000 tons; of this, two-thirds pertain to the cities and one-third to what we may term the rural districts. Estimating that the freight which enters or leaves the rural districts is subjected to an average highway carriage of four miles, we find 37,259,336 tons of freight hauled one mile per annum as the highway part of the business. Reckoning the difference in the cost of transportation over the road of the first class and that which represents the average condition of Massachusetts highways, it becomes evident that the tax due to the imperfections of these ways amounts to between three and four million dollars a year.

It may be objected to this computation that the reckoning of four miles as the average journey of rural freight in ordinary wagons is excessive; in this connection it should be noted that a very large part of the freight which passes over our highways never enters a railroad carriage. Furthermore, the study of four out of the eight main highways connecting Boston with the surrounding country has shown that these roads give passage to about 8,000,000 mile tons of freight per annum which does not touch the railways. The probabilities are that the estimate as above made much underrates both the disadvantages of transportation and the amount of carriage.

The problem may be approached in another way, — that in which it has been essayed by various European students upon the subject; this is as follows: the statistics of Great Britain show that in that country on the average one horse serves twenty-four people; in Scotland the proportion is one to twenty and six-tenths; in France the proportion is one to thirteen and four-tenths; and in Massachusetts the proportion is one to twelve and three-fourths. Or, in other words, it requires about twice as many horses to perform the work allotted to such animals in Massachusetts as it does in Great Britain. The proportion of pleasure horses to those devoted to economic purposes is probably about the same in these countries, and the general conditions of the relation between the country folk and the cities are approximately alike. It is therefore reasonable to suppose that the difference in the number of horses is due to the needs created by variation in the quality of the highways. An extension of the statistics to other countries bears out this impression. Switzerland, which is probably the best highwayed country in the world, has one horse for each twenty-nine and six-tenths people.

Reckoning the cost of each horse in wear and tear, care and food, at twelve dollars a month, which is probably at least twenty per cent. below the truth, and estimating that the ill condition of the Massachusetts roads doubles the number of horses employed within the State, we find that the tax which these imperfect ways imposes on the people of the Commonwealth is very large. It appears that, as compared with Great Britain, we are bearing a loss of about ten million dollars a year; if the comparison is made with Switzerland, the same would be twelve and one-half million dollars per annum.

Some light may be thrown upon this problem by the facts relating to particular highways which have been gathered by the commission, only a few of which can be set forth here. First, to take the instance of the Salem Turnpike, a careful examination has shown that the present cost of transporting a ton of freight from Revere to Boston is about thirteen cents per mile ton, while on the section of the road from Revere to Lynn the cost is twenty-four cents per mile ton. As the whole of this road now under consideration is practically without grades, all the difference in the cost of transportation is due to the variation in the condition of the roadway.

Carefully verified statistics concerning the cost of hauling from the house formerly occupied by Geo. A. Hall, in Revere, to Boston, make it clear that, in the original unimproved condition of the road during the early part of this century, the cost per mile ton was sixty cents; at present the cost over the well-paved way is about eighteen cents per mile ton.

An instance of equally striking nature is represented by Plate A in this report, showing two roads, where in the one case a load of four tons is upborne by a good macadam road five years in heavy use, and in the other a load of six and a quarter tons is supported in the ruts of an ordinary country road. In the lower figure the weight encounters practically no resistance from the condition of the road; in the upper, the principal part of the labor of hauling is brought about by the state of the way itself. The cost of teaming in the lower figure is reckoned about twenty-one cents per mile ton, and in the other forty-three cents per mile ton. It is eminently probable that the actual cost of each of these roads on an average of ten years' use does not vary in any important measure, the difference being that the one is well constructed and needs little repairs; the other was never built, in any proper sense, and is really irreparable.

It may also be added that the statistics, as in Table J, show that the amount of weight drawn per horse in different parts of the Commonwealth varies in a striking manner and evidently in proportion to the condition of the roads; thus, in Boston the average weight of coal drawn per horse is 3,393 pounds, in Pittsfield it is 2,063 pounds, in Northampton 2,375 pounds, in Greenfield 2,678 pounds, in Holyoke 2,133 pounds, in North Adams 1,917 pounds. The table in general shows that the load per horse in Boston is about one-third more than in the other cities in which statistics were taken. It appears to be safe to reckon that the weight of the load which can be hauled by one horse in the rural districts in Massachusetts is only about half that which can be conveyed in the better-conditioned cities and richer towns. It takes twice as many horses to do the work as it would if the roads were in first-class condition.

Although these methods of attaining the result afford discrepant indications as to the amount of loss due to ill-kept highways, they alike clearly indicate that the direct loss is very great, probably amounts to somewhere between five and ten million dollars per annum. No account is here taken of the indirect damage which occurs through the wearing out of animals, vehicles and harnesses, which probably amounts to a large fraction of the sum above stated.

CHAPTER IV.

Economics of Massachusetts Roads.

The wealth and population of our cities depends to a great extent on their ability to manufacture goods or to exchange the various commodities with the more or less scattered communities of the Commonwealth.

In treating of these ways we have divided them into two classes: —

Class one includes the distinctively city streets which are used almost exclusively for the movement of goods and of people residing within their own borders, and which must be cared for according to the local demand made upon them.

Class two consists of those main thoroughfares which in the earlier times constituted the stage and mail routes, and which to-day furnish the ways of ingress and egress for the scattered villages throughout the Commonwealth.

The needs in the way of comfort and economy of the people constantly using the city streets afford an effective guarantee that every possible effort will be made to secure able and experienced men to build and superintend them, and that they will be maintained in such a manner as to get the best results; in the opinion of the commissioners they should not be considered in any scheme of State work which may be undertaken, except as to the possible benefit of advice which may be given concerning the methods and value of materials used, which would naturally come from a central board whose inquiries shall cover these points.

A study of the city streets of the Commonwealth shows that much work of a permanent character has been performed, and that a perfected system is gradually being evolved. Boston, being the chief city, may be assumed fairly to represent the growth and present condition of this class of highway engineering in the Commonwealth.

A study of Boston streets shows that previous to 1853, with the exception of some few ways paved with granite blocks, each six inches wide, the most of the heavy-traffic streets were laid with coarse cobble stones gathered from the fields or beaches near at hand.

The six-inch wide granite blocks were mostly removed early in the fifties, on account of their slipperiness and inconveniences arising from their use by heavy teams. In 1856 the superintendent of streets reported that the round stones were, in his opinion, "the best, cheapest and most durable for Boston streets," and in 1855 this recommendation not only applied to the common cobble-stone pavements, but to the "kidney stones," which were smaller, smoother and harder, and only obtained from St. Mary's Bay, N. S., and which cost, laid on a gravel foundation, about $1.00 to $1.50 a square yard. In 1865 the available supply of cobble-stones was reported as about exhausted, and the comment was "that at best it made a rough road, and few will regret its discontinuance."

In the mean time experiment had been made with the light and heavy "Terry iron block" and the "cellular iron block." The heavy Terry block pavement was laid in Court Street at a cost of $10.00 a square yard; for a few years it gave satisfaction, but eventually went to pieces and was replaced by granite blocks.

The light Terry block pavement was laid on Washington Street between Court and School streets in 1856, at a cost of $6.00 a square yard; but, owing to the great vibration in the blocks, they would not bind well, and their gradual breaking caused their removal in 1859, when they were replaced by kidney stones. The "cellular iron blocks" were experimental only, being laid by private parties; they were removed in less than two years. The light Terry block was fourteen inches square by four and a half inches deep, weighing thirty-one pounds, while the heavy block was twelve inches square by five and a half inches deep, and weighed thirty-six pounds. The cellular iron block was fourteen inches square by one and two-eighths inches deep, and had spaces filled with gravel, the blocks being laid in lime and sand.

From the time the first Nicholson (wooden) pavement was laid by the city in 1856, it can hardly be claimed that it ever proved satisfactory. Its first cost was about $2.50 a square yard, and the cost of repairs were so great that it was soon condemned for use on heavy-traffic streets. Some of this pavement was made of hard rock maple laid on burnetized boards with coating of tar on the ground, but in a year or two the blocks were reported as so worn down as to be fit only to burn. Later a wood block known as the "Warren" was tried, and another called the "Boston." The "Warren" was laid without a flooring, on a gravel foundation, and the "Boston" was laid on a gravel bed not compacted but shaped, and the blocks rammed to a solid bed after softening the foundation by the use of water passed through the joints.

In 1868 it was reported that wood pavement was "not good to use on narrow, heavily travelled streets. In sections of the city where the traffic is light, wood will no doubt be good and prove satisfactory."

In 1862 the "Belgian" blocks were first used, costing about $2.85 a square yard. The blocks were of trap rock, about four inches square by seven inches deep. They were shipped from the Hudson River, and gave great satisfaction, being described as very hard, and showing but trifling wear after several years of use, even on heavy-traffic streets. Their use was in 1865 recommended on all heavy-traffic streets, while the small granite block, three to four inches wide, six to seven inches long and about seven inches deep, was recommended for lighter-travelled streets. Various other kinds of pavements have been tried in Boston, but, although they have given satisfaction in other cities, their failure here has caused their removal; until at the present time the principal pavements in use are sheet asphalt and granite blocks, although there are a few streets paved with brick or asphalt blocks.

The granite blocks now used are three and one-half to four and one-half inches wide, eight to twelve inches long and seven and one-half to eight inches deep, and cost from $2.07 on a gravel bed to $5.00 a square yard on a concrete foundation. On the heavier-traffic central streets the blocks are used entirely, and are laid on a concrete foundation six inches thick, all the joints between the blocks being filled with gravel and gas tar pitch, making a firm pavement, and one that affords an effective roof over the foundation.

The sheet asphalt which is used is mostly "Trinidad," although two streets in Boston have this year been laid with the Sicilian rock asphalt. All the street asphalt is laid on a six-inch concrete foundation, shaped to carry the water to the catch-basins, and rests on an even thickness of two and a half inches of asphalt. This pavement is used on light-traffic and residential streets, where cleanliness and freedom from noise are essential features. Its cost is about $2.50 to $3.75 a square yard, and it requires regular cleaning and continuous repairs.

Brick and asphalt blocks are used on light-traffic streets, and then only when they can be laid on a gravel foundation, as the use of a concrete foundation adds so much to the cost as to put them in the same class with sheet asphalt; owing to the tendency of these blocks to chip at the edges and more rapid wear, they are not considered an equal in value to sheet asphalt at the price mentioned above.

The experience of Boston has been that pavements which have endured well in other places have in certain instances proved a failure here. It should be observed that we have made a study of the wagons in and about Boston and in several other cities in different parts of the State, and a comparison of these observations shows that no such weights per horse, or per inch in tire, are to be met with in other parts of the Commonwealth as are found in Boston. Whilst the best foreign practice allows of only five hundred to nine hundred pounds per inch in width of tire, we find here many different types of wagons loaded to one thousand, fifteen hundred, two thousand and in cases as high as forty-five hundred and fifty-two hundred pounds per inch of width of tire. This excessive weight, in connection with the numerous street railway tracks and the sharp calks on the horses' shoes, tends quickly to destroy anything but the hardest and toughest granite blocks, and to develop inequalities in the surface of any kind of pavement which is not laid on the firmest of foundations We thus see the reason for gradual development of the expensive pavement now used.

The pavements in other cities of Massachusetts are of much the same character as may be found in Boston, except that no other has yet used a concrete foundation under granite blocks. Some of the older cities, such as Salem, Gloucester and New Bedford, have more or less cobble-stone pavement; but these roadways belong to a past age, and, as fast as the finances of the municipalities will permit, are being replaced by granite blocks.

Where no concrete foundation is used, the granite blocks are laid on a gravel, cinder or broken-stone foundation, and cost completed from $2.00 to $2.50 a square yard. The crown generally used is from one-fourth to one-half inch per foot of width; a gutter grade of at least one-half foot to the one hundred feet is required; on streets with "flat" grades the grade is made by a change in the depth of the gutter below the tops of the curbs, of from five inches at the summit to twelve inches at the catch basins.

Holyoke has laid a short piece of one street with asphalt blocks. During the present year Springfield has laid a residential street with Syracuse bricks on edge, on a foundation of common home-made hard-burned brick, laid flat on a gravel foundation, the bed being firmly rolled with a steam roller. One inch of sand is used between the two courses of brick, and the joints of the top course are "run in" with Portland cement grout. The bricks cost $11.00 a thousand at Syracuse, or $15.00 per thousand on the cars at Springfield. The cost of teaming is $1.00 per thousand, and the cost of the completed street about $2.15 per square yard.

Class Two, or the Main Thoroughfares Connecting the City and the Surrounding Country.

One of the debatable points encountered by the commission which has been left undetermined is how far out from the business centres the city type of paving should be extended, or how far into the great centres the broken-stone highway may be used.

While there might be several rules for guidance in this matter, yet we know of but two which commend themselves to attention, and these are, first, as to the kind of work and the comparative cost in a term of years; second, the method which permits of the maximum load and the least interruption, by repairs, to the traffic that passes over it. The first can only be determined by study of the physical conditions or by a careful study of the traffic. The second must be decided upon after knowing how often the traffic must be disturbed by repairs.

The traffic observations on Salem Turnpike offer a ready means of estimating the cost of repairs on a macadam road over which passes a fair amount of heavy travel. At Revere street in Revere observations were made for three successive days upon the passing teams, and upon the character of the vehicles. There were on the average 99 pleasure carriages, 288 express wagons and 107 heavy wagons passing this point each day; this represents what passed over the country road to Lynn. In percentage the carriages constituted 20.2 per cent., expresses 58.3 per cent., and other wagons 21.5 per cent. of the total, showing that over one-half the traffic is from the express business.

There is no occasion for teams to stand along the sides of such a road as this, and the width of stone used need be only sufficient for passing, or say eighteen feet, leaving the rest of the way gravelled, as at present. The cost of building a road of broken stone twelve inches thick would be ninety-two cents a square yard, or $9,715 a mile. The repairs of such a road, based on a traffic of 484 teams, or 1,089 tons a day, means the use, on an average for a term of years, of 138 cubic yards of broken trap rock a mile per year. The cost of the stone, including teaming, loading, spreading, rolling and supervision, is estimated at $2.75 per cubic yard, making the cost per mile as $379.50 per year. Based on the above figures, the cost per mile for say twenty years will be —

Construction,	$9,715
Repairs,	7,590
Interest, four per cent.,	10,808
	$28,113

The annual cost per mile per year amounts to $1,405.65; such a method of construction affords a good road at all seasons of the year.

The same road, if paved with granite blocks, is estimated to cost $2.10 a square yard, or $23,232 a mile, laid on a gravel foundation.

It is uncertain whether the paving would require relaying in a term of twenty years; but the chances are that, owing to one cause and another, it would. The cost of relaying granite blocks would be about forty cents a square yard, or two cents a yard a year, if relaid in twenty years; or $211.20 a mile a year, or $4,224 a mile for twenty years.

Based on the above figures, the cost per mile for twenty years will be —

Construction, ...	$23,232
Repairs, ...	4,224
Interest on first cost only, four per cent., ...	18,586
	$46,042

The mean annual cost per mile per year amounts to $2,302.10.

Not taking into account the interest, we find the total cost of macadam will be $17,305, or $865 a year, and of the granite blocks $27,456, or $1,372 a year, per mile.

The distance from the point of observation on the road to Lynn is about four miles, and the saving in twenty years by the use of macadam over paving amounts to a little over ten thousand dollars.

A further study of the traffic observations (see Appendix J) on this road shows that the number of teams passing out or in, loaded or unloaded, does not vary a great deal. That is to say, of the empty wagons, 10.35 per cent. were going out and 10.18 per cent. were going in; and of the loaded wagons 32.67 per cent. were going out and 46.80 per cent. were going in; of the combined empty and loaded wagons, 43.02 per cent. were going out and 56.98 per cent. were going in. This close agreement shows that what little difference there is is in favor of the loaded teams going towards Boston; but it is so slight that each end of the road should be capable of giving equally good facilities for hauling the maximum load per horse. This introduces the question of the cost of teaming goods over any highway per ton per mile. From a study of the work done by teams over this same road we can form some estimate of this quantity.

The cost of teaming freight from Chelsea to Lynn, where two-thirds of the haul is made over a badly maintained gravel road, is estimated to be about twenty-five cents a ton per mile, while the cost of teaming from the point of observation to Boston, over a paved road all the way, is about thirteen to fourteen cents a ton a mile, showing that the work can be done on the paved road at a saving of from eleven to twelve cents a ton a mile over what it actually costs over the unpaved road in poor condition. From experiments made by French engineers, it is estimated that a horse will perform about seventy-seven per cent. as much work on a good and well-kept macadam road as on a paved surface; which makes the saving on the paved road about eight and a half cents a ton a mile, against eleven cents a ton a mile on the macadam, as compared with the present road, provided each wagon was at all times, and under all conditions, loaded to its utmost carrying capacity.

It is fair to assume that one-half the volume of freight passing the point of observation will be benefited by a good road. The amount of freight teamed is 270 tons a day, on which a saving of two and a half cents a ton a mile can be effected, amounting to a daily saving of $3.25. Deducting Sundays, holidays and stormy days, a team works about 267 days in a year, and the total annual saving per mile on this basis amounts to $868 in favor of the paved road over the macadam, or $17,360 in twenty years. By our previous figures the macadam costs $10,000 less in twenty years than the granite blocks. By our last estimate, into which we reckon the saving on cost of teaming, we find that the block-paved roadway saves us $17,360, or a net saving in twenty years of $7,360.

There are other matters to be taken into consideration in connection with this study. The paved road is good for the whole twenty years, with no interruption to travel by repairs, while the macadam will need resurfacing probably each two or three years, and this, with the temporary obstruction caused by breaking up the road and using a steam roller at these short periods, inclines us to the opinion that the paved surface is in the long run far the cheapest. The same discussion might be continued on Western Avenue, Beacon Street and Blue Hill Avenue, where similar traffic observations were made; but sufficient has been said to show the line of study that will be needed on such main thoroughfares as lead into our large cities.

The next point we wish to call attention to is the bad condition of this piece of road between Boston and Lynn, and the reason for its lack of care.

Starting at Chelsea bridge, where not only the Lynn and other Essex County traffic crosses the Mystic River, but also the traffic from Chelsea, we find a daily traffic of 1,205 against 494 teams at Revere Street, or 711 teams from Chelsea, divided as follows: 208 carriages, 613 express and 414 loaded wagons; or 16.8 per cent. carriages, 49.6 per cent. express and 33.6 per cent. loaded wagons. The percentages indicate that there are more loaded wagons upon the way as we near the city. The traffic from Chelsea is so much larger than that which passes to Chelsea from Essex County that the Essex County traffic does not enter as a factor into the problem as to the kind of pavement to be used at this point. In fact, at this place the way becomes a distinctively city street, and must be treated as such.

The paving at Chelsea bridge is laid on a gravel foundation, and where undisturbed by excavation retains its shape and crown in good condition for at least twenty years. It is therefore safe to state that such a foundation is sufficient for a traffic of 1,205 teams, or 2,879 tons a day, on a width of 42 feet, or 68 tons per foot in width.

A further study of the traffic observations at Revere Street on Broadway (see Appendix J) shows that all of the 1,089 tons, daily passing our point of observation, benefited Essex County and the city of Boston, except perhaps an occasional team to and from Chelsea or Revere. The town of Revere receives no benefit from this traffic, but is put to the expense of maintaining a granite block pavement, in order to make it possible for her own citizens to receive the full benefit of the good roadway through Chelsea to Boston, whereas without the Essex County traffic a good macadam road would be quite sufficient. Naturally the town of Revere only undertakes such care for the thoroughfares as will satisfy the demands of her own people, and as these demands extend only to Revere Street, we find the permanent work stopped at that point, and a stretch of four miles of road has only so much work done on it as will serve to prevent indictment before the grand jury. One method of procedure, in order to secure a good road on this debatable ground, would be by petition to the county commissioners of Middlesex County, within whose jurisdiction this road lies. We are assured, from the conditions, that Revere people will not petition, as they do not wish to add to their burden, when they know the town will reap no benefit from the increased outlay. Chelsea does not care what state this road may be in, and the chances are that no request will emanate from the people of Essex County to the commissioners of Middlesex County for work to be done in Suffolk County. The result is, no petition is likely to reach the county commissioners, and the work will surely not be done without a petition, as that is the only legal way of bringing the subject before those authorities. If this were an isolated case, it must be passed by, but unfortunately it is but one of many.

The parties directly benefited by a good road at this point are the city of Boston and a part of Essex County. Indirectly Chelsea and Revere receive a benefit, but it comes only through an increase in the prosperity of Boston, or on the general principle that what benefits any one town of the State must benefit the whole State. As cases similar to this frequently occur, it can readily be seen that the general welfare of the Commonwealth is affected, and it becomes a question of State policy to furnish relief.

The question of how near the business centre of our larger cities the main thoroughfare should extend is one that will have to be decided by public hearings, at which all parties interested are invited to appear, and after a thorough study of the facts has been made.

The natural conclusion of the above statements is that certain cases arise in the management of public ways which cannot be overcome under the present system of county commission supervision, and that the arbitrarily defined county lines are an obstacle in the way of a perfected general scheme.

A Comparison of the Cost of Well-made and Poorly Made Roads.

There is an almost entire lack of any records as to cost of constructing the roads of the poorer class in all parts of the State. A discussion of the comparative cost between well-constructed roads and those on which less skill has been exercised in the selection and proper arrangement of materials is thus rendered very difficult. Only those cities and towns which are doing the best work as a rule keep such a record as will enable them to know what each part of the work costs.

We are inclined to the opinion that one of the leading causes of poor work in many cities and towns is an entire lack of knowledge of its cost. It would seem that some general provision should be made, looking toward a system of uniform records of the expense incurred in building different kinds of work. There can be no question but that such a scheme would tend to organize a friendly rivalry between different roadmasters in the State, which would be of great advantage to the different municipalities.

There seems to be among our highway authorities a general feeling that with a certain appropriation in hand the only thing to be done is to expend it. It does not occur to most of the roadmasters that there are different ways of planning work, or that they can ever perform good work without larger appropriations. It can clearly be shown that in many cases much is left undone that might well be accomplished without greater expenditures than are incurred.

There prevails a mistaken idea that good work must necessarily be beyond the reach of the average city or town. The object of this chapter is to show that even in first cost good work need not demand a much greater outlay than poor, while poor work in a term of years will call for a much greater expenditure than good.

It must first be carefully noted that comparisons of different classes of roads can be made only after a sufficient study of every detail of the structures which are under consideration. The first cost is necessarily determined by the proximity of suitable materials. The value of the materials can only be ascertained after a full knowledge of the character and amount of the travel. The methods adopted can be decided upon only after a careful survey of the ground. It may be necessary, even when good materials requiring a long haul exist, to accept a poor material as on the whole the cheaper.

An ordinarily poor gravel may be used to advantage on a road with light carriage traffic, and require but little repairs, when, under heavy teaming, it would go to pieces in a week. In fact, we know of a case in Chelsea where a gravel road stood in good shape for six years under the ordinary travel of a suburban cross street, and failed entirely in a few days with the traffic of the main road from Boston to Lynn diverted through it. This street was easily repaired after the extra travel ceased, and has since been in perfect condition, with a smooth, hard surface. We can readily see that it would be folly to cover a road, under such conditions as it originally had to meet, with broken stone at an expenditure of fifty cents a square yard, or with granite blocks at a cost of two dollars a square yard, when the gravel cost but ten cents. If, on the contrary, the heavy traffic had been continued, we should estimate the cost, first, of putting down some material that would last for a term of years, and then compare it with the cost of the poorer material for the same time.

We assume that the gravel road would cost ten cents a square yard, which in the case referred to is a reasonable estimate, and that a macadam road could be constructed for fifty cents, which is also a safe reckoning. The gravel road must be renewed once a year; the macadam will last for five years, at the end of which time it will cost twenty-five cents a square yard to rebuild it. We easily estimate the cost of the gravel road as one dollar a square yard during the ten years, or ten cents a square yard for each year.

In the case of the macadam road, we reckon the first cost to be fifty cents and the cost of repairs for the second term of five years twenty-five cents; this makes the cost seventy-five cents a square yard for a term of ten years, or seven and one-half cents a square yard a year, a saving of two and one-half cents a square yard annually in favor of the macadam road. The above estimates are made with a full knowledge of the facts, and are reasonably accurate.

Next let us assume that the traffic has increased on the above road until the macadam will last but three years, while granite blocks can be put down for two dollars per square yard, and will last for twenty years. In this case the granite will cost ten cents a square yard annually, and the macadam about sixteen and one-half cents for repairs, a saving of about six and one-half cents a yard annually in favor of the highest first cost. If we should take into account the interest on the outlay, at say four per cent., the granite would cost eight cents a square yard a year additional, or eighteen cents a square yard in all.

In the case of the gravel road the interest would apply to the first fifty cents for twenty years, or eight per cent. of the whole, while the last fifty cents would be an interest for but two years. The mean interest would amount to seven and nine-tenths cents a year on each square yard, thus bringing up the annual cost of gravel, including interest, to twenty-four and two-fifths cents, against eighteen cents for the granite, or an annual saving of six and two-fifths cents a square yard in favor of the granite.

In a large part of Plymouth and Bristol counties the surface is covered with sand. Attempts have been made, and with varying degrees of success, to harden these roads by the use of clay. An effort was made at the hearings held by the commission to ascertain the cost of this class of work. No exact information was to be had, but a fairly accurate estimate has been made from the quantity of material used, the length of haul and cost of labor and teams; this we find to be fifteen cents a square yard for first cost, with renewal in about five years, or three cents a square yard annually. A good macadam road can be constructed for sixty cents a square yard; taking into consideration the small amount of travel, and that the road is estimated to last twenty years with hardly any repairs, the annual cost will be three cents per square yard, or the same in each case.

Through certain parts of the Connecticut River valley a poor quality of sandy gravel is hauled for considerable distances, and its cost when delivered on the road must be almost as much as broken trap rock, from Mt. Tom or Mt. Holyoke. No just comparison can be made between these gravel roads and macadam, as at no time is the gravel road in a condition to give first-class results. From testimony given at the hearings, a two-horse load of gravel delivered on the road costs from one dollar to one dollar twenty-five cents a load of about one and a quarter cubic yards. A road made six inches in depth at this price would cost from thirteen to twenty-five cents a square yard. More or less new gravel has to be put on each year, and it is safe to say that at the end of each five years an amount equal to the original depth has been used. This brings the total cost from about ten and six-tenths to five cents a square yard annually. If a macadam road could be built of broken stone that will cost two dollars sixty-eight cents per cubic yard of metal on the road, including steam rolling, the cost for each square yard would be about forty-seven cents. A road built in such a manner would easily withstand the traffic common to localities removed from the business centres for twenty years, with slight repairs during that time. This would make the annual cost per square yard about two and one-third cents. By these estimates the macadam road in a term of twenty years will cost from about one-quarter cent to two and thirteen-twentieths cents per square yard less annually than the gravel road.

The same argument could be continued by a comparison between trap rock as the best metalling for macadam roads, or mica schist the poorest. With light traffic in a district abounding in the poorer material it might be shown to be economy to use it. On the other hand, if the traffic was known to be heavy, it would probably cost less in a term of years to use the best of trap rock, although it might have to be shipped a long distance by rail.

Illustrations such as those already given could be indefinitely multiplied, but a sufficient number have been presented to make the meaning clear.

The advantage of a good road as to conveniences, and the increased work which can be performed by each horse, we have left to be discussed in another part of this report.

The Effect of Traffic upon the Endurance of the Roadway, and the Legislation pertaining thereto. — Study of Tires.

As the main aim of a road is to withstand the destructive effect which wheels may bring upon it, it is obvious that it is important to consider the conditions of these instruments of destruction. There is a general opinion to the effect that the state of our roads may be improved by compelling the adoption of wider tires. Many persons have suggested to the commissioners that the first step towards the improvement of our roads should be taken through legislation having this end in view.

Fortunately for the consideration of this problem, the subject is one of the oldest and most thoroughly discussed of all those which pertain to highways. More than a century ago the authorities of Great Britain undertook to improve their public roads, which were then in much the state of our own at the present day, by legislation concerning the width of tires. This earlier legislation proceeded on the theory that the roads can be preserved, and in a certain measure improved, by insisting upon wheels so wide upon the tread that they would not make deep ruts even in a soft roadway.

The prevailing sentiment throughout our State at the present time corresponds to the belief in England at that early day. The weight of evidence is, however, strongly opposed to the supposition that any benefit results by the use of wide tires as a road-building agency. Mr. Homer, writing in 1767, said: "Broad-wheeled carriages are found to be so unadapted to the purposes of husbandry, the number of horses requisite for their draught so great, and the beneficial

Ore Team, Charlemont, 1892.

Four-inch tire, 956 pounds' weight on each inch of width of tire.

PLATE A.

Coal Team, Chelsea, 1892.
Three-inch tire, 1,333 pounds' weight on each inch of width of tire.

effects of them to the roads so questionable, that neither the encouragements on the one hand, or the discouragements on the other, have been sufficient to bring them into general use."

Macadam, writing in 1822, said: "The advantages of many existing regulations respecting wheeled carriages may very well be questioned. There can be no doubt that many of these regulations are oppressive to commerce and agriculture by compelling an inconvenient construction of carriages. When the Legislature shall have provided the means of putting all the roads in the United Kingdom into the best and fittest state for the accommodation of the agriculture and commerce of the country, they will naturally consider the most proper modes of protecting them from injury."

Thomas Codington, for twenty-five years in charge of the roads in Wales, said: "Increased toll on narrow wheels did not prevent their use, nor the carrying of heavy loads on them."

"The general laws were repealed in Wales in 1844, and in 1878 the 'Highway and Locomotive Act' gave power to county authorities to make by-laws regulating the width of wheels in proportion to the weight carried, and the power has been generally exercised. Effort has been made restricting the weight carried on wheels of less than four and one-half inches. It is certain that narrow wheels cause the greatest damage to roads, but it is difficult to enforce by-laws against them."

In the opinion of the commission, broad tires cannot be considered in the light of road-building engines, though they may certainly be reckoned under the head of preservers of good roads. As an illustration of this, we wish to call especial attention to the two pictures herewith presented (see Plate A). The first represents a four-inch tire bearing up a load of 956 pounds per inch in width of tire, the second a three-inch tire loaded to 1,348 pounds per inch in width on the rear wheels. In the first case the ruts are about sixteen inches deep, while in the second case the heavy load per inch rests directly on the surface. The first road was not properly built, and failed to bear up the load. The heavy wheels press down the gravel until a solid bearing is secured, and the wheels must pass in a single rut. The second road is built of broken trap rock properly laid and firmly rolled, and has stood this continuous wear with no repairs for nearly five years. This illustration is given simply to show that the road must be first properly built in order to receive any benefit from wide tires.

An extended experience in Great Britain and in other European countries has led the trained roadmasters of the old world to the conclusion that with roadways of poor surface, made up of materials so imperfectly united that they will not uphold a considerable weight, it is advantageous to have the tires of wagons which are to carry a heavy burden of a width to a certain extent commensurate with the load hauled; on a well-constructed road the width of the tire is a matter of relatively small importance.

The French engineers, Morin and Depuit, agree that on a solid macadamized road, in a good state of repair, there is no difference due to the work of tires in the amount that can be hauled by a given team. Macadam, writing in 1822, said that "when roads are properly made very few regulations are necessary for their preservation." He further said, "I have never observed any great difference of effect of a well-made road by narrow or broad wheels;" and still further, "a well-made road may wear thin and weak, but never rough, stony or uneven." On the other hand, the same authorities unite in saying that when the surface is uneven and stony the wider tire offers less resistance to the passage of a wagon.

From our own observation and from the testimony in different parts of the State the wider tires offer many advantages which should commend their use to teamsters in general. There can be no question but that on the ordinary roads larger loads can be hauled with less strain upon the horses and less outlay for repairs on the equipments.

In this connection it may be well to refer to the evidence given by Mr. George W. Gale, lumber merchant of Cambridge, which is set forth in the report of testimony given before the commission at its Middlesex County hearing.

It seems to be commonly believed that the most important element in the form of wheel is the width of tire. In general, however, the diameter of the circle of the wheel is probably equally important, as indicated by the following statements. The French engineer, Morin, has shown by a series of experiments that with an equal load and on the same roadway a wheel six feet eight inches in diameter made but slight trace on its passage over the section of the road, while a wheel four feet nine inches in diameter cut deep ruts, and one ten and a half inches in diameter yet deeper ruts.

A further experiment, in which the diameter of the wheel and load were the same, but with different widths of tires, shows that the tire two and four-tenths inches wide caused nearly double the wear of the four and six-tenths inch tire. These experiments also show that a tire four and six-tenths inches wide causes no more damage than one seven inches wide. The general testimony on this point is that above four and one-half inches in width often there is no special advantage or saving in wear on the road.

Experiments at the Royal Agricultural Show at Bedford, England, in 1874, showed that it required a pull of one pound in moving thirty-five and one-tenth pounds resting on wheels three feet five inches in diameter, and the same force moved fifty-eight and seven-tenths pounds on wheels five feet in diameter. This shows that the resistance increases very nearly inversely as the diameter; that is, a load on a wheel six feet in diameter can be moved with one-half the force needed to move the same load on a wheel three feet in diameter. This difference is very largely caused by the greater bearing surface offered by the large wheel, and the consequent less sinking down into the road. As the sinking down is what destroys a road, the above agrees with our former statement. It appears probable that an additional foot in the diameter of the wheel is in general of much more importance as regards the effect on the roadway than an additional inch on the width of the tire.

The reason for this difference in the wearing effect in wheels of different diameters will be apparent on the inspection of the appended diagram (Figure 1), from which it will be perceived that a wheel of small diameter has to cut very much deeper into the road to win a certain amount of bearing surface than the broad wheel. In general, it may be said that on ordinary roads every vehicle has to bear down the surface to a certain depth as it passes, and this in order to bring enough of the tire in contact with the road to uphold the load. On a well-constructed road this down bearing may not exceed the elasticity of the road-bed, so that it quickly springs back to its place as the wheel goes on. On an ill-constructed road the same weight brings about crushing, or displacement of the road materials, in which case the bed does not return to its previous position. It is easily seen that this effect concerns not only the endurance of the road, but the cost of pulling a given weight over it. In any case, the progress of a wagon over a road, even if the road be perfectly level, is a process of going up hill. The aim is to make this grade as little as possible, and this can only be effected by having a road-bed so firm that it will only sink beneath the tread of the wheels to the measure of its elasticity; this, be it said, it would do even though the surface were of cast steel.

A good illustration of the point above made is to be found in the familiar experience of how much greater load a given pulling force will move on a railway than on an ordinary road. On a level surface a pair of horses will pull, if the load rests on a railway, several times as much as on a stone-paved surface, the difference in the two cases being determined in the main by a sinking of the wheels under the weight.

It is also important to note the fact that, although with roads in fair condition a considerable width of tire is desirable, both from the point of view of the man who owns the team and the people who have to pay for the repairs, when the road is very soft the narrow tire may be advantageous. When a road is in the soft condition so common in imperfect ways, when the frost is leaving the ground, it is best that the wheel should cut down to whatever hard foundation there may be, rather than to struggle with the soft material, which is in its way; even with the wide tire, the bearing surface is pretty certain to descend to the base of the softened mass. In these conditions the narrow tire, because of the small section it presents to the mud, cuts its way more easily, and moreover it lifts relatively little mud in the spaces between the spokes as it revolves. On the other hand, the broad tire, because of the width of its sections, the large amount of mud lifted up and in general its adhesion thereto, is very disadvantageous. It is indeed often possible to take a load over a muddy roadway on narrow-tired wheels, where it would be almost impossible to drag a broad-tired wagon.

It appears to your commissioners a matter of doubtful expediency to endeavor, in the present state of our highways, by general legislation to control the width of tires or the diameter of wheels. It is clearly in the power of the cities and towns to pass ordinances which shall be suited to their particular conditions, if it appears to them well to do so. Thus, as in the case of many of our towns where the roads are worn by excessively heavy loads drawn from particular manufactories, the local government can practically at its discretion pass limitation acts. Experience, however, shows that such laws are rarely enforced.

In view of the exceeding diversity in the conditions of the roadways of the Commonwealth, it seems to the commissioners almost impossible to frame a general law concerning vehicles which would suit the needs of the Commonwealth, and which can be enforced. By reference to the tables, which set forth the character of the wagons in the various cities of Massachusetts, it will be seen that the owners of teams have adopted a great many locally peculiar arrangements, which clearly suit the conditions which they have to meet. In other words, the work of teaming in the Commonwealth has attained a very remarkable specialization, which represents a great deal of unconscious labor, skill and experiment, and which has brought the industry of conveying burdens by means of teams to a higher state than it appears to have reached in any other country. In fact, one of the most noteworthy features in the present situation is that with this great skill as applied to carriages so little has been done in the way of roads. It may be worth while to extend this digression by calling attention to the point that the reason why the wagons and other carriages of Massachusetts have obtained a perfection of development unknown elsewhere, the roads at the same time remaining in deplorable condition, is to be found in the fact that the wagon is, as regards its qualities, determined by the skill and foresightfulness of one or two individuals, by the manufacturer who builds it and the teamster who uses it, while the roadway depends upon considerations which in all cases demand a difficult kind of co-operation on the part of the whole community.

In considering the question of changing the width of tires on our wagons, attention should be given to the fact that the cost of effecting this change, even if a good many years were allowed for its accomplishment, would be considerable. There are probably not less than fifty thousand wagons now in use in this Commonwealth which would have to undergo alteration, at a cost of about twenty dollars each, or a total of somewhere near a million dollars, — a sum sufficient to construct about two hundred miles of road of the kind which would not be likely to suffer from any width of tires used upon them.

In view of the facts above set forth, which can be almost indefinitely amplified, your commissioners do not think it well to recommend any legislation concerning the conditions of the tires of vehicles. They are of the opinion that in proportion as our roads are brought into a proper state the tire question will become unimportant.

CHAPTER V.

Methods of Construction.

City Streets.

It is not the purpose of the commission, as it was evidently not the intention of the Legislature, that any great amount of its work should be devoted to the discussion of city ways. This subject is one of exceeding complication, and in general it can be said to have been elaborately and effectively dealt with by the engineers of the municipalities within the Commonwealth. The types of construction which are now in use in our high-traffic ways, and which are for one reason or another worth consideration in this report, may be generally classified as follows: —

First. Sectional pavements, including stone blocks, wood blocks, brick and asphalt blocks.

Second. Sheet pavements, including macadam, asphalt and concrete.

In general it may be said that there are three classes of highways in this Commonwealth, each of which is characterized by several general conditions which may be made the basis of some advice as to plans of construction. These classes are as follows: —

First. City streets on which traffic is of the first order, and where the action of the weather, on account of the necessary methods of construction, may be represented by zero and traffic by three.

Second. Main rural highways occupied by traffic of the second order, where the action of the weather on the highway may be represented by one and that of the traffic by two.

Third. By-ways or town roads, where the effect of the weather may be represented by three and that directly due to the traffic by zero.

1. *City Streets, with Traffic of the First Order, where the Wear due to the Weather is Zero, and that due to the Traffic is Three.*

These streets are divided into three grades, viz., heavy business traffic, light business traffic and residential street traffic.

The heavy-traffic streets are those which carry heavily loaded teams, and require a pavement which will not only withstand the direct wear of the wheels and horses, but which shall have a foundation sufficiently strong to uphold the heaviest loads that may be hauled over it.

A study of city streets will show that as we pass from the business centres the volume of traffic diminishes, although its character remains the same. When the only question to be considered is the most economical pavement, without regard to the comfort of the abutting property owners, granite blocks unquestionably should be used on all streets of heavy traffic. We have already referred to the volume of traffic observations on Broadway or Salem Turnpike where it crosses Chelsea Bridge, and to the fact that the repairs on this pavement were made necessary by constant excavations rather than from the traffic. The street is paved with granite blocks four inches by seven inches and seven inches deep, laid on a bed of gravel seven inches thick. No effort was made to compact the foundation by rolling. With a daily traffic of about 1,459 tons, or forty tons per foot in width of street, this pavement retained its shape very well for nearly twenty years; the wear on the granite blocks, during this term, with a traffic of forty tons per foot per diem, was not such as to affect their value for further use. The gravel foundation was found to be ample to support that burden of traffic.

Taking the above-mentioned facts into consideration, we might say that, up to a traffic of forty tons per foot in width of street, a gravel foundation for granite blocks is sufficient. We are not prepared to state how much beyond this volume of traffic gravel will remain safe to use, but we can affirm that when the traffic is sufficient to wear the blocks so as to make rounded tops in from ten to fifteen years, something more firm and unyielding than gravel must be used for a foundation. We thus find a necessity of dividing our heavy-traffic streets into two grades, — first, those where a gravel foundation may be used; second, those which should be founded on concrete or broken stone.

Method of Constructing with Granite Blocks on Solid Foundation.

All clay or earth should be removed to a depth of fourteen inches below the proposed finished surface. The bed should be carefully graded to the shape of the proposed street; gravel should be spread on the foundation course, if needed to mix with the natural foundation, in order to get a firm bottom, and thoroughly rolled with a heavy roller. Gravel should then be laid on to a depth of seven inches, the upper two inches being free from large stones; the best effect is obtained if it is screened through a two and one-half inch mesh. The blocks are to be laid in parallel rows across the street; they are to be carefully rammed until the bed is solid and the surface even. The surface is then to be covered with sand or gravel sifted through a one-inch screen, which is swept into the joints with a stiff rattan broom. The rammers are again to be used to correct any inequality, and the whole surface is to be covered with sand or screened gravel; it is then ready for traffic.

Where concrete or broken stone is to be used the foundation should be shaped and rolled in the manner as already described, only instead of gravel a bed of concrete or stone six inches thick is to be used. The concrete should be made of good American cement, sharp, clean sand and screenings from gravel banks, or, in place of screenings, broken stone may be used; the mixture should be made by measure, in the proportion of one part cement, two parts sand, five parts stone. The cement and sand are to be first thoroughly mixed while dry, and then water is to be added and the mass turned over and over until it is completely mingled and thoroughly wet. The mortar thus formed is to be carefully mixed with the stone by turning the materials over with shovels. The concrete is then to be thrown into the trench and shaped by the use of "templets" and "straight-edges," and then rammed to the proper grade and until the water "flushes" to the surface. About one inch of sand is then to be spread on the concrete, and on this the granite blocks are to be set, as before. The blocks are to be carefully rammed, so as to give an even surface. The joints are then to be filled to within about one inch of the top with screened gravel which has been passed through a three-quarter inch but will not pass through a quarter-inch screen. The gravel is thoroughly heated just before using, and, while hot, "paving pitch" melted and brought to a temperature of about 300° F. is to be run in until the joint is filled. The street is then ready for travel. Although at times gravel is spread on the paving pitch, its use is not to be recommended.

If broken stone is to be used, the foundation is to be rolled as before, the stone placed in position and rolled with a steam roller until fairly well compacted. Screenings are then to be spread over the surface, thoroughly watered and rolled until a firm, unyielding surface is obtained. One inch of sand is then to be laid on, the blocks set and rammed; the joints filled with hot gravel and pitch as before described. It requires about three to four gallons of pitch per square yard of pavement. The blocks generally used are three and one-half to four and one-half inches wide, eight to twelve inches long and seven and one-half to eight inches deep, requiring on the average about twenty-three to the square yard.

The concrete costs about five dollars a cubic yard, or eighty-three cents per square yard of pavement. The broken stone rolled, in place, will cost about forty-five to fifty cents a square yard of pavement.

The finished pavements on the average will cost as follows: —

Granite blocks on gravel, ...	$2 25
Granite blocks on broken stone, ...	2 75
Granite blocks on concrete (about), ...	3 75

2. Residential Streets with Considerable Traffic.

In selecting the pavement for a residential street, not only the character and volume of traffic has to be considered, but the demands of the residents as to cleanliness and freedom from noise.

The pavements most used for residential streets are sheet asphalt, asphalt blocks, wood blocks and brick.

Sheet asphalt, either "Trinidad" or "rock," affords the nearest approach to an ideal pavement which has as yet been found. It offers the least resistance to travel, and, being jointless, makes but little noise; moreover, it allows all filth to be readily washed off, so as to leave a surface free from mud in wet, or dust in dry, weather. The only fault to be found with this material is its cost and slipperiness. The high cost of construction, as well as the outlay for annual repairs, places it in the list of luxuries, and it will probably only be extensively used in sections closely occupied by well-to-do people.

The slipperiness of asphalt pavement precludes its use on any street with a heavy grade. On a grade of more than one and three-fourths to two feet to the hundred it should not be used. The "Trinidad" asphalt is less slippery than the "rock," for the reason that the sand used in its manufacture does not glaze to such an extent as the limestone which makes up the body of the "rock." Less fault is found on this ground with asphalts in districts where such pavements abound, as the horses then become more used to it, and learn how to keep their feet.

The foundations for both "Trinidad" and "rock" asphalt pavements are to be made by the use of six inches of concrete, in the same manner as already described for granite block pavement. The greatest possible care must be observed in rolling and shaping the earth foundation, as a lack of this support means a possible failure of the whole structure.

The concrete must be allowed to dry for a few days before the asphalt is put on. Trinidad asphalt as used for paving is a mixture of refined asphalt from Pitch Lake in the Island of Trinidad and sand. The refining consists of heating the crude asphalt for five days over a slow fire, at a temperature not too high, expelling the moisture. The roots of trees and other vegetable matter are skimmed from the surface, the earthy matter settles to the bottom, and the refined product is run off into barrels. The mixture when ready for use on the street should be in the shape of a powder heated to a temperature of about 250° F., and contains, besides refined asphalt, residuum of petroleum oil, fine sand and carbonate of lime.

First an asphalt cement is made by mixing the refined asphalt and residuum of petroleum oil in the proportion of one hundred parts of asphalt and thirteen to twenty parts of petroleum. The petroleum must first be freed from impurities, brought to a specific gravity of 18° to 22° Beaume, and a fire test of 250° F. The sand cannot contain more than one per cent. of hydrosilicate of alumina, and must all pass through a No. 10 screen (ten meshes to the inch) and none of it through a No. 80 screen. The asphaltic cement must have a specific gravity of 1.19 at 60° F., and stand a fire test of 250° F. The paving mixture is made up of asphaltic cement, twelve to fifteen parts, sand seventy to eighty-three parts, and carbonate of lime five to fifteen parts. The process of mixing is as follows: the sand, heated to about 300° F., is mixed with the cold carbonate of lime. The sand

and carbonate of lime mixture while hot is to be mixed with the asphaltic cement, heated to about 300° F.

The paving mixture is to be brought in a close cart to the street at a temperature of about 250° F., and dumped where needed. Hot rakes are to be used to level the surface until it is even and of the proper thickness, which should when finished be two and a half inches thick.

The gutter should first be rammed with hot rammers and then ironed with a hot "smoothing iron." The joints should be ironed in the same manner as the gutter. The whole surface is then to be rolled by passing a five-hundred-pound cold hand roller twice over it. To prevent its sticking to the asphalt, the surface of the roller is to be slightly oiled by the use of a rag dipped in kerosene oil and applied by hand as the roller passes back and forth. To prevent the asphalt sticking to the steam roller, and to give a more pleasing appearance, the surface of the street is then swept with Portland cement, or fine clean sand, and afterwards a roller weighing five tons is passed back and forth over the work, first lengthwise and then crosswise, until the asphalt is hard. The surface is to be made perfectly even and true by the use of hot irons and "tamps" between the light and heavy rolling.

The gutters for about two feet in width are to be painted over with hot "paving pitch," applied by ordinary house brooms. During all the processes of rolling care must be taken to "break joints," in order to prevent the formation of ridges and to secure an even surface.

In some work it has been specified that a roller should give a pressure of not less than two hundred and fifty pounds to the inch, and that the surface should be rolled not less than five hours to each one thousand square yards. This requirement is practically abandoned, and the present practice is to roll continuously until no further impression is made on the surface.

The cost of Trinidad sheet asphalt as above described is about $3.50 per square yard in and about Boston. There are three and two-tenths miles of such asphalt now in use in Boston, and none in any other city of the State. Rock asphalt was not used in any part of the State as a street pavement before 1891. During this year one or two streets were paved with natural rock from Kentucky, and in

1892 two streets were paved with the Sicilian rock asphalt. Throughout Europe the rock asphalt is used extensively, and has given considerable satisfaction. It is used in a limited way in one or two American cities. The rock asphalt has all been laid on a six-inch concrete foundation, prepared and laid in the same manner as already described for granite rock pavement.

The method of laying rock asphalt is as follows: the rock is first broken into pieces from two to three inches through by a stone crusher with smooth jaws. These pieces are reduced to a fine granular shape by passing through rollers. The powder is heated to about 250° F. when dumped upon the street. Two scantlings three inches thick are laid down on the concrete foundation about twelve feet apart, their ends being sprung down to the concrete and held there by iron pins driven through the concrete into the ground.

The heap of asphalt is next levelled off with hot shovels, and the surface and thickness regulated by "straight-edges" worked on the scantlings. All hollow places are filled by shovelling on more of the powder. When the top surface is adjusted the junction with finished work is made by the use of hot "joint irons" in the hands of an experienced workman. The whole section is then rolled with a three-hundred-pound roller, usually warmed by a small fire in a pan suspended from the axle inside the roller. The gutters are then made true by a special heated iron. The whole section is then rammed by hot irons weighing about fifty pounds. Eight of these rammers are used, and the men, beginning at the outside, pass around each section four times. The first ramming is light, the others are successively heavier, and in the last the rammers are used with the full strength of the men. A heavy nine-hundred-pound iron roller is then used, and the whole section is thus made smooth. The completed surface is very hard, and can be used as soon as the asphalt is cold. The cost of rock asphalt as laid in Boston was about $3.55 to $3.75 per square yard.

The composition of rock asphalt is so complex that so far time alone has established the value of any particular mine. The usual English and French practice is to specify that the asphalt shall be furnished from some mine the product of which is known to be good.

There is one other kind of sheet pavement which at one time gave great promise, and which was extensively used in Washington and to a less extent in other parts of the country, and that is "tar concrete." This pavement was made of coarse stones coated with coal tar at the bottom, a coat of concrete made of stones and mineral pitch, and a wearing coat of mastic made of a mixture of sand and mineral pitch. This preparation, with slight modification as to thickness and bottom course, is now extensively used for sidewalks and street crossings, where it often gives satisfaction.

The mineral pitch is made by the distillation of coal-gas tar to the point of removing all water and the lighter oils and a certain proportion of the heavier oils. If the process is carried too far the product becomes hard and brittle, and during cold weather is liable to break up. If it is not carried far enough it is soft and sticky, and a pavement containing it will become irregular; this is particularly the case in warm weather. The tendency of the present practice is to remove a little more of the oils than was the practice heretofore, and correct by adding crude coal tar.

All products of coal tar are subject to oxidation by the atmosphere, which renders them brittle and devoid of cementing qualities. They are also affected by changes of temperature, and become friable in cold weather and soft in warm. In the present stage of manufacture, where water gas is being substituted largely for coal gas, the quantity of coal-gas tar produced is diminishing, its price is increasing and its quality is deteriorating. Under these conditions the chances of poor work are much greater than in former years. In view of the failures when relatively good materials were easily obtained at a lower price than at present, it will readily be seen that the slight possible saving in cost arising from the use of tar-concrete will hardly warrant its application to street work. (Specifications for tar-concrete paving are to be found in the Appendix.)

Asphalt blocks are used to a slight extent, and in many respects make a good pavement. In our cold climate the blocks do not run together, as they are often found to do in a warmer climate. The edges are very liable to chip off under the horses' shoes, and a general tendency of the blocks to crack has been observed; the roughening of the surface thus produced tends to make the footing for horses more secure, but it is slightly more noisy and less cleanly than sheet asphalt.

The experience with this class of pavement in Chicago was that it gave a firm footing but was not satisfactory, being too expensive and uncertain, and no more of it is being laid. In Washington asphalt blocks laid on coarse gravel and sand, thoroughly compacted, are still good after an almost continual use of twelve to fourteen years, and will last a long time.

In Boston certain streets have been paved with asphalt blocks, and one advantage claimed for them is that they can be easily replaced after openings for any kind of pipes have been made through the surface. It is asserted in Boston that it is not so durable as is the sheet asphalt.

Two methods have been employed in laying this class of pavement in Massachusetts, viz., on a gravel and on a concrete foundation.

When laid on a gravel foundation, the same method of procedure should be employed as in the case of granite blocks, only more care should be exercised in compacting the bottom; "barring" and tamping have to be resorted to, in order to thoroughly settle doubtful spots, in addition to the heavy steam rolling. There should be laid on the gravel a layer of sand three to four inches deep, which is to be brought to the exact form of the proposed street surface by the use of short strips of board placed about six feet apart across the street. The blocks are to be then laid in parallel rows across the street, and rammed to a solid bed by two rammings. The first ramming is done before any sand is spread on top of the blocks. The second ramming is done after covering the surface with sand and sweeping it into the joints. The whole surface is then covered with about a half inch of sand, which the travel works into the joints. The ramming is done with the lighter wooden rammers, the blow being delivered on a plank, which is laid crosswise of the street during the first ramming and lengthwise during the second.

In the case of a concrete foundation being used, the methods and materials are the same as used in laying the granite blocks, except that the concrete bed is but four inches thick. There should be a layer of sand laid on the concrete, carefully shaped as before described. The blocks are to be laid and rammed, as on the gravel bed.

The cost of paving with asphalt blocks on a gravel foundation is about \$3.40 to \$3.60 per square yard; on the concrete bed its cost is about \$4.15 per square yard.

So far as the commission has been able to ascertain, there does not at the present time exist any wood pavement on a public way in Massachusetts. The city of Boston has from time to time since 1848 tried experiments with different kinds of such pavement, but gradually these have been replaced by other materials.

The abandonment of wood pavements is not peculiar to Massachusetts, but is characteristic of the eastern portion of the United States. Wood was once more or less used as paving material in New York City, Philadelphia and Washington, as well as the greater part of the large cities of this country. In the above-named cities its use has ceased; in the central and western portions of the country it has diminished, and only in Chicago do we find that this material still remains in favor to any extent. The continuance of wooden pavements in Chicago is doubtless to be explained by the fact that the material which could be used for macadam roads which lies near that city is of poor quality; good stone blocks are hard to procure, having to be brought from a great distance; while wood, which can be brought by water carriage plentifully, exists in that part of the country.

Experience has shown that wooden pavements to have any permanent value must be constructed with great care and at much cost. The expense of such construction, at least in this Commonwealth, makes it undesirable that any further essays in its use should be undertaken.

In general, it may be said that in this part of the country asphalt, either in the sheet form or in that of blocks, is less costly, both as regards original construction and maintenance, and quite as satisfactory, as the wooden pavement.

Below will be found a somewhat detailed statement, setting forth the conditions under which a cedar block pavement, of the highest grade of the wood types, should be prepared: —

The foundations for the cedar block pavement are to be made by the use of concrete in the same manner as already described for granite block pavement.

Upon the foundation prepared as above set forth, a cedar block pavement consisting of one course of blocks is to be laid. Each block shall be of the best quality of selected, sound red cedar, entirely free in all cases from loose knots, cracks and any signs of decay. They shall be entirely stripped of bark, trimmed truly cylindrical in shape, and shall measure not less than five inches nor more than nine inches in diameter. They shall be sawed at right angles to their central axes, making parallel faces, and uniform lengths of six inches. A sufficient number only of the largest blocks shall be split in halves and used along the lines of the curbs and longitudinal crosswalks.

In forming the pavement the blocks must be carefully set in place, properly resting on their bases in close contact with each other, and must be kept well driven together, that each block may be firm in its position. The pavement must be carried uniformly across the entire width of the roadway, and to that end the blocks must be selected, using an average mixture of the various sizes.

Blocks having the same diameter should in no case be set in rows across the street; the various sizes are to be alternately intermingled with each other, and each block shall have a full-length close contact with at least three other adjoining blocks.

After the blocks have been placed in accurate positions, they must be thoroughly settled to the correct grade of the surface of the completed pavement, by a system of ramming or tamping with mauls weighing not less than fifty pounds, each having a flat bottom not less than twelve inches in diameter. Each block must be driven to a firm and solid bed, and when they have been thoroughly settled into place, the surface of the pavement thus completed must be even and smooth throughout and moulded to conform to the different structures, street, alley and driveway intersections, drainage details, and the properly established grade lines. No split blocks should be used except along the line of curbstones and crosswalks.

All spaces existing in the pavement shall be filled with gravel, thoroughly rammed in with iron rammers, to a point three inches below the surface of the pavement. The remaining portion of the various spaces shall then be filled with hot gravel, also thoroughly rammed with iron rammers, and immediately thereafter, before the gravel cools, each and every joint existing in the pavement must be filled full to the surface of the pavement with hot paving cement, the same being carefully poured from a vessel having a small spout. The gravel to be used will consist throughout of clean, screened material, not less than one-fourth inch and not more than three-fourths inch in diameter.

The pavement shall be then swept clean, and the entire surface be covered with hot paving cement to a depth limited by the amount required to fully cover the same, followed immediately thereafter, while the cement is yet hot, with a coating of clean, coarse sand, to a uniform depth of one-fourth inch in thickness.

The paving cement is best when made of ten per cent. of refined Trinidad asphalt mixed with coal-tar cement distilled at a temperature of not less than 600° F. The composition is to be used at a temperature of not less than 300° F., determined by a gauge constantly attached to the cement tank while in use on the street.

The wood pavement as above described will cost about $3.30 to $3.60 per square yard. The cost of wood pavement without concrete foundation will be about $2.50 to $2.75 per square yard.

Many wood pavements are laid on gravel or plank foundations, but such practice is, in face of past experience, hardly safe to follow. A special commission, appointed by the city of Boston, reported in 1873 that "the foundation is indispensable for making good pavement. A flooring of one or two inches thick is not stiff enough to carry heavy loads over loose places, and when there are soft places the pavement soon cripples. No wood flooring will keep the pavement in permanently good condition."

A. M. Hirsch, civil engineer and engineer for Board of Public Works, Chicago, in a recent report has said: "The life of wood pavement depends to an important extent on the foundation; and I venture to say that live oak, white pine or cedar, on a hydraulic concrete foundation not less than six inches thick, with water-tight joints, made by a grouting composed of three parts of clean sand and one part Portland cement, judiciously laid and taken care of, will give good economic results. Unless the foundation is rigid, it is impossible to preserve a sound pavement."

The city of Berlin has practically discontinued the use of wood pavements, on account of slipperiness.

The Board of Public Works of New York City in their report of 1891 said, "Wood pavements are an expensive luxury."

Col. Wm. Heywood, engineer and surveyor to the commission, London, in his report of 1888 said: "About forty years ago many of the principal thoroughfares of the city were paved with wood, most of which pavements, from a misplaced ingenuity, and complication in design, proved unsatisfactory. Nearly the whole of them were taken up a few years afterwards. In 1853 but eight streets remained which were paved with wood." By the same report there appears to have been in 1888 six miles of wooden pavement.

Brick Pavements.

Very little brick pavement has been constructed in Massachusetts. Boston has three streets and Springfield one which are paved with this material. The work has been done for so short a time that no judgment as to its fitness for this region can as yet be passed upon it. During the past few years a great many cities throughout the country have been using brick pavements, and the general report seems to be that this method of construction has given satisfaction.

It appears likely that on streets which have to bear a heavy traffic pavements made of brick will be found insufficiently enduring. On light-traffic streets, whenever proper care has been exercised in the construction, it has given thoroughly satisfactory results throughout the entire West and South. When there has been a lack of care in preparing the foundation or in selecting the bricks, an uneven, chipped surface has been the result.

From Bloomington, Ill., and Charleston, W. Va., we have statements that brick pavements have been in constant use for sixteen and eighteen years, with but slight repairs, and are still in good condition.

It is generally believed, but without sufficient inquiry, that clay which is fit for making paving brick does not exist in Massachusetts; experiment alone can determine this; as yet, only those have been used which were either made outside the State or of clay which was brought from other parts of the country. These conditions add nearly forty per cent. to the first cost of the brick, and, as will be shown in the case of Springfield, this amounts to nearly thirty-two cents per square yard of pavement. Unless suitable clay can be found in our own State, the cost of brick pavement will be very nearly if not quite as great as that of granite blocks. The uncertainty of securing brick which have been burned to an equal hardness and the comparatively high cost of the completed pavement will limit its use to purely residential streets, where cleanliness and noiselessness are desired, at a comparatively low cost.

We give below a description of a street in Springfield, which last year was paved with brick, together with the cost of the work.

Description of Brick Pavement as Constructed in Springfield by W. L. Dickinson, Superintendent of Streets (1892).

The pavement was laid on a street occupied by residences only; the grade was slight. Two courses of brick were put down; those used in the bottom course were made in Springfield; those of the top course in Syracuse, N. Y. The bottom course was laid flat, and the top course on edge. The area covered was 1,697 square yards. The bed, which was quartz sand, was first graded so as to conform to the proposed surface, and rolled with a fifteen-ton steam roller until it was solid and even. Sand was then laid on to the depth of one inch; on this was placed a course of hard-burned, common brick, laid flatways. These were rammed with wooden "rammers," weighing about thirty pounds each.

On top of this course of brick, and lengthwise of the street, three strips of inch battens were placed, — one in each gutter and one in the centre. The whole surface was then covered with sand; this was brought to an even thickness of one inch by means of wooden "templets," which were cut on a curve to fit the shape of the proposed street, and guided as they were moved, by the strips already referred to. The strips were then taken up and the spaces thus left carefully filled in with sand. The top course of brick was then laid, on edge so as to break joints, and was firmly rammed by a wooden "rammer" weighing eighty pounds, worked by two men; the blow was given on a two-inch plank (eight feet long and ten inches wide), which was moved along by two men.

The whole surface was then swept clean and the joints filled in with Portland cement, with enough water to allow it to run easily.

Cost of Syracuse brick (per thousand),	$11 00
Cost of freight,	4 00
Cost of teaming,	1 00
Cost delivered on street,	$16 00

Cost of common brick on street (per thousand),	$7 00
Cost of sand per cubic yard,	60
Pay of pavers per day,	2 00
Pay of rammers per day, and other labor,	1 50

Cost of Completed Work.

	Total Cost.	Cost per Square Yard.
Syracuse brick (number to square yard), 79.5,	$2,127 58	$1 253
Common brick (number to square yard), 44.79,	532 00	313
Excavating and grading, ...	287 28	170
Cement, 78 barrels, ...	191 10	1126
Cementing, ...	33 75	02
Labor in paving, etc., ...	481 87	283
	$3,653 58	$2 15

Main Rural Highways.

The art of road building consists mainly in constructing a wearing surface which shall be able at all times to bear up the load that may be hauled over it.

The farmer by using very broad tires may be able to haul small loads for a limited number of times over the greensward. If the amount of the load should be increased, the width of the tire decreased, or the vehicle be made to pass repeatedly over the same place, the wheels would soon cut through the sod and softer soil until they reached a comparatively firm foundation. The depth of the ruts thus formed would depend on the character and number of loads hauled, the condition of the soil and the state of the weather.

The above-mentioned conditions are those which should be most carefully noted by those who have to construct any roadway. A light carriage which might do no injury to a dry road would soon destroy it if wet. Water may reach a roadway either by falling as rain directly upon it, by flowing upon it from either side, or by lateral soakage through the ground.

Rain falling directly on the surface will do little or no harm to a well-constructed road, but if it be allowed to attain to and remain in the foundation the road will soon be destroyed. There are two rules which must be observed in order to maintain a road in good condition: first, take the water out; second, keep the water out. If these simple rules are followed, the foundation will be dry and therefore well fitted to uphold the surface, while the surface, being impervious to water at all times and under all conditions, is fitted to withstand the loads it may properly be called upon to bear.

Where sand or gravel underlies a road which is moderately elevated, no special precaution need be taken to carry off the water, as it will quickly pass downward to where it can do no harm. If a road is constructed over clay or loam foundation, then the only safe method will be to put in a suitable drain or drains; if the ground is level or rises on both sides, one drain should be placed on each side; if the road traverses the side of a hill, one drain constructed on the uphill side will cut off all ground water and prevent its passing under the way.

Whatever method of drainage be used, the channels should be connected with either a main drain or watercourse. The coarse stone used as a foundation to a Telford road has served this purpose of drainage admirably well, and may advantageously be used, unless small blind drains can be built to serve the same purpose equally well, at less cost.

Where the ground is wet and much depth of loam or fibrous soil is encountered, it will probably be the safer plan to use the large stones if they are near by and plentiful, which shall serve the double purpose of foundation and drainage. The sub-grade, or the ground on which the large stones rest, should be thoroughly compacted by rolling. If necessary, gravel should be laid on before rolling, to prevent the soil of the sub-grade from pressing up among the large stone. Blind drains should be built by excavating longitudinal trenches from two and a half to three feet deep and ten to twelve inches wide, to be filled in with broken stone, coarse gravel screenings or pebbles. A small porous drain tile is usually placed in the bottom of the trench, the stone to be thoroughly tamped over it, to prevent any further settlement of the surface. In placing the large stone for a Telford road, it should be borne in mind that these are to act as a foundation, and must transfer the weight of the upborne load to the soft sub-grade. They should therefore be placed as close together as possible, and have a good flat face to rest upon. The smaller end or points of the stone should stand up. The spaces that may be left between the stone should be filled in with wedge-shaped bits placed point downward, and driven in solidly. Such points as may project above the proper line should be broken off by hammers. The foundation course must then be evened up by the use of smaller stone, and rolled until no settlement occurs.

In case the road lies upon a heavy clay, it may be safe not only to put in the Telford bottom as already described, but also to build blind drains which shall quickly remove all water from the sub-grade. The finishing of the road will come under the description of macadamizing.

By careful underdraining an otherwise poor material may make a good roadway. The wearing surface may consist of broken stone or gravel.

Gravels are to be found widely distributed over the State which will make a good road, provided the way is in the main to be used by light spring vehicles. Some of the gravels such as those found in Saugus and Lynn are made up of angular pebbles and material which bind the stones so firmly together that they must be picked from the banks with considerable difficulty and labor. This gravel taken from the bank and used directly on the way with no rolling will shortly make a hard, smooth road. Some light-traveled roads made of this gravel in Saugus have been in continuous use for twelve years, with no repairs, and are yet in good condition. In but few cases can our gravel be economically used on the main roads, over which there is much travel.

Nearly all gravel banks now in use contain more or less stone from the size of an egg upward, with quite a large percentage exceeding two and one-half inches in diameter. No stones larger than two and one-half inches through should be used within four inches of the surface in the construction of a road. The general tendency is for these large stone to work to the surface and to make a very rough, uneven road after it has been in use a short time. A good road often can be built of gravel by first screening out all that which will pass through a one-inch screen and will not pass through a three-inch screen.

The foundation should be prepared if necessary by rolling. Screenings should be placed in this bottom and covered about one or two inches thick with a coating of the gravel that has passed through the one-inch screen. This gravel should contain a small proportion of hard pan or soil of some kind as a "binder." The whole roadway should then be rolled with a heavy roller until it becomes hard and smooth. Fine gravel will not make a good road if the travel is at all heavy. The small stones quickly crush up, and the surface of the roads becomes uneven and muddy. It is very doubtful if in a term of years a gravel road will not cost as much as a macadam road, and it can never be as enduring; the wearing surface receives the shock of all traffic; the materials for its construction must be carefully selected.

The fundamental difficulty with all roads made of ordinary gravel is to be found in the fact that the fragments of the material cannot be made to bind together, however well they may be compressed by the use of the roller; the result is that the first condition of the roadway surface which should shed water like a roof is not obtained. The rain penetrates vertically downward through the mass, breaking up what little adhesion may have been brought about in the mass, so that when a heavy team passes over it it is not upheld. The wheels do not penetrate to any great depth in the roadway, but they form ruts, by loss of material which is ground up by that passage. Moreover, this rut becomes a place in which the water is held, and its penetration downward and consequent softening of the roadway insures its destruction.

It is not only the duty of the roadmaster to build well, but it is as much his duty under his conditions to build economically. As a general rule, the main thoroughfares throughout the State can be built and maintained of broken stone for less money than of any other material. We have already described the methods employed in order to secure a good foundation when the road traverses wet ground. By far the greater part of the main roads of the State will require no special provision to be made for their underdrainage. In many localities they traverse ground that is naturally drained. In other places their surfaces have been covered with gravel until it has mingled with the original soil of the way so as to form a solid surface. In these instances a roadway of broken stone from six to nine inches thick can be easily constructed and cheaply maintained.

It may be necessary to remove the existing top in order to make the proposed roadway conform to a desired cross-section. Under no other condition should a hard surface be broken up. If the surface is found to be hard, the broken stone should be put directly upon it; if loose and rutted, it should be first graded to the shape of the proposed roadway and then firmly compacted by the use of a roller. When the material which is to constitute the foundation is found to be too soft to roll, gravel should be laid on until the roller can be properly worked.

If loose sand or gravel be found, which will not compact under the roller, then hard pan, loam or other suitable material should be laid on to the depth of about one inch, to serve as a "binder." The metal should act in a double capacity: first, it should furnish a firm, smooth-wearing surface; second, it should constitute an impervious roof which will prevent the water that may fall upon its surface from reaching the foundation. About forty-seven per cent. of the volume of the broken stone as ordinarily delivered consists of void space.

The process of rolling tends to move the bits of stone back and forth and downward. This process should be continued until the stones are brought as near together as their shapes will permit. The void spaces should be reduced by rolling, from forty-seven per cent. of the volume of the stone to ten or twenty per cent. These remaining spaces should be filled with some substance which shall prevent the bits from moving after they are once firmly placed. If the bottom soil be properly compacted, it will bear up the broken stone during the process of rolling, and the metal will not be pressed into it. After the rolling has been completed and the interspaces of the metal thoroughly filled with the "binder," the roadway will form a barrier between the surface and the foundation.

Following is a description of the methods of building a macadam roadway: —

Broken stone from one to two and one-half inches in diameter should be placed on the compacted bottom to a depth of three or four inches, and the steam roller passed over it four or five times. Then more broken stone of the same size should be laid on to a depth of three to four inches in the centre of the roadway, and two to three inches at the sides. This should be rolled by the steam roller until a hard bit of stone three or four inches in diameter, if it be placed on the surface of the roadway, will be broken by passing the wheel of the roller over it.

When the rolling on the top layer of stone has been about half completed, it is the custom of some road builders to strew sand over the surface as the roller passes back and forth. This sand should be applied until the interspaces are filled. Other road builders lay on screenings from the crusher varying in size from the dust to one-half inch in diameter, to the depth of about one inch. This material should be thoroughly watered and rolled until the dust and smaller bits of stone are worked into the spaces and bind the stone firmly together. The larger pieces will be mixed with the dust that is left; these, uniting together, will form a hard, smooth-wearing surface.

The surface of a roadway should be so shaped as to allow the water to flow quickly into the gutter. If the rise from the gutter is great, the travel is forced to pass along the centre, and this will soon wear down to such an extent that water will stand on the surface of the way. In addition to this, the water will make gullies in the sides of the roadway, which will at all times be a discomfort and often indeed dangerous to travellers. The crown to be given is not to be determined by any fixed rule, but the best roadmasters allow from one-half to an inch on level ground, and as much more on a hill as will allow the water to reach the gutters before it can attain a velocity that will do any harm.

A macadamized road will endure for a longer time if its surface is sprinkled often enough to keep it damp. The screenings when damp possess greater cementing powers, and the stone will not so easily be kicked out by the horses' feet. It must be borne in mind that the covering of screenings should not be expected to do more than bind the metal firmly together.

The dust and sand which will be formed by the action of the wheels on the smaller bits of stone should be quickly removed. If it be allowed to remain, the water will stand on the roadway instead of flowing rapidly into the gutters. The water thus held back will gradually work into the spaces, and loosen the bond between the fragments. If this bond should be disturbed to any extent, the stone will work loose and the roadway soon be destroyed.

In another part of our report will be found a careful description of the kinds of stone which are suited for road construction. These are placed so as to be generally useful. There are a few plants which now furnish broken stone at points where it is needed. Broken stone can unquestionably be furnished in any part of the State at a price not exceeding $1.30 a ton on the cars. If the demand becomes general from towns near together this price may be reduced. Trap rock broken in Meriden, Conn., has been shipped to Springfield at a less cost than that city could produce it from its own crusher. Towns will be found where the stone delivered by rail will have to be teamed over many miles of country roads. The expense of teaming will probably add so much to the cost of the stone that it will be found to be economy to place a crusher in the town. The work required in such cases will, without doubt, be scattered over a large territory, and a portable crusher can be used. This can be located so as to work a distance of about one mile in each direction, with an average haul of about one-half mile. Field or bank stone can be broken by these crushers, and the cost of delivery on the work will be small. We shall give an itemized list of the cost of breaking stone under the different conditions. It will be found, on close examination of the reports from the different towns, as sent to this commission, that there are many cases where gravel of a poor quality is now being used, and that the cost of maintaining the roads is great. An inspection of these gravel roads shows that they are about as poor as they can be.

Macadam, writing eighty years ago, said, "A well-made road can never wear rough and uneven." The road builder of to-day finds this to be true.

Roads as constructed by Macadam were compacted by the teams that passed over them. The results obtained were good, but expensive. The wear and tear on horse and vehicle during the time they were working over the loose stone was very great. In addition to this, it was necessary to have men constantly at work with rakes and shovels to fill the ruts as they began to appear.

Roads which were compacted by the traffic have been carefully examined, and the materials analyzed. In certain instances where metal had originally been used, in pieces varying from one to two inches through, it was found to have been ground up under the wheels and horses' feet so that forty per cent. of it was mud, and less than ten per cent. of the mass was composed of fragments which retained the size they had when originally built into the roadway. The loss incurred from the reduction in the size of the bits which were in the end to be compacted in the roadway has to be added to the other elements of waste incurred where the rolling was left to be done by the wheels. It seems probable that this loss is sufficient to repay the cost of compacting by rollers especially adapted to that purpose.

Road rollers are divided into two essentially different types, — those which are propelled by horses and those which are driven by steam power. The effects arising from the use of these two diverse contrivances differ in an important way. Where a roller is driven by horses, the effect arising from the tread of the animals is to break up the road, or, in other words, neutralize the work for which the roller is used. Where the machine is of sufficient weight to do good work, it requires from four to six horses to keep it in motion, and the consequent disturbance of the way before it has become thoroughly compacted is a very serious hindrance to the prosecution of the work. Moreover, experience shows that a road thus finished by horse roller is pretty sure to have at many points depressions which, though they are for the time filled by fine material, shortly reappear and break the desired perfect smoothness of the way.

In the case of the steam roller, where the power is applied directly to the wheel, we have the advantage that a weight greater than that which can be conveniently drawn by horses can be used, and there are, of course, no such difficulties as are brought about by the action of the horses' feet. Experience, moreover, shows that the cost of running a roller of sufficient weight to compact a surface in a reasonable time is greater where it is propelled by horses than where it is moved by steam. An element of importance is the time required with the two classes of engines. Owing to the relatively great weight of the steam roller, it requires fewer movements over the surface to insure the necessary compaction.

The cost of rolling with a steam roller may, in general, be estimated at from five to ten cents per square yard of the way, while the expense of the same work performed with horses will in most cases be from twenty-five to seventy-five per cent. more than that estimate.

Grades of Massachusetts Roads.

So far as the grades are concerned, the roads of Massachusetts have been generally neglected. In many cases this neglect has been enforced by legislative provisions, as in the case of the Newburyport Turnpike. Nearly all the old turnpikes are in this condition, and as these in their present state of our public ways constitute the larger part of the important avenues of the Commonwealth, the effect of these provisions has been very detrimental.

In general, the alignment of our roads with reference to natural conditions, such as the nature of the under-earth or access to construction materials, has been to a great extent neglected. The information which the commission feel it possible to give in this report concerning the matter of grades is but limited, and this for the reason that all such questions need to be discussed with reference to the particular geographical and physical conditions of the site where the proposed road is to be built.

Very carefully made experiments show that on perfectly level surface the character of the way may very much affect the amount of power required to move a given load: thus, on a smooth paved surface of ordinary character, 33.4 pounds of traction will start a load weighing one ton; on a first-class macadamized road, 44 pounds of traction; on a thin macadam road, with a foundation of somewhat springy nature, 62 pounds; while on a gravel road of good character 140 pounds is required to start the load.

The same facts may be otherwise expressed by the statement that where one horse would pull a load on a good pavement four are required on a gravelly road. These differences in the pulling power required on roads apparently level is in fact due to the existence of slight irregularities, which are in fact grades; that is, they require a load to be drawn up hill. When a road has a measurable incline, the effect is to give a constant element of grade or of difficulty which may be definitely measured by the following rule: to obtain the power necessary to draw any load up any incline, divide the weight of the load by the length of the road with a rise of one foot.

It has been experimentally determined that on a grade of two and one-half per centum, that is, with a rise of two and one-half feet in elevation in a hundred feet of length, the load on ordinary wheels will not run down hill, or, in other words, the team can be stopped without chucking. This seems also to be the grade at which a horse can pull, while moving at a walk, a load of given weight as easily as he can draw it at a trot on a level surface. On these accounts the above-mentioned grade has been accepted by the best roadmasters as that which should be used wherever the expense involved in so doing is not likely to be excessive.

In a similar way, though from less definite sources of determination, engineers have come to the conclusion that grades as steep as five feet in the hundred are about the maximum which should be allowed on any high-class roads.

It is a well-recognized fact that with the increased steepness of road the difficulties arising from the fall of rainwater over its surface are rapidly augmented; it is easily understood that on a sloping roadway the water flowing to the gutter tends to make a longer journey than on one which follows a level. On this account skilled engineers always give a steeper crown on the slope than on the level part of the highway which they are constructing; thus a crown of one-half inch to the foot is deemed sufficient for roads which are on a horizontal surface; the crown is increased to an inch or an inch and a half where the grade exceeds five feet in a hundred.

The only question concerning alignment which has other than local and immediate interests is the relation of the line of the way to the grades which are to be encountered and to the materials to be used in its construction. In general, it may be said that the roads in Massachusetts have had their position determined without a proper consideration as to the course which it was best for them to follow. A large part of the cost which the present ill condition of our highways imposes upon our people is due to bad defects of position.

Width of Highways.

In view of the considerable cost which is necessarily incurred in building the most economical roadway, it becomes a matter of importance to determine the necessary width of the section which is to be made conveniently passable by wheels. The result of the inquiries made by the commission is to show that in ordinary country roads the metal part of the road need not exceed fifteen feet in width.

The shoulder of the way on either side should, however, have additional width, and from two and one-half to three feet.

In the less-used parts of village ways the streets should be wide enough to permit two teams to pass each other while at the same point one team is standing on the side of the roadway; for such needs a width of twenty-one feet is quite sufficient. In the business portion of a village it seems desirable to have the way afford room for two teams to pass each other with vehicles standing against the sidewalk on either hand; thirty feet in width is sufficient to provide these conditions.

In the cities, and even in the parts of some of the larger villages where the amount of traffic is large, it is necessary to increase the width of the way; but the measure of this has to be determined by the local conditions.

Maintenance of Highways.

The first point concerning the system of repairs of our highways to which the commission would draw attention is the importance of immediately remedying, as they occur, slight defects of the way. As soon as an irregularity has in any way occurred in the surface of the road, the tendency of each wheel which passes it is to extend the defect; thus, while the amount of labor involved in effecting the reparation may at first be simple, each day of delay commonly adds much to the expense; on this account it is very important to have methods of supervision so arranged that defects will be immediately observed and at once repaired.

It appears to the commission most desirable that the towns should be held legally responsible for all accidents to the ways within their limits, and that they should be required through their authorities to care for the work of repairing, so long at least as those reparations are of a slight nature. In case the towns fail of their own motion to do such work, there should be some means whereby they may be effectively urged to accomplish it whenever attention to the need has been called by the officers of the State Board; in this way the need of having a large force of men under the direction of the State commission could be avoided.

In the course of a term of years, the length of which will depend upon the plan of construction and the amount of travel which affects the road, the way will need to have the surface which has been worn away replaced. There are two methods of accomplishing this end; the one longest in use consists in breaking up the roadway by picks, or by spikes on the wheel of the roller; new metal is then put on and the surface again thoroughly rolled. In a newer practice it is becoming the custom, where the metal remaining on the road at the time when repairs are needed does not exceed three inches in depth, to leave the latter undisturbed, and to apply the new material upon it, this new material to be thoroughly watered and rolled down in the manner previously described.

In the commissioners' opinion, the specific repairs of this nature should be done by contract. The cost of such general repairs, including the placing of from two to three inches of new metal on the road, may in general be estimated at from twenty to thirty cents per square yard. In most cases, with a well-constructed stone highway, repairs of a general sort will be required at intervals of from eight to twenty years, as determined by the amount of travel over the way.

Routes and Approximate Cost Thereof.

In section 2 of the act establishing the commission, the phrase "routes and the approximate cost" occurs. It is not quite clear to the commission what the Legislature intended by this clause to command; they have, however, carefully considered the possible meanings of the phrase, and beg to report as follows.

So far as relates to the materials to be used in construction, it is the opinion of the commission that, where it is in anywise possible, macadam roads should be built, experience having shown that, measured by the term of years, ways of this nature are more economical than any other, — it being understood that where the conditions demand the peculiar features of the construction, the Telford foundation of the way should be used. Details concerning the cost of such construction are given in the preceding sections of the report. It may in general, however, be said that the original cost per mile of such roadways laid down on the line of previously existing routes will be from $2,500 upwards, according to the amount of traffic which the road is to be called upon to endure and the peculiarities which may exist with the character of the underlying earth. Taking the Commonwealth as a whole, it seems likely that the average cost of such ways will be about $4,500 to $5,500 per mile.

So far as the routes to be selected for improvement are concerned, the commissioners beg to report that they have not been able specifically to determine what particular highways should be recommended for such improvement; they would state, however, that the total number of miles of public way in the Commonwealth, outside of the cities, is about 18,000, of which total about 1,500 miles may be considered as of leading importance in the way of intertown routes. In the opinion of the commission, the improvement of this length of ways would provide a tolerably good system of communication between the centres of population, the cities and towns of the Commonwealth. At an annual expense of $500,000 it would probably require about fifteen to twenty years to bring this system of main highways into the desired condition. It is probable that the sum above noted would also prove sufficient for all the larger repairs, such as the resurfacing the ways which would be from time to time called for. This estimate is on the basis that the ways have been previously graded, and that any alterations demanded in the alignment of the ways should be effected at the cost of the counties.

NOTE ON BRIDGES.

In the act constituting the commission it is not evident that it was intended to have any study whatever given to the bridges in the Commonwealth. The only mention made of these structures is in section 4, where it is stated that "county commissioners, boards of selectmen and aldermen, and other officers having authority over public ways, roads and bridges throughout the Commonwealth, shall at reasonable times, on request, furnish the commissioners any information required by them concerning public ways, roads and bridges within their jurisdiction." In view of this fact, the commission has given only incidental attention to the public bridges throughout the Commonwealth.

The total number of structures in the Commonwealth which are classed as bridges is 3,950; in addition to this there is a large number of culverts, which, in the ordinary use of the term by engineers, may not be so classed.

All matters concerning the small culverts, which are intended to carry the temporary stream of water on its way to a main water course, properly relate to questions of highway construction. Such culverts are commonly reckoned as part of the ordinary expense of highway construction, and will be so treated in the estimates on cost of building. The passages of larger size which are intended to convey the road over streams which are permanent may receive brief consideration.

In general, it may be said that the present tendency is to disuse wood for short bridges and larger culverts, and to replace this material with stone, either in the form of horizontal slabs or arches, both of which forms of construction are of a permanent nature. Experience seems to show that for culverts of moderate size, vitrified clay pipe, now much in use, is well adapted to the needs.

As far as the methods of construction of bridges in Massachusetts are concerned, the commission deems it best to make no report whatever, the matter being one of exceeding difficulty; its discussion would require expenditure of time and money, which are at the present time not available. From an economic point of view, however, it may be noted that the tax imposed upon many of the towns in this Commonwealth for the construction and repair of bridges which do not in the main serve their own citizens is very great; this burden is particularly heavy on those municipalities which border on the navigable tide-waters of the Commonwealth. The towns along the Merrimac and other large rivers are also subjected to a considerable tax, made still more serious within the navigable limits of those streams by the interests of commerce, which not only comes from beyond their borders, but is really of an interstate character.

In general, bridges on the line of a main highway are for the use of many towns rather than for the town in which they may happen to be placed, and it is often the case that they are a direct loss to that town.

In view of this fact, it would seem a matter of justice that the cost of building and maintaining all bridges on main water ways should be borne directly by the county or counties in which they lie.

APPENDIX.

Containing a Number of Separate Tables and Other Sources of Information which from their Nature have not been deemed a Necessary Part of the Foregoing Report, and therefore have not been embodied in it, yet which will afford Special Information of Much Value to the Citizens of the Commonwealth.

APPENDIX A.

A request was sent to all the city engineers of Massachusetts to furnish the commission with descriptions of the methods used and results obtained on the highway work of their several municipalities. Owing to the limited time at the disposal of the commission, only one of these reports has been secured. Fortunately for the end in view, this concerns a city of the rural type, where the roadways afford excellent illustrations of high-grade construction.

REPORT ON HIGHWAY WORK.

CITY HALL, WEST NEWTON, MASS., Jan. 6, 1893.

To the Honorable Board of Massachusetts Highway Commissioners.

GENTLEMEN: — In reply to your request for information on all kinds of pavements, gravel and macadam work with the crown, foundation, drainage, grades, depth of gravel or stone, methods of doing work, and cost of different kinds of work throughout the city of Newton, I herewith respectfully submit the following report on the practice in the city of Newton, together with a map of Newton, showing location of different kinds of work.

The city of Newton is situated from six to twelve miles west of the State House. It has an area of about 20 square miles. It has 114.2 miles of accepted streets, and about 55.4 miles of unaccepted streets, ranging in width from 30 to 70 feet. It is composed of fourteen villages, under one municipal government, and having a population of from five hundred to five thousand each.

The main line of the Boston & Albany Railroad passes through the north section of the city, and the Highlands branch, connecting with the Woonsocket division of the New York & New England Railroad at Cook Street, passes through the south section of the city. The two sections are connected by the recently constructed Newton circuit line of the Boston & Albany.

Three of the villages have large manufacturing industries, while the rest are what would be called residential villages, which have been located and built up about the various stations on the lines of railroad as a centre. The central portion of the city is but sparsely populated, but it is cut up by main avenues connecting the various sections. But a small percentage of the streets are what may be called country roads.

The construction and maintenance of the highways, streets or roads are under the general supervision of a superintendent and the city engineer, acting in a consulting or advising capacity. There are three distinct foremen, who have the immediate supervision, under the super-intendent of streets, of from three thousand to five thousand acres of territory, representing a nearly equal mileage of streets.

Ledge or gravel lots of large area have been purchased or leased in the various sections of the city, so that the haul for material to any one section is rarely over a mile. The ledges of the south section of the city are composed largely of conglomerate, in which the rounded or angular stones form a large percentage of the whole mass; the stones are trap or granite in character, and when broken make excellent roads. In the central portion of the city the ledges are largely a green variety of trap, resembling Hudson River trap in hardness, but not so desirable. In the north part of the city there are but few ledges; but the gravel banks are full of trap and granite, cobble-stones of a superior quality.

Two of the districts have two and one district has three stables, in which are kept from one to nine horses, or a total of thirty-six horses, which are ready for immediate or constant use for any repairs which may be needed.

Wages paid per day of nine hours are as follows: —

District foreman,	$3 50 to $5 00
Engineer or road roller,	3 00
Masons,	3 50
Pavers,	2 50
Ledgemen,	$2 00 to 2 50
Drivers (double team),	2 25
Drivers (single team),	2 00
Sub-foremen and graders,	2 00
Laborers,	1 75

The charges made by the city on the highway books in determining the cost of any special work are, in addition to the foregoing: —

For double team and driver (per day),	$5 00
For single team and driver (per day),	3 50
For single load of broken stone of 26 to 28 feet, at crusher,	1 05
For double load of broken stone of 40 to 42 cubic feet, at crusher,	1 75
For rubble stone for foundation for Telford road, per cubic yard, except when obtained in work,	50

At the above rates, Telford macadam roads 12 to 14 inches deep, having from 8 to 9 inches of rubble-stone foundation placed, 4 to 6 inches of broken stone and from one-fourth to one-half inch of surfacing material, have been constructed for from 63 to 83 cents per square yard; macadam roads 6 to 8 inches thick at 40 to 55 cents per square yard; macadam roads 4 to 6 inches thick at 25 to 40 cents per square yard.

The stone-breaking plant consists of one stationary and one Farrel Marsden, portable, 9 by 15 inches stone breaker, operated respectively by one Atlas engine with horizontal boiler, and one portable Lidgerwood double cylinder engine with vertical boiler. The stationary plant is placed near a ledge of hard green trap stone. The stone is drilled with a Rand drill (steam) and blasted with forcite powder. The drill is operated by steam from a separate boiler; the stone is broken to a size to go in the breaker by hand drilling or with sledge-hammers, and taken by horses and carts to the breaker, a distance of about five hundred feet, and delivered on a platform level with the top of the hopper. It is fed into the hopper by two laborers. From the breaker the stone is delivered in four sizes into bins through revolving cylinders with casing of perforated boiler iron. The first is what is known as dust; second one inch, third two and one-half inch, stone; fourth, tailings, that have passed by the meshes and out at the end of the cylinder. The portable crusher is operated at the various gravel lots and some of the ledges at the south part of the city.

The following is a record in detail of the cost of the various items of labor and material which go to make up the total cost of breaking stone of different classes.

The stone is measured in the carts, as drawn or shovelled from the bins. The units of weight of the stone of the different classes are obtained by weighing several cart-loads which have been carefully measured, and found to be as follows: —

	Dust (lbs.).	No. 2 (lbs.).	No. 3 (lbs.).	Tailings (lbs.).
Greenish trap rock, . .	95¾	84⅓	88¼	91
Conglomerate, . . .	101*	–	87.7	94.4
Cobble-stone, . . .	101½*	–	98	99.6

* Dust and No. 2 not separated by screening.

During the fall of 1891 a careful record in detail was kept of the cost and quantity of stone of various qualities broken with plant as above described.

DETAILED COST FOR BREAKING STONE.

	Greenish Trap Ledge, resembling Hudson River Trap in Hardness.	Conglomerate Ledge-stone.	Cobble-stone, largely Trap Stone.	Cobble-stone, largely Granite.
Hours run,	412	144	101	198
Cubic yards broken (total),	3,155	1,288	1,178	1,785
Long tons (2,240 pounds) broken (total),	3,398	1,446	1,417	2,142
Short tons (2,000 pounds) broken (total),	3,805	1,620	1,587	2,399
Cubic yards broken (per hour),	7.7	8.9	11.8	9.0
Long tons broken (per hour),	8.2	10.0	14.0	10.8
Short tons broken (per hour),	9.0	11.2	15.7	12.1
Number cubic yards tailings,	1,004	378	205	365
Per cent. of tailings,	31.8	29.3	17.5	20.4
Number cubic yards two and one-half inch stone,	1,618	668	672	994
Per cent. two and one-half inch stone,	51.3	51.9	57.0	55.7
Number cubic yards one inch stone,	323	–	–	–
Per cent. one inch stone,	10.2	18.8	25.5	23.9
Number cubic yards one-half inch stone or dust,	210	242*	300*	427*
Per cent. one-half inch stone or dust,	6.7	–	–	–
Average number of hours worked per day,	9	9	9	9

* Dust and two and one-half inch stone not separated by screening.

Wages Paid per Day.

Foreman,	$3 00	$3 00	$3 00	$3 00
Operator of steam drill,	3 00 1 75	– 2 50	–	– –
Engineer of boiler operating steam drill,	1 25	–	–	–
Engineer operating stone breaker,	2 00	2 25	2 00	3 00
Blacksmith,	2 50	2 25	–	–
Watchman,	–	1 75	1 75	1 75
Common laborer,	1 75	1 50	1 50	1 75
Water boy,	–	1 00	1 25	–
Two one-horse carts and one driver,	5 00	5 00	–	5 00

Cost of Material.

Coal (per ton 2,000 pounds),	$5 25 65	$5 25 65	$5 25 65	$5 50 65
Oil (per gallon),	15	15	15	15
Powder (per box 50 pounds),	11 34	11 34	–	–
Waste (per pound),	091½	09½	09½	09½
Cost per cubic yard broken stone in bins or at crusher,	898	1 113	445	447
Cost per long ton,	834	991	37	372
Cost per short ton,	745	885	33	332

Cost and Percentage of Whole Cost in Units of Labor and Material.

	Greenish Trap Ledge, resembling Hudson River Trap in Hardness.	Conglomerate Ledge-stone.	Cobble-stone, largely Trap Stone.	Cobble-stone, largely Granite.
Steam drilling: —				
Labor, cost per cubic yard,	$0 092	–	–	–
Per cent. of cost,	10.3	–	–	–
Coal, oil, waste, powder and repairs, cost,	$0 084	$0 018	–	–
Per cent. of cost,	9.4	1.6	–	–
Hand drilling: —				
Labor, cost per cubic yard,	–	$0 249	–	–
Per cent. of cost,	–	22.3	–	–
Sharpening drills and tools: —				
Labor, cost per cubic yard,	$0 069	$0 023	–	–
Per cent. of cost,	7.7	2.1	–	–
Breaking stone for crusher: —				
Labor, cost per cubic yard,	$0 279	$0 42	–	–
Per cent. of cost,	31	37.8	–	–
Total cost of preparing stone for crusher: —				
Labor, cost per cubic yard,	$0 525	$0 71	–	–
Per cent. of cost,	58.4	63.8	–	–
Filling carts: —				
Labor, cost per cubic yard,	$0 098	$0 127	–	$0 144
Per cent. of cost,	11	11.4	–	32.4

Carting to crusher:—				
Labor, cost per cubic yard,	$0 072	$0 062	$0 314	$0 098
Per cent. of cost,	8	5.6	70.6	22
Feeding crusher:—				
Labor, cost per cubic yard,	$0 053	$0 053	$0 033	$0 065
Per cent. of cost,	5.9	4.7	7.4	14.5
Engineer of crusher:—				
Labor, cost per cubic yard,	$0 031	$0 038	$0 029	$0 036
Per cent. of cost,	3.4	3.5	6.5	8
Coal, oil, waste and repairs:—				
Labor, cost per cubic yard,	$0 079	$0 05	$0 015	$0 044
Per cent. of cost,	8.8	4.5	10.1	9.9
Repairs:—				
Labor, cost per cubic yard,	$0 041	–	–	$0 011
Per cent. of cost,	4.5	–	–	2.4
Moving and setting up portable crusher:—				
Labor, cost per cubic yard,	–	$0 023	–	$0 019
Per cent. of cost,	–	2.1	–	4.2
Watchman:—				
Labor, cost per cubic yard,	–	$0 049	$0 024	$0 029
Per cent. of cost,	–	4.4	5.4	6.6

The volume and character of the traffic over the streets of Newton has not been such as to warrant paved surfaces except for gutters or street crossings. Street gutters are usually laid from three to five feet wide. If laid to a curbstone, its slope is slightly in excess of that of the street, the lowest part being next to the curbstone. If laid to a grassed border, it is laid with a depth of from two to four inches, extending up slightly on the slope of the border.

Until recently street gutters have been constructed with rounded cobble-stones, obtained from the local gravel banks, laid on a bed of coarse sand or fine gravel, and cost from seventy-five cents to one dollar per square yard. The cost of keeping gutters of this class free from weeds is so great that there has been laid to a considerable extent a tar concrete of superior quality, which has given general satisfaction, with but little cost for maintenance. Gutters of this class of an inferior quality are in a fair condition after twelve or fourteen years of use.

The laying of street crossings and sidewalks surfaced with tar concrete has been the practice for some twenty-two years. There are now laid in the city about fifty-two miles of sidewalk of this class. The durability of these sidewalks depends upon the quality of the tar and the care used in mixing with the gravel base. Some of the first sidewalks laid are still in fair condition.

A copy of the specifications for laying concrete sidewalks and street crossings I have sent you. The cost as per contract for 1892 was as follows: —

For laying tar concrete sidewalks (per square yard), . .	$0 75
For laying street crossings (per square yard), . .	1 05
For laying gutters (per square yard), ...	1 15
For surfacing concrete sidewalks, one coat, ...	40
For surfacing concrete sidewalks, two coats, ...	50
For surfacing concrete crossings, one coat, ...	58
For surfacing concrete crossings, two coats, ...	65

In addition to the above should be added the cost of grading and preparing the sidewalk or street to receive the surfacing material, which is performed by day work, at an average cost of about ten cents per square yard.

The streets are constructed with either gravel macadam or Telford-macadam road-beds. Gravel road-beds are maintained in streets upon which the travel is small in volume. As the amount of travel increases and the surface of the street wears off, it is repaired or rebuilt with a macadam surface. The thickness of the macadam surfacing depends upon the character of the travel and the foundation under it; it is usually from four to eight inches in depth. Telford-macadam road-beds are constructed on streets upon which the travel is large in volume and heavy in character, or the foundation under the road-bed wet or quaggy.

The question of the availability of and the means for handling economically materials of different classes and qualities affects largely the decision as to the character of the road-bed to be made.

It is desirable to reduce the grades of the streets as much as possible, and the laying out of new streets with grades exceeding five per cent. is discouraged, although sometimes difficult to avoid.

The standard cross-section of a road as adopted in Newton is shown on an accompanying cross-section plan, with the slopes of one-half inch per foot for both sidewalk and road-bed.

In practice the crown of the streets with less than three per cent. grade is reduced, and increased when the grade is over four per cent. In all cases the crown should be greater than the longitudinal slopes, in order to shed quickly to the gutters the water falling upon the street.

No general set of specifications can be made for the construction of all classes of road-beds, or for each particular class, as each would have to be studied by itself, and modifications made to take advantage of the local conditions.

The following is a form of contract and specifications for the construction of a new street, which provides for a gravel road-bed, a drain in which to take off the surface water, and so laid as to intercept the ground water, thereby drying out the foundation of the road-bed.

CITY OF NEWTON.

CONTRACT AND SPECIFICATIONS FOR BUILDING STREET, FROM STREET TO STREET, ABOUT FEET.

This agreement, made and concluded this day of by of the city of Newton, county of Middlesex and Commonwealth of Massachusetts, as part of the first part, and of as part of the second part, *witnesseth:* —

That the said part of the first part, in consideration of the covenants and agreement hereinafter mutually entered into, does for himself, his executors and administrators, covenant and agree to and with said part of the second part, that he shall and will in a good and workmanlike manner, at own proper cost and expense, according to the best of art and ability, do and perform all work, and provide all material required for the work hereinafter named, in accordance with the plans and directions made, and to be made, from time to time, as the work proceeds.

SPECIFICATIONS.

1. The contractor is to furnish all material, labor and tools, except as herein otherwise specified, necessary to the full completion and construction of the street, drain and catch-basins, in accordance with these specifications.

2. The street is to be built to a width of feet, and to conform accurately to a cross-section plan attached hereto.

3. The site of the street is first to be cleared for its entire length of all stumps, roots, brush, and of all trees except those that may be designated for preservation.

4. Such a portion of the trees and brush as may be considered by the engineer suitable for firewood shall be cut into four-foot lengths and properly piled outside of the line of the road, as directed. All bushes, limbs of trees, stumps and roots so removed shall be placed outside of the line of the road, as directed, and burnt. No roots or stumps will be allowed as filling on any part of the work.

5. All trees that have been saved are to be properly protected from injury by teams, or otherwise, during the progress of the work.

6. All loam and loamy material is to be removed from the surface of the ground within the lines of the street.

7. Such ledge and boulders as may be necessary shall be removed to the sub-grade, to the satisfaction of the engineer.

8. The street shall then be graded accurately to a sub-grade eight inches below the finished grade, as shown on a profile and cross-section of said street, made by the city engineer of said city of Newton.

9. In all cases where it is necessary to fill in, the contractor shall fill with such material as is satisfactory to the engineer.

10. The sub-grade of the sidewalk shall be at least four inches below the finished grade.

11. A coating of good binding gravel, of a quality approved by the engineer, shall then be added, and graded to conform to the finished grade of said street, except upon the edge of the sidewalk, where loam shall be placed, as shown on the cross-section hereto annexed.

12. The surface of the street as sub-graded, and each successive layer of gravel or stone surfacing, shall be thoroughly wet, if necessary, and thoroughly compacted by being rolled over with a ring horse-roller weighing not less than 4,300 pounds, or with a steam road-roller; and all depressions in the surface or sub-surface resulting from said rolling shall be filled with suitable material, and compacted by the continued use of the road-roller, until the wheels of a heavily loaded wagon will not leave a rut or depression on the finished surface.

13. Where cutting is to be done, the earth is to slope upon the adjoining land, upon a slope of one and one-half horizontal to one vertical.

14. In case of filling, the earth shall be sloped upon the adjoining land upon a slope of two horizontal to one vertical. Said slope both in cuts and fills shall be covered with at least twelve inches of good loam, so applied as to insure against slipping, and carefully rolled with a hard roller. Where necessary, the earth is to be removed to the proper sub-grade for the slopes.

15. The loam filling along the edge of the sidewalk is to be covered with good fresh sods, laid in the best manner.

16. The slopes at the side of the streets are to be thoroughly sown with the best lawn grass-seed, mixed with a proper proportion of the best barley, and properly rolled. The sowing of the seed and the laying of the sods are to be done at such times and seasons as shall be directed by the engineer.

17. The contractor shall construct catch-basins, man-holes, and a drain shall be laid of such size and in such location as shown on the plan and profile of said street.

18. All drain pipe must be first-quality salt-glazed vitrified clay socket pipe, equal in quality to the best Ohio River or Akron pipe; and to be laid with uncemented joints, strictly in accordance with the lines and grades of the engineer.

19. The contractor shall fill the trench about, and at least four inches above, the top of the pipe with a screened gravel from one-quarter to three-quarters inch in dimension, which shall be thoroughly compacted about the pipe.

20. The rest of the trench shall be filled to within one foot of the surface with clean screened gravel not exceeding three inches in diameter, which shall be covered with a layer of jute bagging, or sod laid with the grass side down, and the top foot of the trench will be filled with gravel.

21. The man-holes shall be built of the best quality hard-burnt sewer brick, wall to be eight inches in thickness, laid up in cement mortar, one part American hydraulic cement and two parts of clean screened sharp sand, to be four feet in diameter at the bottom, and provided with the standard iron man-hole cover used by city of Newton.

22. The catch-basins shall be built of the best quality hard-burnt sewer brick, wall to be eight inches in thickness, to be laid up in cement mortar, one part American hydraulic cement and two parts clean screened sharp sand, to be six and one-half feet deep, to be five feet in diameter at the bottom, and provided with a No. 18 Concord grate. Each basin to be connected with the main drain by an eight-inch pipe. Bottom of basins to be paved with brick laid dry.

23. All said work to be completed in a thorough and workmanlike manner, in accordance with the lines and grades furnished by the engineer, to be satisfactory to and with the approval of the said engineer.

24. No claim for extra work shall be made unless the same shall be done in pursuance of a written order from the engineer, and the value of any extra work is to be determined by the said engineer.

25. The work under this contract is to be commenced within ten days of the award, and is to be completed on or before

26. The engineer will make monthly estimates of the amount of work done under this contract during the preceding month; upon the delivery of this certificate the contractor shall be entitled to receive ninety per cent. of the value of the work certified to have been performed.

27. It is further mutually agreed that whenever this contract, in the opinion of the said engineer, shall be completely performed upon the part

of the said contractor, he shall certify the same to the said part of the second part, who shall pay the contractor, within thirty days after receiving said certificate, the amount that may be due, excepting therefrom such sum or sums as may be lawfully retained to protect said part of the second part from liens or attachment; that nothing herein contained shall be construed to affect the right hereby reserved of said part of the second part to reject the whole or any portion of said work, should said certificate be found or known to be inconsistent with the forms of this agreement, or otherwise improperly given.

28. In consideration of the full and proper completion of the work, the part of the first part agree to receive, and the part of the second part agree to give, the following price for building said street, including clearing, grubbing, grading, loaming and sodding, also including said drain, man-holes and catch-basins, the sum of dollars.

IN WITNESS WHEREOF the parties hereto have signed and sealed this contract this day of A.D.

(Signed)

City of Newton, by its mayor,
Witness,

The above specifications can be adapted to all classes of road construction, by making the unit depth of surfacing material required the depth below the finished surface the road shall be sub-graded.

If a macadam road-bed of sufficient depth is required, the surfacing can be put on in two layers, and tailings from the screen at the stone breaker, or an inferior quality of stone, may be used for the bottom course; and clause 11 of the specifications would read: "A layer not more than four inches thick of tailings from the screen at the stone breaker, or screened stone of approved quality having no dimensions over four inches, shall then be added. After being compacted by the road-roller, a layer of broken stone or screened gravel stone of approved quality, not more than two and one-half inches and not less than one inch in dimension, shall then be added, and the surface graded to conform to the finished surface of the street, except on the edge of the sidewalk, where loam shall be placed as shown on the cross-section hereto annexed."

If a Telford-macadam road-bed is desired, the first part of clause 8 in the specifications would read: "The street shall then be graded accurately to a sub-grade twelve or fourteen inches below the finished grade, as shown on the profile and cross-section of said street, made by the city engineer of the said city of Newton."

Clause 11 of the specifications would read: "A layer of ledge stone of approved quality, eight or nine inches high, four to eight inches thick and eight to fourteen inches long, shall be placed on the edge, bedded on the widest edge, and placed closely together in courses set at right angles to the curb line. The surface to be levelled off, and the stone wedged securely together by the use of stone hammers."

The clause for macadam surfacing on the Telford foundation may be the same as for macadam road-bed. When the stone or gravel will not bind by continued rolling over them without a binding surfacing material, the following clause may be added after clause 11 of the specifications: "A thin coating of hard pan or binding gravel of approved quality, which will make a coating after being rolled not exceeding one-quarter inch in thickness, shall be added to the top layer of stone or gravel. To this a single layer of stone screenings, not exceeding one inch in dimension, shall be added, and the whole thoroughly wet. This gives a smooth and durable surface, and we find it to be one of the best on streets having somewhat sharp grades."

Where a drain for intercepting the ground water only is necessary, an unglazed clay tile of size from one-half to six inches in diameter, depending upon the distance necessary to lay without an outlet, may be substituted for the vitrified clay pipe of larger size, and the depth to be laid below the surface may be reduced to three feet.

I prefer in practice a depth of five feet of trench, from being more nearly below the frost line, as giving more satisfactory results.

For a number of years previous to 1891 the streets were maintained and cleaned by the district system. They were cleaned three or four times a year, usually repaired in spring and fall. The method employed gave fairly satisfactory results. In 1891 the section system of maintaining and cleaning the streets was tried. Briefly described, the method employed is as follows:—

Plans showing the streets of the city were prepared. They were classed as principal and secondary streets and country roads, and were shown on the plans in a color for each class. Twenty-two and four-tenths miles of the principal streets were selected upon which to make a trial of the method proposed, and were divided into ten sections, in such a way that the work on each would be as equally divided as possible; that is, sections having the most traffic and wear, and those in the least perfect condition, were selected with less superficial area to be cared for than those sections recently put in condition and receiving less traffic.

The men assigned to each section were selected from the most reliable and efficient on the force, and were called section men, and remained under the charge of the district foreman. Their duty was to keep their section in proper condition; that is, to keep the gutter clean of weeds, trim the grass, patch all gullies and ruts in the road-bed, look after the sidewalks, etc., in fact, do all the small repairs necessary as soon as needed, the regular street force being called upon only for large repairs and renewal of road-beds, etc.

They were not to be called off from their regular work except on emergencies, such as snow-storms, etc., when the entire force are needed clearing the roads. Each man was supplied with a wheel-barrow, a pick, a shovel and wooden rake, hoe, lantern, sickle, edging knife and cord line. The wheelbarrows were painted blue, with the section number clearly painted on the handle, so as to be easily seen by the foreman or superintendent when on the rounds of inspection.

At convenient places on each section piles of crushed stone and gravel were located, from which material was obtained for patching up whatever holes or ruts which might appear in the road-bed or in the sidewalks. The other streets were cleared up at stated intervals by the rest of the highway force.

The improved appearance and condition of the streets thus cared for was quickly noticed by the citizens. The men appeared to take a pride in their work, and their efforts were attended with nearly equal results, considering the varying condition, namely, original condition, of the road-bed; level or hilly streets, stone curbing or sodded edging, concrete or cobble-paved gutters, amount of traffic, etc.

The total expenditure in 1891 by this method was $4,414.14, or a little less than one cent a square yard of road-bed, exclusive of side-walks cared for on each section.

The system was extended in 1892 by the addition of ten section men to the force, making a total of 45.5 miles, or 787,230 square yards, of road-bed, exclusive of sidewalk, thus cared for; and it is anticipated that in a short time all of the streets will be cared for in this way.

The watering of streets contributes largely to comfort in their use and economy in their maintenance. The work is performed in the following manner: —

The city contracts with various contractors for watering the streets, at the rate of $100 per month per cart. They keep the sections to which each cart is assigned well watered and free from dust. The watering of the streets begins as early in April as may be necessary, and continues until the first of December. During the months of April and November the streets require watering but few days; the payment for these months is based on day-service rather than month-service. The number of teams contracted for is 14; the number of miles of street watered is 40.5.

In the city of Newton the actual frontage available for assessment is 72 frontage miles, or 36 street miles; there being 4.5 miles of street made up of frontage not available for assessment, and street intersections which have no frontage. The watering department are paid a gross sum of $2,100 for water. The cost during the year for teams was $9,238.62, and for clerical hire $199.95, making a total expenditure for watering streets of $11,538.57. This sum, divided equally by the number of miles of street whose frontage is available for assessment, will equal $326 per mile, making a cost of 6 cents per foot of street available for frontage assessment, and 3 cents per foot of frontage. It is estimated that the city pays about half, or, in order that there should be no legal question raised, the assessment made on the estates was at the rate of 1½ cents a front foot, or a sum estimated not to exceed 60 per cent. of the cost. At the above rate of assessment, the net income was 49 per cent. of the cost.

Respectfully submitted,

ALBERT F. NOYES,
City Engineer.

A GENERAL CROSS-SECTION of MACADAM STREETS.

Newton, Mass. Albert F. Noyes. City Engineer.

AA = Gravel Sidewalks.
BB = Loam Embankments.

APPENDIX B.

CITY OF NEWTON.

SPECIFICATIONS. — CONCRETE SIDEWALKS AND CROSSINGS.

1. The work consists in laying new tar concrete sidewalks, street crossings and gutters, and repairing old work, in the streets of the city of Newton, Mass., during the year 1892, as may be from time to time required by the highway committee.

2. The areas ordered to be concreted will be excavated and prepared by the superintendent of streets, ready to receive the concrete.

3. The contractor to furnish all transportation, labor, tools and materials for preparing, heating, mixing, spreading and rolling the concrete, and finishing the surface ready for use.

4. The materials used for concrete to be coarse, clean gravel, clean screened sharp sand, the best quality of coal tar distillate, containing its original oils free from all petroleum compounds or water, and the best quality pitch, mixed so as to form the best as paving cement, and the whole mixed in proportions to make the best quality durable concrete.

5. Each class of work to consist of three layers: a foundation of cobbles or broken stone and tar composition; a binding course of fine gravel and tar composition; a wearing surface of sand and tar composition, — each layer to be thoroughly consolidated and rolled separately.

6. *Foundation.* — The foundation course to consist of coarse gravel from two inches to four inches in greatest diameter, according to the class of work, thoroughly coated with hot coal-tar paving cement before the delivery on the work, spread evenly and well tamped and rolled until the stone cease to creep under the roller, and are thoroughly compacted.

7. *Binding Course.* — The binding course to consist of clean screened gravel not exceeding one inch in greatest diameter, heated to 230° to 250° F., and mixed while hot with hot coal-tar composition, in proportion of about one gallon composition to one cubic foot of gravel. This material to be spread while fresh over the

foundation course already prepared, to a depth of two inches, well tamped and rolled down into the foundation course.

8. *Wearing Surface.* — The wearing surface to be composed of clean screened sharp sand, free from all vegetable matter, clay, loam or quicksand; of such size that not over twenty per cent. shall remain on a sieve of twenty meshes to the inch, or more than five per cent. will pass through a sieve of sixty meshes to an inch, about sixty per cent. to be coarser than forty meshes to an inch. This sand to be thoroughly heated and mixed with coal-tar composition previously heated in a separate caldron, in the proportions of eighty-six per cent. sand and thirteen to fifteen per cent. composition. This material to be spread while hot over the binding course, in an even layer, and thoroughly compressed and rolled before cooling. The surface will then be sprinkled with fine sand or hydraulic cement, well rolled in.

9. All materials used, as well as the plant and method of manufacture, will be subjected to the inspection and approval of the city engineer and superintendent of streets, who may order changes in the proportions of the compositions as occasion may require.

10. *Sidewalks.* — These are to be laid out with a foundation course of not less than two and one-half inches in thickness, having no gravel over two inches in greatest diameter. The binding course to be not less than one-half inch thick, unless otherwise directed. The concrete to extend from face of property line, fence or wall to the inside line of curbstone, or sod line where there is no curbstone, or sod line where there is no curbstone on the walk.

11. *Street Crossings.* — These are to have a foundation course of four inches, to extend six inches each side beyond the other courses. The binding course to be not less than one inch in thickness, and the wearing surface to be not less than one and one-half inches in thickness. When the crossing is properly rolled, the contractor shall repack the road material over the projecting sides of the foundation course, and roll it down even with the crossing.

12. *Gutters.* — In case of gutters, the foundation course of not less than four inches will extend six inches beyond the surface courses toward the street, and the tar composition for the binding course and the one and one-half inch wearing surface will contain more pitch, and be mixed so as to give a harder surface, to stand the wear of heavy truck wheels; and the surface to receive an additional wash of hot tar composition. The road metal to be replaced over the projecting foundation course, and to be rolled as in case of crossings. The cross-section of the gutter to be dished without exaggerating the slope from the centre of the street. Where no curbing is set, the foundation course to extend also under the sods as well as the road-bed.

13. *Measurements.* — The contractor shall furnish the city engineer, as required, a list of the concrete sidewalks, crossings and gutters completed, and the city engineer shall cause the same to be measured. Unless otherwise ordered, crossings will be built eight feet wide on the foundation course, and nine feet will be allowed for measurement. Gutters will be built four feet wide on the surface, and four and one-half feet on the foundation course, and will be measured as four and one-half feet wide. Sidewalks, unless otherwise directed, will be built and be measured according to the width of the streets, as follows: —

30 foot street, with curbing, sidewalk 4 feet 6 inches; without curbing, 3 feet 6 inches

35 foot street, with curbing, sidewalk 5 feet 4 inches; without curbing, 4 feet 4 inches.

40 foot street, with curbing, sidewalk 6 feet; without curbing, 5 feet 6 inches.

50 foot street, with curbing, sidewalk 7 feet 8 inches; without curbing, 7 feet.

60 foot street, with curbing, sidewalk 9 feet 6 inches; without curbing, 8 feet 6 inches.

No allowance will be made where the concrete has been run out over these widths, owing to carelessness or the omission of guide strips by the contractor; but actual widths will be taken wherever the concrete has not been carried out to the full width. All repairs to be measured actual size of patch as marked out by pick before laying.

14. *Repairs.* — These are to be made on the different class of work as may be required, and to consist either of skim coat, that is, a binding course and a wearing surface. In doing this work the old surface will be painted over with a light coat of tar oil, in order to soften it up, so it will bind with the new material.

15. The prices for the work are to be made out per square yard for each class, as follows: —

Sidewalks, new work, ...
repairs, skim coat, ...
repairs, two-layer work, ...
Crossings, new work,. . . . .
repairs, one-layer work, ...
repairs, two-layer work, ...
Gutters, new work, ...

16. *Settlement.* — All work on the streets to be done by orders of the highway committee. All new sidewalks to be paid one-half by the city, and the other half by the abutters that have petitioned for the

work; this half to be collected by the contractor. If, after due application, the bill is not paid by the abutter within one year, the city will, at the request of the highway committee, pay the bill and collect it from the estate. All the repair work and all work on crossings and gutters are paid by the city.

17. *Payments.* — At the end of each month the city engineer shall cause all the work finished during the month to be measured, and shall issue a certificate of the measurements and the amount due to the contractor, and forward a copy to the contractor and to the highway committee for approval. All bills approved will be paid by the city treasurer on the tenth day of the next succeeding month.

18. All work to be performed in the order and at the time that the superintendent of streets may notify the contractor. All work to be done to his satisfaction, and satisfactory to the city engineer.

APPENDIX C.

DESCRIPTION OF A TELFORD-MACADAM ROAD, AS CONSTRUCTED IN HINGHAM, MASS., BY A. H. KIMBALL, SUPERINTENDENT OF STREETS.

The part of the road described passed through a cut where the land rose on either side, and the ground was a heavy wet clay.

A drain twelve inches square was first constructed, the bottom of which was about three feet below the surface, in the centre of the proposed street. This drain was made of rough slabs of stone on the two sides and top. The depth from the top of the covering stone to the bottom was about twenty inches. Coarse field stones from five to sixteen inches in diameter were tilled in over the drain, eight inches thick in the centre of the roadway and ten feet wide; this was then rolled with a fifteen-ton steam roller until no further settlement occurred; the grade and cross-section were maintained as the work of rolling progressed. The soil on both sides of the coarse stone was then removed to the full width of twenty-five feet, and the bed so prepared carefully rolled with the fifteen-ton steam roller. Metal, from which had been removed all that would pass through a one-inch screen, was then laid on to a depth of six inches in the centre of the roadway, thinning to two inches at the sides. After this had been carefully rolled, metal from three-eighths inch to one inch in diameter was laid on, to a depth of one inch in the centre of the roadway, thinning out to nothing at ten feet on each side of the centre. The whole surface of the road was then spread with sand, watered and rolled, until all voids in the stone were filled. Screenings from the crusher which had been passed through a three-eighths inch screen were then laid on to the depth of about one inch over the surface of the whole road; these were thoroughly watered and rolled with the steam roller until they formed a hard, smooth surface.

The centre of the finished road was twelve and one-half inches above the gutters.

The coarse stone used was brought from fields near the work; they cost thirty-four cents per load and forty-one and two-thirds cents a load for teaming. The broken stone was bought at one dollar and twenty-five cents a ton at the crusher, and was teamed about one and one-quarter miles. The sand cost sixty-two and one-half cents a double load, delivered on the road.

The total length of the road, of which the above forms a part, was 2,882 feet; 440 feet of it was built as above described (see diagram), the balance was constructed on top of the old road surface.

The cost of the completed work was as follows: —

Average cost per mile,	$5,465 00
Average cost per linear foot,	1 03½
Cost per square yard macadam,	1 35¾
Cost per square yard Telford,	46

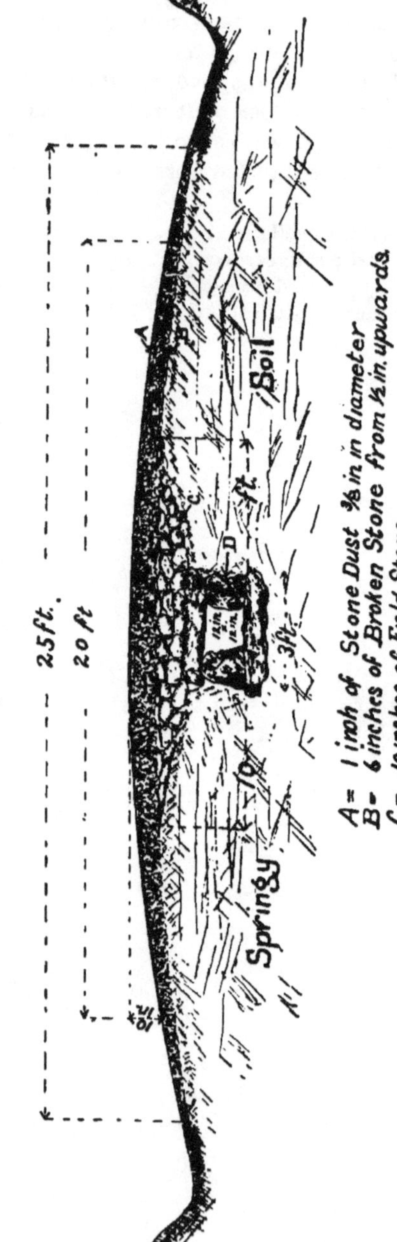
Type of Road on Wet Foundation.
A.H Kimball, Supt. of Streets.
Hingham, Mass.
25 ft.
20 ft
A
B
C
D
Soil
Springy
10 ft
3 ft.
A= 1 inch of Stone Dust 3/8 in in diameter
B= 6 inches of Broken Stone from ½ in. upwards.
C= 10 inches of Field Stone
D= Stones of Drain 6 to 8 inches thick.
Total depth from surface 3 feet.
Scale 1 in.=8 ft.

APPENDIX D.

Specifications for Macadam Road, Franklin, Essex County, New Jersey.

Specifications as per title heretofore mentioned for macadamizing said streets in the township of Franklin, Essex County, New Jersey: —

The roads and streets named in the title aforesaid are to be amended and repaired solely of broken trap rock and clean trap screenings, unless the engineer shall permit the use of clean hard sand in place of trap screenings.

The macadam shall have the uniform width of fifteen feet, and will in no instance be less than four inches thick when compacted. When ordered in writing by the party of the first part, the thickness shall be increased by the contractor, who shall be paid twenty per cent. over contract price for each additional inch of trap rock, said inch not to include the finishing cost hereinafter particularly specified. If from any cause the thickness shall be less than four inches, the contractor shall, at any time when required to do so, pick up the surface and add sufficient broken trap and screenings to make the required thickness, at his own cost.

The trap rock shall be broken to pass through a two-inch ring, all stones of less than one inch diameter being screened out. It shall be free from dust, dirt or loam, free from flat pieces or spawls, and free from splinters or pieces in which the greatest diameter is more than twice the smallest. All broken stone that is of poor quality, from the presence of small stones or any of the above-mentioned defects, or that is found not to conform with the sample deposited by the contractor, shall be rejected, and wherever or whenever found shall be removed by the contractor from the road or street.

Screenings shall be such fragments of trap rock as will pass freely through a one-inch ring free from loam or other dirt. They shall not contain more dust from the crusher than the sample deposited by the contractor.

The whole width of the road-bed shall be rolled by a steam road-roller weighing not less than four hundred pounds on each inch in width of the driving wheels, until the road-bed is compacted to the satisfaction of the engineer. Any settlement that may be developed shall be made good by the addition of sufficient strong earth or gravel to bring the compacted road-bed to the engineer's lines and profiles.

After the road-bed has been accepted by the engineer, clean broken trap shall be spread and levelled by the contractor so that it shall have a width of fifteen feet on top, and the compacted road-bed shall be fully four inches thick.

The shoulders or berms of the road-bed shall then be made up of strong earth or gravel, free from muck or vegetable matter, of such thickness that, on being rolled consecutively with the broken stone, they will conform to the transverse profile of the road.

All stones when in place shall be rolled with a steam road-roller of the weight specified above until they are compacted; when screenings shall be added and rolled in until all spaces between the stone are thoroughly filled. This will be determined by water "flushing" on the surface of the road, and not sinking through it.

When the road is thoroughly compacted to the satisfaction of the engineer, a coating of screenings shall be spread over the road to the uniform depth of one inch. This coating of screenings, which is not to be rolled, shall not be counted as a part of the thickness of the road-bed, which shall be four inches thick before the above-mentioned top-dressing is applied.

The contractor will provide and maintain signs by day and lights by night, warning people against passing over streets he is constructing, and assumes all responsibility for accidents in default of such signs or lights.

The contractor shall remove all debris and excess of materials from the streets as they are furnished, and, on the completion of his work, leave all the streets or roads he has constructed free from dirt or obstruction.

The contractor undertakes by this instrument, in return for the payments to be made to him, to build a hard, clean road of uniform thickness and profile, in conformity with the above specification, that will not rut under traffic, and to maintain the same for one year for the prices above mentioned, without claims against the party of the first part on account of any negligence of its servants.

APPENDIX E.

DESCRIPTION OF A FIVE-INCH MACADAM ROAD, AS CONSTRUCTED BETWEEN THE TOWNS OF FLUSHING AND JAMAICA, LONG ISLAND, N. Y., BY G. A. ROULLIER, CIVIL ENGINEER, 1892.

The road was about seven miles long, and in this distance passed over several brooks and a number of hills. The culverts over the brooks were substantial sand-stone arches, with parapets about three feet high of the same material.

The maximum grade as established was generally five feet to the hundred; in one case it was for a short distance six feet in a hundred.

Trap rock alone was used for metalling; part of it was obtained by breaking boulders found along the line of the road, the rest was shipped from the palisades of the Hudson.

No figures could be obtained giving the cost of breaking the stone from the neighborhood. The palisades rock cost as follows per ton: —

Broken trap rock on boat at Flushing,	$1 50
Unloading,	15
Teaming,	35
Total cost per ton delivered on road,	$2 00

The stone was laid on about seven inches thick, and rolled to about five inches. A cubic yard of stone covered about five square yards of road. A cubic yard of the broken stone weighed about 2,500 pounds, and at $2.00 per ton cost $2.50. By the above figures the broken stone that was used to cover one square yard would cost about fifty cents when dumped on the road.

The ground traversed by the road was a light sandy loam, which allowed the wheels to sink to the hubs in the fall of the year.

The ground was first shaped to conform to the surface of the proposed road, and rolled with a ten-ton steam roller until it was firm and even; the grade and cross-section were maintained as the work of rolling progressed. When, owing to the original nature of the earth, it was impossible to roll it with the steam roller, the sub-grade was lowered three inches and the space filled in with broken stone; this was covered with a light layer of sand, and then rolled "to a bearing."

Broken stone, the fragments from one inch to two inches in diameter, thoroughly mixed, was then laid on to a depth of seven inches in the central half of the roadway, thinning on either side to four and one-half inches. The stones were spread broadcast by shovels.

After the requisite depth and cross-section were obtained, the metal was rolled "to a bearing" by passing the roller at least four times over every portion of the surface. Clean, coarse sand was then spread over the surface as the roller worked back and forth, and watered and rolled until all the voids in the stone were filled. Trap-rock screenings were then added in small quantities at a time, and rolled and sprinkled until they ceased to sink into the macadam, and the water flushed before the roller.

While this surface was still wet it was covered with a layer of clayey earth not exceeding one-eighth of an inch in thickness; over this gravelly sand not exceeding one inch in thickness was spread. There were places where a small quantity of clayey earth was spread over the broken stone before the screenings were applied.

The broken-stone roadway was made eighteen feet wide, but the earth was shaped to a regular crown of one-half inch to the foot, and rolled for a width of twenty-four feet.

The gutters were two feet below the level of the centre of the finished road, and were paved with bank stone found on the line of the construction.

The total cost of this admirable roadway was about $15,000 a mile, which included all grading, culverts and paving, as well as macadamizing. The macadamizing cost 66 cents a square yard, or about $6,969 per mile.

Streets built exactly as that above described are to be found in Flushing which have been in use for several years, yet show hardly a wheel mark, much less a rut of any kind, on their surface.

SECTION of the FLUSHING and JAMAICA ROAD. QUEENS COUNTY, N.Y.

G.A. Roullier, Engineer.

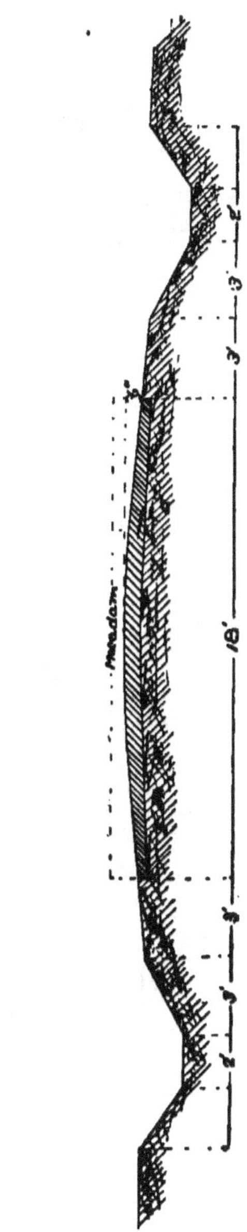

Warren St., Boston, 1892.

Showing method of resurfacing over a hard road without breaking it up.

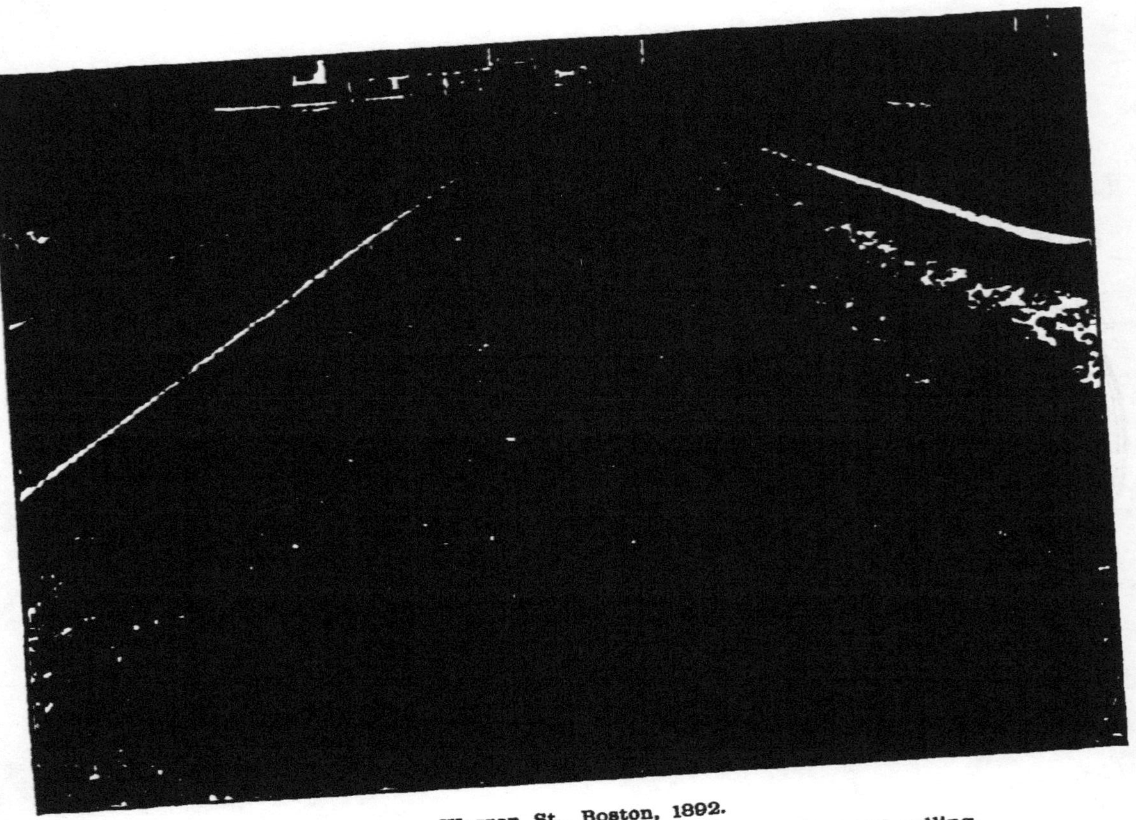

Warren St., Boston, 1892.

Repairs on a macadam road; showing method of binding and rolling.

LIBRARY
OF THE
UNIVERSITY
OF
CALIFORNIA.

APPENDIX F.

DESCRIPTION OF A MACADAM ROAD AS CONSTRUCTED UPON AN OLD GRAVEL STREET IN CHELSEA, BY W. E. McCLINTOCK, CITY ENGINEER, 1887.

The street was about 2,200 feet long, 30 feet wide between the curbs, and was shaded by a row of elms on each side; a large amount of light and some heavy travel passed over it. The old surface was generally flat, yet full of hollows, very wet and muddy, not drying for several days after a rain. Granite curbs were on each side of the street, and catch-basins were at the intersection of each cross street.

Trap rock broken to sizes from one inch to two and a half inches was laid on, so as to give a crown of about one-half inch to the foot; the depth of stone varied from three to four inches at the gutter and from five to eight inches in the centre, averaging about six inches. The stone was rolled with a fifteen-ton steam roller until it was firmly compacted; the surface was then covered with trap-rock screenings, which had passed through a one-half inch mesh, to a depth of about one inch. The screenings were watered and rolled until the surface was hard and smooth. In about six weeks the dirt was scraped off from the roadway, and in a few weeks more it was cleaned a second time. In about six months the surface while damp was swept with a machine sweeper.

At the present time, after nearly six years' wear, the street is in good condition, the surface remaining hard and smooth.

The total cost of the work, including stone, breaking, teaming, spreading and steam rolling, was about 44 cents a square yard. The broken stone cost about $1.25 a ton at the crusher, one mile distant from the place where it was used.

There have been several miles of streets in Chelsea built on the same plan, at prices varying from 33 to 55 cents a square yard. These streets have not been repaired since they were macadamized, and will not need attention for several years to come.

CHESTNUT ST. CHELSEA

Built in 1888 by W. E. McClintock.

Showing method of macadamizing over old gravel road, without breaking it up. From dust to 2½ in. in diameter broken stone, 6 in. deep in centre to 4 in. on the sides.

APPENDIX G.

Description of Method of repairing a Road, situated in Belmont, which had been Macadamized for about Fifteen Years without requiring any Repairs, by W. E. McClintock, 1892.

The road as originally macadamized was thirty-two feet wide. The top of this road had worn off, leaving the large stones which were used in the original construction projecting up in such a manner as to create a very rough, uneven surface.

A strip fifteen feet wide through the centre was broken up by the use of picks in the steam-roller wheels. Men with picks followed the roller, and loosened up the surface already broken by it. The surface was then rolled with the fifteen-ton steam roller, and a coating of broken trap rock, the fragments from one-half inch to one inch in diameter, was laid on to a depth of two inches, and rolled. This was covered with trap-rock screenings varying in size from fine dust to a half inch in diameter, watered and rolled till the surface was solid and even.

The cost of this work was twenty-five cents a square yard. This amount, averaged over the time since the road was built, shows the annual cost for repairs to have been three-fifths of a cent per square yard. The amount of vertical wear was in the fifteen years of use about one-seventh of an inch per year. The stone used in the repairs was trap rock, shipped about thirty miles by rail, and hauled about one and one-half miles over the road.

APPENDIX H.

TABLES SHOWING THE COST OF BREAKING STONE FOR HIGHWAY USE IN MASSACHUSETTS AND ELSEWHERE.

Newton, Middlesex County. (A. F. NOYES, *City Engineer.*)

Material: broken cobble-stone.		Cu. Yds.
Amount broken,		1,177
Amount broken per hour,		11.8
Divided as follows: —	Cu. Yds.	Per Cent.
Tailings,	205	17.50
Two and one-half inch,	672	57.00
Dust and one inch,	300	25.50
Total,	1,177	100.00

Total cost per cubic yard in bins at crusher,		$0 44½
per ton of 2,240 pounds,		37
per ton of 2,000 pounds,		33
Divided as follows: —	Cost.	Per Cent.
Teaming to crusher,	$0 314	70.60
Feeding to crusher,	033	7.40
Engineer of crusher,	029	6.50
Repairs, waste, oil, etc.,	045	10.10
Watchman,	024	5.40
Total,	$0 445	100.00

Material: broken stone (conglomerate).			Cu. Yds.
Amount broken,			1,288
Amount broken per hour, on an average,			8.9
Divided as follows: —	Cu. Yds.	Per Cent.	Weight, Cu. Yds.
Tailings,	378	29.30	2,549
Two and one-half inch stone,	668	51.90	2,368
Dust and one inch stone,	242	18.80	2,727
Total,	1,288	100.00	

Total cost per cubic yard in bins at crusher,	$1 112
per ton of 2,240 pounds,	991
per ton of 2,000 pounds,	885

Divided as follows: —

	Cost.	Per Cent.
Powder and repairs,	$0 018	1.60
Labor, drilling,	249	22 30
Sharpening drills and tools,	023	2.10
Breaking stone for crusher,	420	37.80
Loading stone for crusher,	127	11.40
Teaming stone for crusher,	062	5.60
Feeding stone for crusher,	053	4.70
Engineer for crusher,	038	3.50
Coal, oil, waste for crusher,	050	4 50
Moving and setting up portable crusher,	023	2.10
Watchman portable crusher,	049	4.40
Total,	$1 112	100.00

	Cost.	Per Cent.
Total cost preparing stone for crusher,	$0 71	63 80
Total cost delivering to crusher and breaking,	402	36.20
Total,	$1 112	100.00

Material: broken stone (greenish trap).

	Cu. Yds.
Amount broken,	3,155
Amount broken per hour, on an average,	77

Divided as follows: —

	Cu. Yds.	Per. Cent.	Weight, Cu. Yds.
Tailings,	1,004	31.80	2,457
Two and one-half inch stone,	1,618	51.30	2,383
One inch stone,	323	10.20	2,277
One-half inch stone or dust,	210	6.70	2,585
Total,	3,155	100.00	

Total cost per cubic yard in bins at crusher,	$0 898
per ton of 2,240 pounds,	834
per ton of 2,000 pounds,	745

Divided as follows: —

	Cost.	Per Cent.
Labor, steam drilling,	$0 092	10.30
Steam drilling, including coal, oil, waste, powder, repairs,	084	9.40
Sharpening drills and tools,	069	7.70
Breaking stone for crusher,	279	31.00
Loading stone for crusher,	098	11.00
Teaming stone for crusher,	072	8.00
Feeding stone for crusher,	053	5.90
Engineer of crusher,	031	3.40
Coal, oil, waste and repairs of crusher,	079	8.80
Repairs,	041	4.50
Total,	$0 898	100.00

	Cost.	Per Cent.
Total cost preparing stone for crusher,	$0 525	58.40
Total cost delivering to crusher and breaking,	373	41.60
Total,	$0 898	100.00

Description of Stone-breaking Plant with Cost of Breaking, for Years 1887 and 1888, Chelsea, Mass. (W. E. McCLINTOCK, *City Engineer.*)

The crusher is a 9 by 15 Farrell and Marsden, with a 10 by 12 portable engine rated at twenty horse-power. The crusher is set on a platform on the side of a hill, so arranged that the stone can be delivered at the jaws of the crusher without a second handling. The stone passes from the jaws of the crusher into a rotary screen, which is made to revolve by the same power that runs the crusher. From the screen it falls into shutes which carry the stone of different sizes into four bins. The bins are of sufficient capacity to hold the stone of two days' breaking. It takes two men to feed the crusher and one man to run the engine. The city does not own the ledge, and was obliged to contract with the lessee, who quarried out the stone and delivered it on the platform at a certain price; this price in 1887 was seventy-five cents a ton, in 1888 a dollar a ton.

Itemized cost (per ton) of breaking 1,718 tons of stone during the year 1887 (trap rock): —

Tools,	$0 013
Oil and cans,	016
Stone at the crusher,	75
Crushing, labor,	194
Fuel,	05
Total cost per ton,	$1 023

Cost of stone-breaking (3,853 tons) during the year 1888, including every item of expense at and around the crusher, engine and bins, and stone, quarrying, breaking to go into crusher, teaming to crusher, etc.; the price is given per ton of stone broken: —

Running,	$0 051
Repairs and putting in pump,	055
Feeding,	078
Stone, quarrying, etc.,	967
Clearing screen and bins,	025
Fuel,	048
Oil and waste,	007
Chills,	020
Water,	005
Total cost per ton,	$1 256

Total amount expended in crushing, ... $4,847 14

APPENDIX I.

Description of the Holyhead Road, as built by Sir Thomas Telford.

Section Built on Foundation of Large Stone.

The crown was two-fifths of an inch per foot. The bottom layer consists of quarry-stone pavement, seven inches deep in centre, thinning to three inches on sides, laid in by hand. The middle layer consists of broken stone, two and one-half inches in diameter, six inches in the centre, thinning to four inches on sides. The top layer consists of gravel one and one-half inches deep.

Section Built on Foundation of Gravel.

Crown, one-half inch per foot. The bottom layer consists of gravel six inches deep in centre, thinning to three inches on sides. The middle layer consists of broken stone, two and one-half inches in diameter, eight inches deep in centre, thinning to four inches on sides. The top layer consists of gravel one and one-half inches deep.

SECTION OF HOLYHEAD ROAD

Built by Thomas Telford.

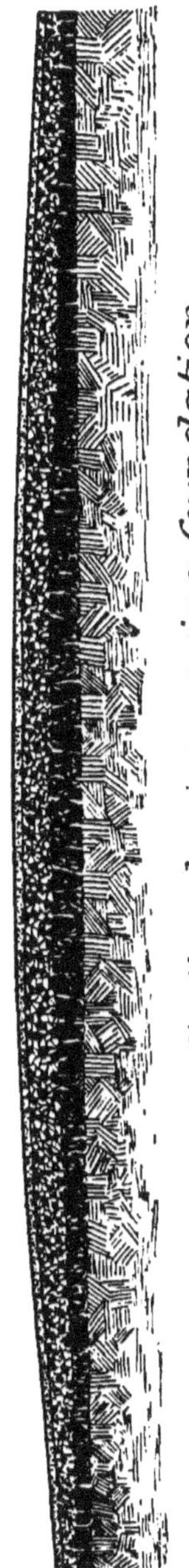

Section showing paving foundation.

Section showing gravel foundation instead of pavement.

GREENFIELD, MASS.

Macadam road on side-hill showing drains

8 ft

20 ft

3 ft

3 ft

Bottom layer consists of large broken stones, 3 to 4 in. in diam. 4 in. deep in centre.

Top layer consists of broken Stone from dust to 2½ in. in diam. 6 in. deep in centre.

APPENDIX J.

Table H gives the results of a study of the different types of wagons used in and about Boston, Holyoke, North Adams, Northampton, Pittsfield, Greenfield and Springfield. In this table are shown the length of axle, width of tire, weight of wagon and load, and the load per inch in width of tire. The average load per inch of tire of each type of wagon is also given. A condensed statement of the load hauled by each horse on the different types of wagons in the different municipalities referred to will be found in Table J.

TABLE II. — *Statistics showing the Kinds of Wagons, Loads per Horse, Width of Tires and Weights on Each Inch of Width of Tires.*

Boston, Mass., 1892.

KIND OF WAGON.	No. of Wagons observed.	No. of Horses.	Gauge. Front.		Gauge. Rear.		Width of Tires. Front.	Width of Tires. Rear.	Weight (Pounds). Wagon.	Weight (Pounds). Wagon and Load.	Distribution of Load.	Load per Inch on Width of Tire (Maximum).
			ft.	in.	ft.	in.	in.	in.				lbs.
Tip-cart,	1	1	5	8	5	8	2¼	2¼	2,300	10,300	Even.	1,145
"	1	1	5	3	–		3	–	1,900	6,700	"	1,117
"	1	1	5	3	–		3	–	1,900	4,800	"	800
"	1	1	5	3	–		3	–	1,900	4,800	"	800
"	1	2	5	3	5	6	2¾	3	2,650	13,650	4-5 rear.	1,820
"	1	2	5	2	5	2	2	2¾	2,600	9,100	"	1,320
"	1	2	5	2	5	2	2	2¾	2,500	8,500	"	1,240
"	5	2	5	2	5	2	2	3	2,700	7,300	"	975

	lbs.
Average load per inch of width of tire for all one-horse wagons,	965
" " " " two-horse wagons,	1,339
" " " " types observed,	1,147
" " " " wagons observed,	1,152

TABLE H. — Continued.

Boston, Mass., 1892 — Continued.

KIND OF WAGON.	No. of Wagons observed.	No. of Horses.	Gauge. Front.		Gauge. Rear.		Width of Tires. Front.	Width of Tires. Rear.	Weight (Pounds). Wagon.	Weight (Pounds). Wagon and Load.	Distribution of Load.	Load per Inch on Width of Tire (Maximum).
			ft.	in.	ft.	in.	in.	in.				lbs.
Beer, ...	3	1	5	2	5	2	2¼	2¼	2,300	4,200	Even.	466
"	4	1	5	8	5	8	2¼	2¼	2,350	4,600	"	510
"	1	2	6	2	6	2	3	3	5,500	13,500	"	1,125
"	1	2	5	7	5	7	3	3	3,000	12,000	"	1,000
"	1	2	5	7	5	7	3	3	2,500	7,500	"	625
"	2	2	5	10	5	10	2¼	2¼	2,800	8,800	"	977
"	3	2	6	2	6	2	3	3	3,700	11,700	"	975
"	10	2	5	4	5	4	3	3	2,700	10,700	"	892
"	12	2	5	9	5	9	3	3	3,800	8,000	"	666
"	2	2	5	7	5	7	2¾	2¾	4,300	8,800	"	800

	lbs.
Average load per inch of width of tire for all one-horse wagons, ...	488
" " " " two-horse wagons, ...	883
" " " " types observed, ...	804
" " " " wagons observed, ...	758

Caravan, ...	1	1	5	6	5	6	2¼	2¼	2,000	6,000	Even.	666
"	1	1	6	0	6	0	2½	3	2,800	8,800	"	880
"	3	1	5	3	5	3	2	2¼	2,500	8,500	3-4 rear.	1,410
"	1	2	6	3	6	3	3	3	4,200	9,700	Even.	810
"	1	2	5	10	5	10	3¼	3¼	3,700	12,700	"	977
"	2	1	6	3	6	3	2⅞	2⅞	3,600	10,100	"	880
"	5	2	6	0	6	0	3	3¼	3,600	14,600	3-4 rear.	1,685
"	10	2	5	10	5	10	2¾	2¾	4,000	13,000	Even.	1,180
"	1	2	6	1½	6	2	2½	3	4,300	12,300	3-5 rear.	1,230
"	1	2	5	8	5	8	2½	2½	3,600	12,600	Even.	1,260
"	5	2	5	8	5	8	2	2¼	3,600	13,600	"	1,700
"	1	2	5	8	5	8	2¾	2¾	3,600	14,600	"	1,330
"	1	2	6	0	6	0	2½	3	4,400	18,400	"	1,840
"	1	2	5	10	5	10	2⅞	3	3,500	13,500	3-5 rear.	1,350
"	4	2	6	3	6	3	3	3	4,500	14,500	Even.	1,210
"	1	2	5	6	5	6	2¼	3	2,500	14,500	"	1,610
"	1	2	5	0	5	0	2⅝	3	3,500	13,500	3-4 rear.	1,690
"	1	4	6	0	6	0	4⅛	4⅛	5,500	25,000	Even.	1,510
"	1	4	6	3	6	0	3	3½	4,700	11,500	"	960
"	1	4	5	2	5	2	3¼	3¼	4,500	24,500	"	1,880
"	1	4	5	6	5	6	3	3¼	3,650	22,650	2-3 rear.	2,320
"	1	4	5	6	5	6	3	4	6,350	38,250	3-4 "	3,590
"	1	4	6	5½	6	7½	3	3½	6,300	30,300	Even.	2,520

	lbs.
Average load per inch of width of tire for all one-horse wagons, ...	959
" " " " two-horse wagons, ...	1,375
" " " " four-horse wagons, ...	2,130
" " " " types observed, ...	1,499
" " " " wagons observed, ...	1,434

TABLE H. — Continued.

Boston, Mass., 1892 — Continued.

KIND OF WAGON.	No. of Wagons observed.	No. of Horses.	Gauge. Front.		Gauge. Rear.		Width of Tires. Front.	Width of Tires. Rear.	Weight (Pounds). Wagon.	Weight (Pounds). Wagon and Load.	Distribution of Load.	Load per Inch on Width of Tire (Maximum).
			ft.	in.	ft.	in.	in.	in.				lbs.
Coal, ...	1	1	–		4	8	–	2⅛	1,480	4,780	Even.	956
"	1	1	5	2	5	0	2¼	2⅝	2,400	6,400	"	710
"	1	1	5	6	5	3½	2	2	1,580	5,580	"	700
"	1	1	–		5	6	–	2¾	1,500	5,500	"	1,000
"	1	1	5	7	5	9	2¼	2¼	1,450	4,450	"	495
"	1	1	–		5	1	–	2½	1,900	5,900	"	1,180
"	1	1	5	5	5	5	2¼	2¼	1,750	5,750	"	640
"	1	2	5	5½	5	3½	2½	2⅝	4,000	10,500	"	1,050
"	1	2	5	8	5	6½	2¾	3	3,000	10,000	"	910
"	1	2	5	9	5	8	3	3	3,000	10,000	"	830
"	1	2	5	9	5	10	3	3	3,000	9,500	"	790
"	1	2	5	5½	5	5	3	3	2,800	8,800	"	730
"	1	2	6	0	6	0	3	3⅛	2,900	9,900	"	830
"	1	2	5	6	5	5½	3	3	3,150	10,150	"	846
"	1	2	5	2	5	2	2¼	2¼	3,100	8,900	"	990
"	1	2	6	0½	6	0	2½	3	3,730	12,730	"	1,270
"	1	2	5	5	5	5	2¼	3⅛	3,150	11,150	Tip-cart.	1,430
"	1	2	5	6	5	8	3	3	3,580	10,580	"	1,410

"	1	2	5	6	5	6	3	3	3,420	9,420	Even.	785
"	1	2	5	2	5	7	2⅝	3	2,800	8,800	Tip-cart.	1,170
"	1	2	5	10	5	9	2¼	2¼	2,000	8,000	–	890
"	1	2	5	4½	5	5	2⅛	3	3,900	10,400	Tip-cart.	1,390
"	1	2	5	7½	5	7½	2⅞	2⅞	4,150	11,150	Even.	970
"	1	2	5	4	5	4	2¼	3	3,220	11,220	2–3 rear.	1,250
"	1	2	5	0½	5	1	2	2	2,250	6,250	Even.	780
"	1	2	6	6	6	4½	3	3	4,580	16,580	"	1,380
"	1	1	5	5½	5	8½	2⅛	2⅛	1,500	4,500	"	530
"	1	1	5	3	5	5	2	2	1,500	5,500	"	690
"	1	1	5	4	5	3	2	2	1,500	5,500	"	690
"	1	1	5	3	5	2	2	2	1,700	4,700	"	590
"	1	1	–		4	6½	–	2½	1,400	3,600	"	720
"	1	1	–		5	5	–	3	1,800	4,800	"	800
"	1	1	5	6½	5	5½	2	2	1,400	4,400	"	550
"	1	1	5	4½	5	0	2	2	1,325	4,825	"	600
"	1	1	5	6½	5	6	1⅞	1⅞	1,180	3,880	"	520
"	1	1	–		4	8	–	2½	1,480	4,780	"	960

	lbs.
Average load per inch of width of tire for all one-horse wagons, ...	725
" " " " two-horse wagons, ...	1,018
" " " " types observed, ...	824

Note.—In tip-carts used for hauling coal it is assumed that four-fifths of the weight is borne by the rear wheels.

TABLE H. — Continued.

Boston, Mass., 1892 — Continued.

KIND OF WAGON.	No. of Wagons observed.	No. of Horses.	Gauge. Front.		Gauge. Rear.		Width of Tires. Front.	Width of Tires. Rear.	Weight (Pounds). Wagon.	Weight (Pounds). Wagon and Load.	Distribution of Load.	Load per Inch on Width of Tire (Maximum).
			ft.	in.	ft.	in.	in.	in.				lbs.
Express, ...	1	1	5	6	5	6	2½	2½	2,300	4,800	Even.	480
"	1	1	4	6	4	6	1⅜	1⅜	1,000	2,500	"	455
"	1	1	4	6	4	6	1⅜	1⅜	1,200	2,700	"	490
"	1	1	4	6	4	6	1⅜	1⅜	1,000	2,500	"	455
"	1	1	4	6	4	6	1⅜	1⅜	1,200	2,700	"	490
"	1	1	4	6	4	6	1½	1½	1,500	4,000	"	670
"	1	2	5	11	5	11	1¼	3¼	3,600	11,600	"	890
"	1	2	6	4	6	4	3	3	5,700	20,000	"	1,670
"	1	2	6	1	6	1	3	3	4,700	15,700	"	1,310
"	1	2	4	6	4	6	1½	1½	2,500	6,000	"	1,000
"	1	2	4	6	4	6	1½	1½	3,000	7,000	"	1,165

	lbs.
Average load per inch of width of tire for all one-horse wagons, ...	507
" " " " two-horse wagons, ...	1,207
" " " " types observed, ...	825

Grain, ...	1	1	5	5¼	5	6½	2⅜	2⅜	1,900	6,300	Even.	665
Carriage, ...	1	1	4	8	4	8	¾	¾	225	725	"	240
"	1	1	3	10	3	10	[illegible]	[illegible]	90	240	"	120
"	1	2	4	8	4	8	[illegible]	[illegible]	600	1,800	"	520
"	1	4	5	4	5	4	1½	1¼	2,000	4,500	"	750

	lbs.
Average load per inch of width of tire for all one-horse wagons, ...	180
" " " " two-horse wagons, ...	520
" " " " four-horse wagons, ...	750
" " " " types observed, ...	410

Lime and cement, ...	1	1	5	10	5	10	2¼	2¼	2,500	8,500	Even.	945
" "	1	2	5	1	5	1	2	3	2,500	8,500	"	1,060
" "	1	2	5	1	5	10	2¼	3	3,200	10,200	"	930

	lbs.
Average load per inch of width of tire for all one-horse wagons, ...	945
" " " " two-horse wagons, ...	995
" " " " types observed, ...	978

TABLE H. — Continued.

Boston, Mass., 1892 — Continued.

KIND OF WAGON.	No. of Wagons observed.	No. of Horses.	Gauge. Front.		Gauge. Rear.		Width of Tires. Front.	Width of Tires. Rear.	Weight (Pounds). Wagon.	Weight (Pounds). Wagon and Load.	Distribution of Load.	Load per Inch on Width of Tire (Maximum).
			ft.	in.	ft.	in.	in.	in.				lbs.
Lumber, ...	5	2	5	2	5	2	4	4	2,900	7,900	Even.	495
"	3	2	5	6	5	6	2½	2½	1,600	6,600	3-4 rear.	990
"	1	2	5	6	5	6	2¾	2¾	1,900	10,900	Even.	990
"	1	2	5	0	5	0	2¾	3	3,200	16,000	3-4 rear.	2,000
"	1	3	5	3	5	3	3	3	1,600	13,600	Even.	1,135
"	1	3	5	6	5	4½	2⅝	2⅝	1,500	13,500	"	1,285
"	1	3	5	6½	5	5	3	3	4,000	16,000	"	1,335
"	3	3	5	2	5	2	2½	2½	2,500	11,500	3-4 rear.	1,725
"	4	3	5	2	5	2	3	3	3,000	13,000	"	1,625
"	1	4	5	2	5	2	3	3	3,800	18,000	"	2,250
"	1	1	5	6	5	6	2¼	2¼	2,000	6,000	Even.	670
"	1	1	5	6	5	6	2	2	1,800	6,300	"	790
"	10	2	5	9	5	9	3¼	3¼	3,600	11,600	"	890
"	1	2	5	5	5	5	3¼	3¼	3,000	10,000	"	770
"	1	2	5	6	5	6	2¼	2¼	2,200	6,200	"	690
"	1	2	5	6	5	6	3	3	2,200	6,200	"	520

	lbs.
Average load per inch of width of tire for all one-horse wagons, ...	730
" " " " two-horse wagons, ...	918
" " " " three-horse wagons, ...	1,421

" " " " four-horse wagons, ... 2,250
" " " " types observed, ... 1,135
" " " " wagons observed, ... 1,068

Ice, ...	1	2	5	7	5	7	2⅜	2⅜	4,100	10,700	Even.	980
"	1	2	5	7	5	7	2¼	2¼	4,000	10,300	"	940
"	7	2	5	6	5	6	2¼	2¼	3,750	10,500	"	955

Average load per inch of width of tire for all two-horse wagons, ... lbs. 958
" " " " wagons observed, ... 956

Milk, ...	1	1	5	3	5	2½	1⅞	2	1,200	3,100	Even.	415
"	1	1	5	4	5	3	1⅞	1⅞	1,050	2,650	"	355
"	1	2	5	4	5	4	2¼	2¼	1,850	6,850	"	760
"	1	1	5	2	5	2	1⅞	1⅞	900	1,600	"	215
"	1	1	5	5	5	5	2	2	1,400	5,150	"	645
"	1	1	5	2	5	2	1½	1½	700	1,200	"	200
"	1	1	5	3	5	4	1⅞	1⅞	1,260	4,000	"	535
"	1	1	5	5	5	5	2¼	2¼	1,600	5,600	"	660
"	1	1	5	3	5	3	1¼	1¼	1,050	2,170	"	310
"	1	1	5	4	5	3	2¼	2¼	1,400	4,150	"	460
"	1	1	5	4	5	3½	2	2	1,200	3,700	"	460
"	1	1	5	5	5	4	1⅞	1⅞	1,100	3,600	"	480
"	1	1	5	4	5	3½	2	2	1,200	2,100	"	260
"	1	1	5	3½	5	5	2	2	1,500	5,200	"	650
"	1	1	5	3	5	3	1⅞	1⅞	1,150	2,750	"	365

Average load per inch of width of tire for all one-horse wagons, ... lbs. 429
" " " " two-horse wagons, ... 760
" " " " types observed, ... 451

TABLE H. — Continued.

Boston, Mass., 1892 — Concluded.

KIND OF WAGON.	No. of Wagons observed.	No. of Horses.	Gauge. Front.		Gauge. Rear.		Width of Tires. Front.	Width of Tires. Rear.	Weight (Pounds). Wagon.	Weight (Pounds). Wagon and Load.	Distribution of Load.	Load per Inch on Width of Tire (Maximum).
			ft.	in.	ft.	in.	in.	in.				lbs.
Meat,	20	1	5	6	5	6	2½	2½	2,300	6,800	Even.	680
"	19	2	5	6	5	6	3½	3½	4,200	12,200	"	870
"	1	3	5	6	5	6	3½	3½	5,500	25,000	"	1,780
Average load per inch of width of tire for all types observed,												lbs. 1,110
" " " " wagons observed,												798
Stone,	1	1	5	2	5	2	2	2	1,800	5,800	Even.	725
"	1	1	5	6	5	6	2½	2½	2,000	7,000	"	700
"	1	1	5	6	5	6	2½	2½	2,500	7,500	"	750
"	1	2	5	0	5	0	4	4	2,600	10,600	"	665
"	1	2	5	2	5	2	2½	2½	2,400	13,600	3-5 rear.	1,630
"	1	2	5	2	5	2	3	3	3,800	10,800	Even.	900
"	1	2	5	3	5	3	2½	3	3,100	10,100	"	1,010
"	1	2	6	6	6	6	2½	2½	3,500	12,500	"	1,250
"	1	3	5	6	5	6	2¾	3	3,000	23,000	"	2,090
"	1	3	5	6	5	6	2¾	3	3,000	23,000	"	2,090
"	1	4	5	2	5	2	3	3	5,200	35,200	3-5 rear.	3,520
"	1	4	5	2	5	2	3	3	4,900	30,000	Even.	2,500

"	1	4	5	2	5	2	3	3	3,800	25,800	3-5 rear.	2,580
"	1	4	5	2	5	2	3	3	3,800	25,800	Even.	2,150
"	1	4	5	10	5	10	2½	3½	4,300	15,250	2-3 rear	1,450
"	1	4	5	3	5	6¾	3¼	3½	4,300	15,250	" "	1,450
"	1	8 to 16	5	2	5	2	5	5	8,400	68,400	3-5 rear.	4,100
"	–	–	–	–	–	–	–	–	–	88,400	–	5,300

	lbs.
Average load per inch of width of tire for all one-horse wagons, ...	725
" " " " two-horse wagons, ...	1,091
" " " " three-horse wagons, ...	2,090
" " " " four-horse wagons, ...	2,275
" " " " eight-horse wagons, ...	4,100
" " " " sixteen-horse wagons, ...	5,300
" " " " types observed, ...	1,938

Holyoke, Mass., 1892.

Caravan, ...	1	1	4	10	4	10	2	2	1,300	4,800	Even.	600
"	8	2	5	2	5	2	3	3	2,500	11,500	"	960
"	1	2	4	8	4	8	3	3	1,740	7,200	"	600
"	4	2	5	2	5	2	2¾	3¾	2,850	12,000	"	800
"	1	2	5	2	5	2	3¾	3¾	2,600	11,500	"	765

	lbs.
Average load per inch of width of tire for all two-horse wagons, ...	781
" " " " types observed, ...	745
" " " " wagons observed, ...	856

TABLE H. — Continued.

Holyoke, Mass., 1892 — Concluded.

KIND OF WAGON.	No. of Wagons observed.	No. of Horses.	Gauge. Front.		Gauge. Rear.		Width of Tires. Front.	Width of Tires. Rear.	Weight (Pounds). Wagon.	Weight (Pounds). Wagon and Load.	Distribution of Load.	Load per Inch on Width of Tire (Maximum).
			ft.	in.	ft.	in.	in.	in.				lbs.
Coal,	2	2	5	2	5	2	2	4	2,000	6,000	Tip-cart.	600
"	3	1	5	1	5	1	4	4	1,000	3,200	"	320
"	4	1	4	6	4	6	1¾	1¾	1,000	3,200	"	730
Average load per inch of width of tire for all types,												lbs. 550
" " " " wagons observed,												564
" " " " one-horse wagons,												525
Lumber,	1	2	5	4	5	4	3	3	2,000	6,500	Even.	540
North Adams, Mass., 1892.												
Caravan,	1	1	5	0	5	0	1¾	2	1,200	4,700	Even.	670
"	6	2	4	11	4	11	2¾	2¾	1,100	7,000	"	640
"	4	2	5	4	5	4	2¾	2¾	2,180	8,700	"	790
Average load per inch of width of tire for all two-horse wagons,												lbs. 715
" " " " types observed,												700
" " " " wagons observed,												697

Coal, ...	1	2	5	2	5	2	3	3	1,670	5,170	Even.	430
"	1	2	5	2	5	2	3	3	1,740	5,740	"	480
"	2	2	5	2	5	2	3	3	1,860	5,860	"	490
Average load per inch of width of tire for all one-horse wagons, ...												lbs. 455
" " " " types observed, ...												467
" " " " wagons observed, ...												473
Lime and cement, ...	7	2	4	11	4	11	3	3	1,600	5,300	Even.	440
" "	2	1	4	10	4	10	2	2	800	2,800	"	350
Average load per inch of width of tire for all types observed, ...												lbs. 395
" " " " wagons observed, ...												420
Tip-cart, ...	2	1	4	8	4	8	3	3	1,000	4,000	Even.	335
Northampton, Mass., 1892.												
Caravan, ...	1	1	4	6	4	6	2¼	2¼	1,100	3,300	Even.	370
Grain and coal, ...	1	1	4	6	4	6	1½	1½	900	2,900	"	485
" "	1	2	4	11	4	11	2	2	1,200	6,700	"	840
Average load per inch of width of tire for all types observed, ...												lbs. 663

NOTE. — In tip-carts used for hauling coal it is assumed that four-fifths of the weight is borne by the rear wheels.

TABLE H. — Continued.

Northampton, Mass., 1892 — Concluded.

KIND OF WAGON.	No. of Wagons observed.	No. of Horses.	Gauge. Front.		Gauge. Rear.		Width of Tires. Front.	Width of Tires. Rear.	Weight (Pounds). Wagon.	Weight (Pounds). Wagon and Load.	Distribution of Load.	Load per Inch on Width of Tire (Maximum).
			ft.	in.	ft.	in.	in.	in.				lbs.
Ice, ...	6	2	5	0	5	0	2½	2½	2,300	7,300	Even.	730
Lumber, ...	2	1	5	0	5	0	2	2	1,300	5,300	"	665
"	1	2	5	4	5	4	2¼	2¼	1,600	6,300	"	700
Average load per inch of width of tire for all types observed,												lbs. 683
" " " " wagons observed,												677
Tip-cart, ...	1	2	5	4	5	4	2	4	1,800	4,300	–	430
"	1	2	5	0	5	0	2½	2½	1,300	4,300	–	690
Average load per inch of width of tire for all types observed,												lbs. 560

Pittsfield, Mass., 1892.

Lumber,	1	2	5 2	5 2	2¾	2¾	1,150	7,400	Even.	675
"	2	2	5 0	5 0	2½	2½	1,200	7,700	"	770
"	2	1	4 8	4 8	2	2	900	5,400	"	675
"	1	1	4 6	4 6	1½	1½	700	2,700	"	450
Average load per inch of width of tire for all one-horse wagons,										lbs. 563
" " " " two-horse wagons,										723
" " " " types observed,										643
" " " " wagons observed,										669
Milk,	1	1	4 6	4 6	1½	1½	700	2,500	Even.	420
Stone,	1	1	4 0	4 0	2	2	800	2,800	"	350
"	1	2	4 4	4 4	2½	2½	1,500	8,500	"	850
"	1	2	4 6	4 6	3	3	1,300	4,800	"	400
Average load per inch of width of tire for all two-horse wagons,										lbs. 625
" " " " types observed,										533
Grain,	1	1	4 6	4 6	1¾	1¾	700	2,700	Even.	385
Flour, etc.,	2	2	5 0	5 0	2¼	2¼	2,000	7,000	"	640
Average load per inch of width of tire for all types observed,										lbs. 513
" " " " wagons observed,										555

TABLE H. — Continued.

Pittsfield, Mass., 1892 — Concluded.

KIND OF WAGON.	No. of Wagons observed.	No. of Horses.	Gauge. Front.		Gauge. Rear.		Width of Tires. Front.	Width of Tires. Rear.	Weight (Pounds). Wagon.	Weight (Pounds). Wagon and Load.	Distribution of Load.	Load per inch on Width of Tire (Maximum).
			ft.	in.	ft.	in.	in.	in.				lbs.
Ice,	2	1	4	8	4	8	1½	1½	900	2,900	Even.	480
"	2	2	4	10	4	10	2	2	1,300	5,300	"	660
Average load per inch of width of tire for all types observed,												lbs. 570
Lime and cement,	1	1	4	6	4	6	2½	2½	1,200	4,300	–	430
Beer,	4	1	4	6	4	6	2	2	900	2,500	Even.	310
"	1	2	5	3	5	3	2½	2½	1,500	6,500	"	650
"	1	2	4	10	4	10	2½	2½	1,900	7,900	"	790
"	4	2	4	8	4	8	2	2	1,000	4,500	"	560

	lbs.
Average load per inch of width of tire for all two-horse wagons,	667
" " " " types observed,	578
" " " " wagons observed,	492

Caravan,	6	1	4	10	4	10	2	2	1,000	4,000	Even.	500
"	2	1	4	6	4	6	1¾	1¾	1,200	4,200	"	600
"	1	2	5	2	5	2	2¼	2¼	2,000	11,000	"	1,000
"	8	2	5	0	5	0	2½	2½	1,900	7,000	"	700
"	1	4	5	0	5	0	3	3	2,400	10,400	"	866
Average load per inch of width of tire for all one-horse wagons,												lbs. 550
" " " " two-horse wagons,												850
" " " " types observed,												733
" " " " wagons observed,												648
Coal,	2	2	5	2	5	2	2¼	2½	1,900	6,000	Even.	667
"	1	2	4	6	4	6	3	3	1,750	6,750	"	563
"	3	1	5	0	5	0	2¾	3	950	3,150	"	290
"	3	1	5	0	5	0	2	2	1,200	2,700	"	340
Average load per inch of width of tire for all one-horse wagons,												lbs. 315
" " " " two-horse wagons,												615
" " " " typos observed,												465
" " " " wagons observed,												421
Farm,	1	1	4	5½	4	5½	1¼	1¼	700	2,500	Even.	500
"	1	2	4	5	4	5	2 1/16	2 1/16	1,200	4,200	"	510
Average load per inch of width of tire for all wagons observed,												lbs. 505

TABLE H. — Continued.

Greenfield, Mass., 1892.

KIND OF WAGON.	No. of Wagons observed.	No. of Horses.	Gauge. Front.		Gauge. Rear.		Width of Tires. Front.	Width of Tires. Rear.	Weight (Pounds). Wagon.	Weight (Pounds). Wagon and Load.	Distribution of Load.	Load per Inch on Width of Tire (Maximum).
			ft.	in.	ft.	in.	in.	in.				lbs.
Coal,	3	1	4	10	4	10	1¾	1¾	970	3,500	Even.	500
"	2	1	4	10	4	10	2	2	1,175	4,000	"	500
Average load per inch of width of tire for all one-horse wagons,												lbs. 500
Ice,	2	2	5	0	5	0	2	2	1,500	6,000	Even.	750
"	1	1	5	0	5	0	2	2	1,030	4,030	"	505
Average load per inch of width of tire for all types observed,												lbs. 628
Lumber,	1	2	4	11	4	11	3	3	1,500	4,700	Even.	390
"	1	1	4	11	4	11	2	2	1,225	2,800	"	350
Average load per inch of width of tire for all types observed,												lbs. 370

	1	1	4	8	4	8	1½	1½	650	2,650	Even.	440
	1	1	4	8	4	8	1½	1½	800	3,300	"	550
Average load per inch of width of tire for all types observed,												lbs. 495
Dirt, sand and stone,	2	2	5	0	5	0	3	4	1,600	4,600	Even.	390
Springfield, Mass.; 1892.												
Beer,	–	2	4	8	4	8	2¼	2¼	2,700	11,200	Even.	1,245
"	–	2	5	4	5	4	2	2	2,200	8,200	"	1,025
"	–	2	5	2	5	2	2½	2¾	2,800	9,000	"	900
"	–	2	5	2	5	2	2½	2¾	2,600	7,900	"	790
"	–	2	5	2	5	2	2¾	2¾	3,000	9,200	"	836
"	–	1	4	6	4	6	1½	1½	900	3,100	"	517
Average load per inch of width of tire for all one-horse wagons,												lbs. 517
" " " " two-horse wagons,												959
" " " " types observed,												886
Caravan,	–	2	5	6	5	6	2¾	2¾	2,450	5,450	Even.	495
"	–	2	6	4	6	4	2½	2¾	2,500	9,000	"	900
"	–	2	6	2	6	2	2½	2¾	3,000	10,000	"	1,000
"	–	2	5	0	5	0	2	2¼	1,900	7,900	"	988
"	–	1	4	11	4	11	2	2	1,500	5,000	"	625
Average load per inch of width of tire for all one-horse wagons,												lbs. 625
" " " " two-horse wagons,												846
" " " " types observed,												800

TABLE H. — Concluded.

Springfield, Mass., 1892 — Concluded.

KIND OF WAGON.	No. of Wagons observed.	No. of Horses.	Gauge. Front.		Gauge. Rear.		Width of Tires. Front.	Width of Tires. Rear.	Weight (Pounds). Wagon.	Weight (Pounds). Wagon and Load.	Distribution of Load.	Load per Inch on Width of Tire (Maximum).
			ft.	in.	ft.	in.	in.	in.				lbs.
Express,	–	1	4	6	4	6	2	2	1,000	2,300	Even.	287
"	–	2	4	10	4	10	1¾	1¾	1,200	5,400	"	770
Average load per inch of width of tire for all types observed,												lbs. 529
Grain,	–	1	5	8	5	8	1¾	1¾	1,000	3,300	Even.	470
"	–	1	6	1	6	1	1¾	2	1,200	3,700	"	530
Average load per inch of width of tire for all one-horse wagons,												lbs. 500
Stone,	–	2	6	1	6	1	3	4	1,800	5,800	3-4 rear.	544
"	–	2	5	8	6	1	2¾	2¾	2,000	8,000	Even.	730
Average load per inch of width of tire for all two-horse wagons,												lbs. 637

Lumber, ...	–	1	4	4	4	4	2	2	900	3,650	Even.	456
"	–	2	5	1	5	1	3	3	1,600	10,600	"	880
Average load per inch of width of tire for all types observed, ...												lbs. 668
Lime and cement, . . .	–	2	5	2	5	2	1½	1½	1,900	6,900	Even.	1,150
Ice, ...	–	2	4	10	4	10	1½	1¾	1,380	5,380	"	897
"	–	2	5	0	5	0	3	3	2,300	7,300	"	608
Average load per inch of width of tire for all two-horse wagons, ...												lbs. 753
Coal, ...	–	2	5	0	5	0	3	4	2,000	8,500	Even.	708
"	–	2	5	0	5	0	3	4	2,300	7,000	"	583
"	–	1	4	2	4	2	3	4	2,800	5,800	"	483
"	–	1	5	0	5	0	1½	1½	1,150	3,650	"	608
"	–	1	5	0	5	4	1¾	2	1,600	4,700	"	670
"	–	1	5	2	5	4	1¾	2	1,600	4,700	"	670
"	–	1	5	2	5	4	1¾	2	1,700	5,000	"	715

Average load per inch of width of tire for all one-horse wagons, ...	lbs. 630
" " " " two-horse wagons, ...	646
" " " " types observed, ...	634

TABLE I. — *Giving the Number of Tons of Freight hauled One Mile, per Day and per Year, over the Roads on which Traffic Observations were made.*

PLACE OF OBSERVATION.	Total Number of Tons of Freight hauled in Three Days.	Number of Tons hauled per Day.	Average Haul in Miles.	Number of Ton-miles per Day.	Number of Ton-miles per Year of 330 Days.
Beacon Street, at Brighton Road,	2,592	864	3.3	2,851	94,083
Beacon Street, at Coolidge's Corner,	1,685	562	3.0	1,686	55,638
Blue Hill Avenue, at Washington Street,	611	204	3.9	796	26,268
Blue Hill Avenue, at Mattapan,	703	234	3.0	702	23,166
Broadway, at Chelsea Bridge,	2,777	926	2.3	2,130	70,290
Broadway, at Revere Street, Revere,	1,437	479	4.0	1,916	63,228
Western Avenue, Cambridge Bridge,	2,028	676	1.6	1,082	35,706
Western Avenue and Arsenal Street,	2,290	763	3.3	2,518	83,094
Totals,	14,123	4,708	-	13,681	451,473
Averages,	-	-	3.0	-	-

TABLE J. — *Statistics showing the Average Load (in Pounds) per Horse for Different Kinds of Wagons in Various Cities of the Commonwealth.*

CITIES.	CHARACTER OF TEAMS.								
	Coal.	Lumber.	Caravan.	Stone.	Ice.	Tip-cart.	Cement and Lime.	Milk.	Meat.
Boston,	3,393	3,611	5,089	5,205	3,275	4,081	4,167	2,184	5,000
Pittsfield,	2,063	3,219	3,010	2,417	2,000	-	3,100	1,800	-
Northampton,	2,375	3,175	2,200	-	2,500	1,375	-	-	-
Greenfield,	2,678	1,588	-	1,500	2,625	-	-	-	-
Holyoke,	2,133	2,250	3,951	-	-	-	-	-	-
North Adams,	1,917	-	3,237	-	-	3,000	1,925	-	-
Springfield,	2,917	3,625	2,950	2,500	2,250	-	2,500	-	-
Average outside Boston,	2,347	2,771	3,070	2,139	2,344	2,188	2,508	1,800	-
Per cent. of average values to Boston values,	69	77	60	41	72	54	60	82	-

An average of these percentages gives the load per horse outside of Boston as sixty-four per cent. of the Boston value.

APPENDIX K.

Table B shows the answers to Schedule B, which contained the following interrogatories: —

Number of miles of roads of all description? Of the above total miles of roads in your town, will you please state how many miles of roads connect with the adjoining towns. Give the names of county roads. How many miles of roads are local only? Of the above total miles of roads, will you please state, as near as possible, the —

Number of miles of dirt roads; average width of travelled roadway.
Number of miles of gravel roads; average width of travelled roadway.
Number of miles of macadamized roads; average width of travelled roadway.
Number of miles of granite block paving; average width of travelled roadway.
Number of miles of wood paving; average width of travelled roadway.
Number of miles of brick paving; average width of travelled roadway.
Number of miles of asphalt paving; average width of travelled roadway.
Number of miles of concrete paving; average width of travelled roadway.
Number of miles of cobble paving; average width of travelled roadway.

This table gives the number of miles of different kinds of pavements and roads in the Commonwealth outside of Boston.

A brief study will show that there are 5,548 miles of gravel roads, 469 miles of macadam, 49 miles of granite blocks, 26 miles of cobble, 6 miles of concrete, $\frac{3}{4}$ mile of asphalt, 1,643 square yards of brick and 10 miles of shell. Outside of Boston there are about 20,000 miles of streets and roads in the Commonwealth. The above figures show that nearly 30.5 per cent. of them are either paved, macadamized or gravel. The remaining 69.5 per cent. are what we class dirt roads, or roads which are made from the soil over which they pass. A large percentage of the 5,548 miles of gravel roads are but little better than the dirt. They are mostly bad during wet weather.

Table C shows the replies to Schedule C, which contained the following questions: —

How much of the appropriation for 1891 was expended for the following purposes: Snow and ice? General repairs? Cleaning streets and gutters? Sidewalks? Gravel roads? Macadamized roads? Paved gutters? Paved streets? Bridges? New roads?

Total appropriations for highways and bridges for 1891? What is the assessed value of real estate? What is the assessed value of personal property? What was the rate of taxation in 1891?

This table contains the reports from the different towns and cities of the Commonwealth, and shows amount of money expended on different classes of work, together with the valuation and tax rate. A study of the table will show that by far the greater part of the money has been expended on general repairs.

In the counties of Dukes, Barnstable and Nantucket, no macadamizing was done. Money was expended on macadam roads during 1892 in the several counties as follows: —

Barnstable, not any.	
Berkshire, one city, four towns,	$22,595
Bristol, two cities, two towns,	67,524
Dukes, not any.	
Essex, one city, four towns,	29,033
Franklin, one town,	4,200
Hampden, one city, two towns,	20,065
Hampshire, none reported.	
Suffolk, outside of Boston, one city,	5,569
Middlesex, four cities, seven towns, about	73,677
Norfolk, one city, four towns,	48,500
Plymouth, five towns,	10,200
Worcester, one city, one town,	22,303
Total,	$303,666

Several cities and towns have failed to return answers; some of these have done considerable macadam work during the past year, but they are necessarily omitted from this report. It appears that a total of eleven cities and thirty towns have expended $303,666 in constructing macadam roads in the year 1892.

Gravel roads have been built in the several counties as follows: —

Barnstable, one town,	$1,000
Berkshire, one city, seven towns,	7,925
Bristol, five towns,	11,474
Dukes, one town,	53
Essex, one city, six towns,	9,834
Franklin, one town,	100
Hampden, two cities, five towns,	15,103
Hampshire, two towns,	4,400
Suffolk, one city, one town,	4,455
Middlesex, four cities, ten towns,	55,668
Norfolk, seven towns,	38,488
Plymouth, ten towns,	14,041
Worcester, sixteen towns,	21,489
Total,	$184,030
Total amount reported as expended in nine cities and seventy-two towns on gravel roads was	$184,030

Several cities and towns have not separated the macadam and gravel work; as a result, these figures do not represent the exact expenditures, but they furnish a good means of studying the character of the work in a general way. Judging from the reports sent to this commission, it is fair to say that roads built of macadam or gravel are the only ones that are in any way permanent. By separating the cities' and towns' expenditures, we find that the macadam work in the cities cost $130,702; in the towns, $172,974; total, $303,676. Gravel work in the cities cost $42,680; in the towns, $141,350; total, $184,030.

It will be seen that the total amount expended on gravel and macadam roads in the different towns throughout the State amounted to $314,324.

By referring to Table L, it will be seen that the average amount expended in the towns per year for the past three years was $1,136,-944. The amount expended on work of a more or less permanent character was about twenty-seven and one-half per cent. of the total expenditure. A further study will show that a considerable amount was expended on bridges, roads, sidewalks, paved gutters, cleaning streets and removing snow and ice.

Schedule D was as follows: —

Have you a steam roller? Weight? Cost? Have you a horse-roller? Weight? Cost? Is the horse-roller solid? Is the horse-roller of the ring pattern? Have you a stone crusher? Size? Cost? Is your crusher set up to take the stone without two handlings? Do you have an elevator to lift stone from crusher to screen or bins? Height? Cost of elevator? Do you have a revolving screen? Do you have plain screens? How many grades of stone do you screen out? Do you have storage bins at crusher for broken stone? How many? Do you load broken stone from bins without shovelling? Do you load broken stone by shovelling? How much per ton does it cost to load broken stone with shovels? How many horses do you use to haul your horse-roller? Do you own a road machine? Cost? Do you own water carts? How many? Capacity in gallons?

These were asked to show the machinery in use for road building throughout the Commonwealth. The road machine or scraper seems to be in general use. They are to be found in the several counties as follows: —

	Number.	Cost.
Barnstable,	13	$2,975
Berkshire,	31	6,712
Bristol,	16	2,825
Dukes,	–	–
Essex,	17	3,418
Franklin,	21	4,775
Hampden,	25	4,900
Hampshire,	25	5,100
Middlesex,	46	9,571
Nantucket,	1	250
Norfolk,	24	5,171
Plymouth,	26	5,490
Suffolk (excluding Boston),	3	735
Worcester,	71	16,800
Total,	318	$54,722

There are only 92 cities and towns of the State that do not own a road machine; the remaining 259 own 318 machines, which cost $54,722. These machines are used to a considerable extent by the cities in clearing snow out of the gutters. They are, however, most generally used for shaping the road surface.

A great many of the towns can manage to work the scraper at least once a year over most of the roads. The results obtained are not what could be desired, but the roads are better than they otherwise would be. Some towns scrape sods, soil and anything back onto the road; others scrape them off, and then fill the ruts. By the use of the scraper a mistake is often made by cutting away the turf which has formed along the sides; when this is removed, the water washes the sides to a certain extent. Many good superintendents rather deprecate the indiscriminate use of this machine, and claim that the general condition of the roads is at a lower standard since their introduction.

But few municipalities own a water cart; this is usually hired when it is needed about any work. There are, however, one hundred and thirty so owned by forty-five different cities and towns. It is well to remember that a careful watering of well-made streets greatly increases the length of time they will wear without repairs. A strong wind will remove the dry binding material from the surface of a road, and leave the stones projecting up so as to form an uneven way, or be kicked out by the horses as they travel over it.

Barnstable, Dukes and Nantucket counties have no stone crushers. There are stone crushers in the several other counties as follows: —

Berkshire,	3
Bristol,	6
Essex,	9
Franklin,	1
Hampden,	3
Hampshire,	1
Middlesex,	16
Norfolk,	10
Plymouth,	7
Suffolk,	5
Worcester,	3
Total,	64

Most of the crushers are set up on a side hill, with bins beneath for two to four grades of stone; in most of these the stone has to be shovelled. Ten cities and towns have elevators and storage screens, with a revolving screen at top of the bins, the stone being loaded into the carts without shovelling. A few bins are arranged to load by means of shutes directly into the carts. There are several cities and towns that buy the broken stone of private parties. This stone is in many cases shipped by rail from ten to one hundred miles, and sold on the cars at destination at $1.25 to $1.40 per ton. The private plants known to the commission are in Salem, Waltham, Boston, Dedham, Hingham, Westfield and Rockport. Some trap rock has been shipped to Springfield from Meriden, Conn. A very few of the crushers are portable.

In reply to the question as to the cost of shovelling broken stone onto the carts, 25 towns answered, "This cost varies from 4 to 20 cents, a mean of about 9½ cents per ton." In this connection it is well to call attention to the fact that an elevator and bins, or bins set up to load without shovelling, will save 9½ cents on each ton of stone on this one item. If the time saved on the team while waiting to be loaded be taken into account, the saving may be estimated to be from 20 to 30 cents a ton, or about $5.00 on 2,000 tons of stone.

Most of the roadmasters believe that broken stone should be screened into sizes nearly equal; but five put the stone on without screening; nine screen into two sizes; seventeen into three sizes; fourteen into four sizes. At several plants the coarse stone that comes out at the end of the revolving screen is passed back through the crusher.

There are 28 steam rollers owned by cities and towns, and 2 owned by private parties; 2 of these weigh 18 tons; 23 weigh 15 tons; 2 weigh 12 tons; 1 weighs 11 tons; 1 weighs 10 tons; 1 weighs 7 tons.

There are 87 horse-rollers owned by different cities and towns, of the following patterns: 72 iron rings, 11 stone, 2 plain iron. These are worked by from two to six horses. The roadmasters who are accomplishing the best results are strongly in favor of a steam roller. They affirm that the work can be done much better and at less cost by steam than by horses. One objection to the use of horse-rollers is that it requires so much time to compact the roadway properly that part of the work lays behind. In order to roll all work a little, none of it is thoroughly compacted.

Schedule E consists of the following questions: —

Do you favor legislation providing for assistance by the Commonwealth in the building and maintaining of certain roads? Do you favor legislation providing for assistance by the county rather than by the Commonwealth, in the building and maintaining of certain roads? Do you favor legislation providing for a State Highway Commission for the purpose of supervising the roads for which the State renders aid in building and maintaining, and for consultation with county or town officials? Having had experience in road work in your own town, will you kindly make any suggestions bearing on the questions submitted that will assist the State Highway Commission in making a careful study of the road question throughout the State?

This schedule is sent out for the purpose of obtaining the sentiment of the cities and towns with reference to assistance by the State, by the counties, and the formation of a State commission. Some valuable information and suggestions were sent in reply to the fourth question; these will be submitted with the other exhibits for further reference and use. The appended table will show the feeling in the different municipalities as expressed by the selectmen or road commissioners.

There is a strong feeling that in the smaller towns there is no practicable way to obtain instruction and guidance other than by a State commission, who shall visit the towns and advise with the road officers. The sentiment is very strong throughout the State that the counties have not assisted the poorer towns. The reasons for this, as expressed, were numerous. Lack of money seems to be the primary cause; politics and local jealousies are in many instances equally to blame. One oft-repeated statement was that a central board would be freer from local influences. A study of the testimony given before the commission at the different county seats will show more clearly than anything else the strength of the feeling.

Questions in Schedule F: —

Do you use rock on your roads? Does your rock come from a ledge? Does your rock come from a gravel bank? Does your rock come from stone walls, or fields? How many ledges do you work? What is the average distance you have to haul rock? What does it cost per ton to blast? What does it cost per ton to team rock? How many gravel banks do you use? What is the average distance you team gravel? What does it cost per single load to team? What does it cost per double load to team? Does your gravel bank have many large stones in it? Is the gravel clean and free from dirt? Is there binding material in the gravel? How does the gravel wear on the roads? Does the gravel crush easily and make the roads muddy? What proportion of your annual appropriation for highways is expended on county roads? What condition are your county roads in; that is, are they dusty in dry weather? Are they muddy in wet weather? Do they bog up in the spring when the frost is coming out? Does the water easily drain off after a rainfall? Are there side ditches? How deep are the ditches below centre of road? Do the roads rut up? In repairing, do you use a road scraper? Do you scrape sods onto the roads in repairing? Do you team on fresh gravel in repairing? What crown do you give the roadway? Do you use broken stone in resurfacing your county roads? Do you screen the broken stone before putting it on the road? What depth do you put on the broken stone? Do you roll your broken stone? Do you roll your gravel? Do you put on any binding material on your gravel roads? Do you roll before putting on your binding? Do you use gravel, or sand, for a binding material? Do you use hard-pan for binding material? Do you use dirt for binding material? Do you screen out large stone from binding material? Do you roll after putting on binding material? Do you use screenings from the broken stone for binding on broken-stone roads? Do you put anything on top of stone screenings when using them for binding material? What? Why? What sized opening do you use in screen when screening road metal out of the broken stone? Do you have a one-inch mesh in your screen? What do you do with the one-inch stone, — do you put it on top of road, or underneath the larger stone, or use it on other work? Do you use the one-inch stone in repairing? How deep do you use it? Do you use a binding material with the one-inch stone? What? How deep? Do you roll before putting on binding material? Do you roll after putting on binding material? What is your rule in rolling?

Is it possible, with your appropriations, to keep your county roads in good repair all the year? If your county roads are put in good condition, is it possible, with your appropriation, to maintain them in good condition all the year? In cases where the road bogs up and becomes shaky in the spring when the frost is coming out, will you kindly describe the material under the roadway, — is it clay? Is it loam? Does the ground slope up on the side? Does the ground slope up on the side? Does the ground slope up on both sides? Is there a ditch on the side? Is there a ditch on the side?

Schedule F covers so many questions that it is impossible to tabulate them so that they will be of any value The principal answers have been taken off, and will be submitted as part of the testimony. They will explain quite plainly the methods that are used throughout the State, and are interesting as a history of the present time.

TABLE B.* — *Mileage of Pavements.*

BARNSTABLE COUNTY.

TOWNS	Total Miles, Roads.	Intertown Roads, Miles.	Local Roads, Miles.	Dirt Roads.		Gravel Roads.		Macadam Roads.		Granite Block Pavement.	
				Miles.	Width.	Miles.	Width.	Miles.	Width.	Miles.	Width.
					Feet.		Feet.		Feet.		Feet.
Barnstable,	164	75	–	164	30	–	–	–	–	–	–
Bourne,	61	61	–	¼ loam.	20	61	–	–	–	–	–
Brewster,	45	–	–	45	35	–	–	–	–	–	–
Chatham,	51	25	–	51	30	–	–	–	–	–	–
Dennis,	76	50	26	76	14	–	–	–	–	–	–
Eastham,	48	12	36	8	–	40	–	–	–	–	–
Falmouth,	108	–	–	108	–	–	–	–	–	–	–
Harwich,	97	35	62	97	40	–	–	–	–	–	–
Mashpee,	46	30	16	46	–	–	–	–	–	–	–
Orleans,	40	15	35	40	30	–	–	–	–	–	–
Provincetown,	19	1	18	19	22	–	–	–	–	–	–
Sandwich,	64	·6	58	64	20	10	–	–	–	–	–
Truro,	80	18	62	60	30-40	20	30-40	–	–	–	–
Wellfleet,	58	40	18	58	20	–	–	–	–	–	–
Yarmouth,	73	6	67	73	30	–	–	–	–	–	–

BERKSHIRE COUNTY.

Becket,	77	60	17	77	12	–	–	–	–	–	–
Cheshire,	52	16	36	52	12	–	–	–	–	–	–
Clarksburg,	13	12.5	0.5	11	10	2	12	–	–	–	–
Dalton,	29	–	–	29	30	–	–	–	–	–	–
Egremont,	42	30	12	34	13	5	12	3	12	–	–
Florida,	36	6	30	36	16	–	–	–	–	–	–
Great Barrington,	82	–	–	7	16	75	14	–	–	–	–
Hancock,	29	16	13	29	12–16	–	–	–	–	–	–
Hinsdale,	41	28	13	41	12	–	–	–	–	–	–
Lanesborough,	47	35	12	47	16	–	–	–	–	–	–
Lee,	55	45	10	43	18	12	18	–	–	–	–
Lenox,	48	32	16	45	20	–	–	3	20	–	–
Monterey,	51	35	16	51	12	–	–	–	–	–	–
Mount Washington,	37	–	37	37	16	–	–	–	–	–	–
New Ashford,	12	5	7	12	12	–	–	–	–	–	–
New Marlborough,	100	–	–	100	12	–	–	–	–	–	–
North Adams,	90	–	–	45	20	45	–	–	–	–	–
Otis,	53	–	–	53	14	–	–	–	–	–	–
Peru,	45	20	25	45	–	–	–	–	–	–	–
Pittsfield,	135	42	93	10	–	124	–	1	–	–	–
Richmond,	39	24	15	39	16	–	–	–	–	–	–
Sandisfield,	85	50	35	85	12	–	–	–	–	–	–
Savoy,	59	30	29	59	12	–	–	–	–	–	–
Sheffield,	94	76	18	74	12	20	–	–	–	–	–
Stockbridge,	43	19	24	3	8	30	14	10	14	–	–
Tyringham,	25	15	10	25	12	–	–	–	–	–	–
Washington,	50	25	25	50	12–16	–	–	–	–	–	–
West Stockbridge,	33	–	–	–	–	–	–	–	–	–	–
Williamstown,	65	48	17	48	16	–	17	–	–	–	–
Windsor,	66	–	–	66	14	–	–	–	–	–	–

* Table A is omitted.

TABLE B. — Continued.

BRISTOL COUNTY.

TOWNS.	Total Miles, Roads.	Intertown Roads, Miles.	Local Roads, Miles.	Dirt Roads.		Gravel Roads.		Macadam Roads.		Granite Block Pavement.	
				Miles.	Width.	Miles.	Width.	Miles.	Width.	Miles.	Width.
					Feet.		Feet.		Feet.		Feet.
Acushnet,	32	25	7	32	35	–	–	–	–	–	–
Attleborough,	65	–	–	–	–	–	–	–	–	–	–
Berkley,	49	49	–	26	18–33	23	18–33	–	–	–	–
Dartmouth,	77	–	–	64	18	3	–	10	–	–	–
Dighton,	49	20	29	39	10	10	–	–	–	–	–
Easton,	67	20	–	57	15	–	–	10	20	–	–
Fairhaven,	38	–	–	–	–	–	–	–	–	–	–
Fall River,	108	–	–	–	20	–	20	–	25	4	30
Freetown,	55	–	–	–	55	30	–	–	–	–	–
Mansfield,	50	20	–	49¼	15	–	–	3-4	–	–	–
New Bedford,	113	10	103	73.12	16–50	–	–	26.39	*	1.25	*
North Attleborough,	66	–	–	–	–	–	–	–	–	–	–
Norton,	57	–	–	57	–	–	–	–	–	–	–
Raynham,	51	18	33	–	–	51	15	–	–	–	–
Rehoboth,	107	54	53	82	15-20	25	15–20	–	–	–	–
Seekonk,	52	25	27	52	16	–	–	–	–	–	–
Somerset,	26	–	–	26	16–30	–	–	–	–	–	–
Swanzey,	44	34	10	7	10	37	14	1,000	16	–	–
Taunton,	160	–	–	147	–	–	20	10	30	3	30
Westport,	78	25	53	78	20	–	–	–	–	–	–

DUKES COUNTY.

Chilmark,	29	16	13	29	8	–	–	–	–	–	–
Cottage City,	–	–	–	–	–	–	–	–	–	–	–
Edgartown,	50	–	39	50	30	–	–	–	–	–	–
Gay Head,	3	–	–	–	–	–	–	–	–	–	–
Gosnold,	18	–	18	–	–	–	–	–	–	–	–
Tisbury,†	69	26	43	67.5	25	–	–	–	–	–	–

ESSEX COUNTY.

Amesbury,	40	–	–	–	–	–	–	–	–	–	–
Andover,	88	–	88	2	15	80	18	6	24	–	–
Beverly,	62	25	37	–	–	51⅘	24	10	–	⅛	–
Boxford,	55	35	15	–	–	55	16	–	–	–	–
Bradford,	23	12	11	4	35	19	35-45	–	–	–	–
Danvers,	55	40	15	5	10	49	15	1	18	–	–
Essex,	28	12	16	10	8	18	–	–	–	–	–
Georgetown,	33	10	23	33	40	–	–	–	–	–	–
Gloucester,	–	–	–	–	–	–	–	–	–	–	–
Groveland,	28	25	3	8	16	20	16	–	–	–	–
Hamilton,	30	‡	5	30	–	–	–	–	–	–	–
Haverhill,	–	–	–	–	–	–	–	–	–	–	–
Ipswich,	60	23	37	–	–	60	17	–	–	–	–
Lawrence,	–	–	–	–	–	–	–	–	–	–	–
Lynn,	–	–	–	–	–	–	–	–	–	–	–

* Three-fifths width of road. † Concrete pavement, 1.5 miles; width, 20 feet. ‡ Nearly all.

TABLE B. — Continued.

ESSEX COUNTY — Concluded.

TOWNS.	Total Miles, Roads.	Intertown Roads, Miles.	Local Roads, Miles.	DIRT ROADS.		GRAVEL ROADS.		MACADAM ROADS.		GRANITE BLOCK PAVEMENT.	
				Miles.	Width.	Miles.	Width.	Miles.	Width.	Miles.	Width.
					Feet.		Feet.		Feet.		Feet.
Lynnfield,	16	–	–	–	–	–	–	–	–	–	–
Manchester,	22	7	15	22	25	–	–	–	–	–	–
Marblehead,	30	12	18	–	–	all.	30	–	–	–	–
Merrimac,	25	15	10	25	22	–	–	–	–	–	–
Methuen,	63	–	–	–	–	61	20	2	40	–	–
Middleton,	29	29	–	29	25	–	–	–	–	–	–
Nahant,	12	–	–	–	–	12	2 rods.	–	–	–	–
Newbury,	43	23	20	15	16	28	–	–	–	–	–
Newburyport,	68	–	–	26	25-60	35	17-50	6	–	1	–
North Andover,	78	25	53	–	–	–	–	1	–	–	–
Peabody,	37	–	–	–	–	–	–	–	–	–	–
Rockport,	25	15	10	25	14	–	–	–	–	–	–
Rowley,	37	21	16	2.5	22	34.5	22	–	–	–	–
Salem,	70	–	–	5	20	45	25	20-25	25	6	25
Salisbury,	31	14	17	13	–	18	–	–	–	–	–
Saugus,	24	12	12	–	–	24	16	–	–	–	–
Swampscott,	18	5	13	–	–	18	45-50	–	–	–	–
Topsfield,	38	20	18	all sup	posed to	be grav	elled at	some tim	e.	–	–
Wenham,	18	15.5	2.5	–	–	18	24	–	–	–	–
West Newbury,	42	20	22	12	15-24	30	15-24		–	–	–

FRANKLIN COUNTY.

Ashfield,	81	22	59	81	14	–	–	–	–	–	–
Bernardston,	43	25	18	22	14	21	14	–	–	–	–
Buckland,	48	17	31	48	15	–	–	–	–	–	–
Charlemont,	52	32	20	52	20	–	–	–	–	–	–
Colrain,	66	40	26	66	16	–	–	–	–	–	–
Conway,	86	35	–	86	16	–	–	–	–	–	–
Deerfield,	81	–	–	–	–	–	–	–	–	–	–
Erving,	23	20	3	23	16	–	–	–	–	–	–
Gill,	32	18	14	29	16	3	14	–	–	–	–
Greenfield,	55	–	–	52	16	–	–	3	15–25	–	–
Hawley,	51	26	25	51	13	–	–	–	–	–	–
Heath,	57	45	12	57	15	–	–	–	–	–	–
Leverett,	43	–	–	43	12	–	–	–	–	–	–
Leyden,	56	16	40	56	14–16	–	–	–	–	–	–
Monroe,	19	11	8	19	16	–	–	–	–	–	–
Montague,	90	50	40	90	20	–	–	–	–	–	–
New Salem,	78	–	–	78	12	–	–	–	–	–	–
Northfield,	65	30	35	62	14	3	18	–	–	–	–
Orange,	83	69	14	83	20	–	–	–	–	–	–
Rowe,	40	22	18	40	12	–	–	–	–	–	–
Shelburne,	51	30	21	51	12	–	–	–	–	–	–
Shutesbury,	48	–	–	48	10–20	–	–	–	–	–	–
Sunderland,	32	23	9	32	–	–	–	–	–	–	–
Warwick,	67	35	32	67	15	–	–	–	–	–	–
Wendell,	64	36	28	64	–	–	–	–	–	–	–
Whately,	48	34	14	48	–	–	–	–	–	–	–

TABLE B. — Continued.

HAMPDEN COUNTY.

TOWNS.	Total Miles, Roads.	Intertown Roads, Miles.	Local Roads, Miles.	Dirt Roads.		Gravel Roads.		Macadam Roads.		Granite Block Pavement.	
				Miles.	Width.	Miles.	Width.	Miles.	Width.	Miles.	Width.
					Feet.		Feet.		Feet.		Feet.
Agawam,	55	40	15	45	3 rods.	10	–	–	–	–	–
Blandford,	93	71	22	93	10	–	–	–	–	–	–
Brimfield,	68	–	–	68	16–18	–	–	–	–	–	–
Chester,	70	60	10	70	3 rods.	–	–	–	–	–	–
Chicopee,	81	45	36	60	20–25	20.5	25–30	0.5	–	–	–
Granville,	76	40	36	76	14	–	–	–	–	–	–
Hampden,	32	29	3	32	18	–	–	–	–	–	–
Holland,	34	25	9	34	12	–	–	–	–	–	–
Holyoke,*	80	–	–	19	25	58	30	–	–	2.5	40
Longmeadow,	60	29½	30½	48	18	12	20	–	–	–	–
Ludlow,	58	58	–	58	15	–	–	–	–	–	–
Monson,	114	76	38	104	18	10	–	–	–	–	–
Montgomery,	29	9	20	29	16	–	–	–	–	–	–
Palmer,	94	64	30	64	20	30	–	–	–	–	–
Russell,	28	12	16	28	16–18	–	–	–	–	–	–
Southwick,	61	25	36	55	20	5	20	–	–	–	–
Springfield,†	125	–	–	25	–	69	25	20	30	1.5	40
Tolland,	40	25	15	40	–	–	–	–	–	–	–
Wales,	26	22	4	26	–	–	–	–	–	–	–
Westfield,	110	38	72	54	22–24	56	–	–	–	–	–
West Springfield,	50	40	10	50	30	–	–	–	–	–	–
Wilbraham,	45	25	20	45	16	–	–	–	–	–	–

HAMPSHIRE COUNTY.

Amherst,	69	50	9	69	–	–	–	–	–	–	–
Belchertown,	127	100	27	102	18	25	–	–	–	–	–
Chesterfield,	59	50	9	59	–	–	–	–	–	–	–
Cummington,	55	–	–	55	12	–	–	–	–	–	–
Easthampton,	42	–	–	–	–	–	–	–	–	–	–
Enfield,	40	20	20	40	18	–	–	–	–	–	–
Goshen,	31	–	–	31	10	–	–	–	–	–	–
Granby,	54	39	15	54	18	–	–	–	–	–	–
Greenwich,	41	27	14	41	16–18	–	–	–	–	–	–
Hadley,	54	25	29	54	–	–	–	–	–	–	–
Hatfield,	37	25	12	37	18	–	–	–	–	–	–
Huntington,	50	30	20	50	20	–	–	–	–	–	–
Middlefield,	39	29	10	39	14	–	–	6	25	–	–
Northampton,‡	108	60	48	–	101	–	–	–	–	–	–
Pelham,	49	15	34	49	15	–	–	–	–	–	–
Plainfield,	47	16	31	47	–	–	–	–	–	–	–
Prescott,	42	30	12	42	12	–	–	–	–	–	–
Southampton,	71	25	46	71	–	–	–	–	–	–	–
South Hadley,	38	18	20	23	–	15	–	–	–	–	–
Ware,	84	25	50 or 60	84	16	1–4	–	–	–	–	–
Westhampton,	46	35	11	46	16	–	–	–	–	–	–
Williamsburg,	47	30	17	47	20	–	–	–	–	–	–
Worthington,	64	–	–	64	12	–	–	–	–	–	–

* Asphalt pavement, ½ mile; width, 40 feet. Concrete pavement, ⅛ mile; width, 30 feet.
† Brick pavement, 1,643 square yards; width, 30 feet.
‡ Concrete pavement, 500 feet.

Table B. — Continued.

MIDDLESEX COUNTY.

TOWNS.	Total Miles, Roads.	Intertown Roads, Miles.	Local Roads, Miles.	Dirt Roads.		Gravel Roads.		Macadam Roads.		Granite Block Pavement.	
				Miles.	Width.	Miles.	Width.	Miles.	Width.	Miles.	Width.
					Feet.		Feet.		Feet.		Feet.
Acton,	60	20	40	27	–	33	–	–	–	–	–
Arlington,	37	12	25	–	–	28	24	9	36	–	–
Ashby,	63	40	23	63	18	–	–	–	–	–	–
Ashland,	38	24	14	20.5	20	17.5	25	–	–	–	–
Ayer,	25	10	15	18	18	7	19	–	–	–	–
Bedford,	34	31¾	2¼	–	–	34	–	–	–	–	–
Belmont,	25	11	14	–	–	18	18	7	–	–	–
Billerica,	57	45	12	–	–	32	–	25	–	–	–
Boxborough,	28	20	8	28	1 rod.	–	–	–	–	–	–
Burlington,	34	24	10	10	2 rods.	24	–	–	–	–	–
Cambridge,	79	–	–	–	–	–	–	76	35	3	40
Carlisle,	37	22	15	17	20	20	–	–	–	–	–
Chelmsford,	77	*	–	25	30	52	–	–	–	–	–
Concord,	56	–	–	†	25	*	25	1	40	–	–
Dracut,	50	35	15	2	17	48	23	–	–	–	–
Dunstable,	36	23	13	21	10	15	20	–	–	–	–
Everett,	40	8	32	–	–	36	40	4	–	–	–
Framingham,	86	32	54	10	12	71	20	5	20	–	–
Groton,	74	50	24	14	15	60	20	–	–	–	–
Holliston,	46	30	16	16	18	30	–	–	–	–	–
Hopkinton,	66	30	36	66	–	–	–	–	–	–	–
Hudson,	48	32	16	48	24	–	–	–	–	–	–
Lexington,	50	40	10	all either dirt or gravel.				–	–	–	–

Lincoln,	38	30	8	3	10–12	35	10–18	–	–	–	–
Littleton,	44	–	–	24	10	20	–	–	–	–	–
Lowell,	109	–	–	–	–	–	–	10	28–36	9.6	28–43
Malden,	70	15	55	22	25	45.5	25	2	30	0.5	30
Marlborough,	–	–	–	–	–	–	–	–	–	–	–
Maynard,	19	12	7	19	2 rods.	–	–	–	–	–	–
Medford,‡	70	25	25	15	20	30	–	25	–	200 yds.	–
Melrose,	36	12.5	23.5	1	15	34	25	1	27	–	–
Natick,	62	35	27	30	15–35	30	–	2	30	–	–
Newton,	169	–	–	40	20–26	79	–	50	26–40	–	–
North Reading,	27	20	7	27	14	–	–	–	–	–	–
Pepperell,	70	32	38	48	2 rods.	62	2.5 rods.	–	–	–	–
Reading,	45	14	31	8	15	37	20	–	–	–	–
Sherborn,	39	30	9	1	15	38	15–25	–	–	–	–
Shirley,	43	25	18	43	–	–	–	–	–	–	–
Somerville,	80	20	60	37	–	1	–	43	–	–	–
Stoneham,	36	–	–	–	–	–	–	–	–	–	–
Stow,	44	–	–	all.	12–15	–	–	–	–	–	–
Sudbury,	66	40	26	21	18	45	–	–	–	–	–
Tewksbury,	50	30	20	5	12	44	12	1	33	–	–
Townsend,	76	–	–	–	–	–	–	–	–	–	–
Tyngsborough,	36	18	18	4	–	32	–	–	–	–	–
Wakefield,	42	–	–	65	–	–	–	700	–	–	–
Waltham,	85	–	–	3	10	–	–	–	–	300	51
Watertown,	32	7	25	–	–	22	–	10	–	–	–
Wayland,	42	27	15	15	20	27	30	–	–	–	–
Westford,	81	40	41	81	20	–	–	–	–	–	–
Weston,	40	30	10	–	–	40	20	–	–	–	–
Wilmington,	44	42	2	10	20	34	25	–	–	–	–
Winchester,	25	15	10	5	10	10	15	10	20	–	–
Woburn,	–	–	–	–	–	–	–	–	–	–	–

* Nearly all. † Very few. ‡ Cobble pavement, 300 yards.

Table B. — Continued.

NANTUCKET COUNTY.

TOWNS.	Total Miles, Roads.	Intertown Roads, Miles.	Local Roads, Miles.	Dirt Roads.		Gravel Roads.		Macadam Roads.		Granite Block Pavement.	
				Miles.	Width.	Miles.	Width.	Miles.	Width.	Miles.	Width.
					Feet.		Feet.		Feet.		Feet.
Nantucket,*	114	–	114	114	50	–	–	–	–	–	–

NORFOLK COUNTY.

TOWNS.	Total Miles, Roads.	Intertown Roads, Miles.	Local Roads, Miles.	Dirt Roads, Miles.	Dirt Roads, Width.	Gravel Roads, Miles.	Gravel Roads, Width.	Macadam Roads, Miles.	Macadam Roads, Width.	Granite Block Pavement, Miles.	Granite Block Pavement, Width.
Avon,	13	3	3	–	–	13	30	–	–	–	–
Bellingham,	44	30	14	24	3 rods.	20	–	–	–	–	–
Braintree,	46	25	21	37	–	–	–	9	20	–	–
Brookline,	54	24	30	–	–	37	26.8	17	33.3	–	–
Canton,	42	25	17	–	–	42	–	–	–	–	–
Cohasset,	23	16	7	23	20	–	–	–	–	–	–
Dedham,	76	54	22	25	20	51	25	–	–	–	–
Dover,	31	–	–	–	–	31	–	–	–	–	–
Foxborough,	52	20	32	52	15	–	–	–	–	–	–
Franklin,	66	34	32	26	15	40	–	–	–	–	–
Holbrook,	19	16	3	–	–	19	30	–	–	–	–
Hyde Park,	40	–	–	33	33	–	–	7	–	–	–
Medfield,	39	25	14	–	–	39	12–35	–	–	–	–
Medway,	37	17	20	17	20	20	–	–	–	–	–
Millis,	37	20	17	–	–	37	23	–	–	–	–

Milton,	47	21	26	5	12	37	20	5	25	–	–
Needham,	45	27	18	–	–	44	–	–	–	–	–
Norfolk,	39	29	10	39	16	–	–	–	–	–	–
Norwood,	30	–	–	–	–	–	–	–	–	–	–
Quincy,	78	15	63	68	–	–	–	10†	–	†	–
Randolph,	31	22	9	–	–	31	–	–	–	–	–
Sharon,	54	34	20	19	22	35	22	–	–	–	–
Stoughton,	50	18	32	26	–	24	–	–	–	–	–
Walpole,	58	20	38	8	10	50	18	–	–	–	–
Wellesley,	32	22	10	32	24	–	–	–	–	–	–
Weymouth,	63	–	–	–	–	63	10–25	–	–	–	–
Wrentham,	85	60	25	25	10	60	20	–	–	–	–
PLYMOUTH COUNTY.											
Abington,	39	25	14	9	16	30	24	–	–	–	–
Bridgewater,	65	42	23	44	22	18	25	3	22	–	–
Brockton,	98	–	–	49	30	40	–	3	–	6	–
Carver,	65	50	15	65	30	–	–	–	–	–	–
Duxbury,	70	40	30	70	20	–	–	–	–	–	–
East Bridgewater,	46	26	20	6	42	40	42	–	–	–	–
Halifax,	31	10	21	22	15	9	8–12	–	–	–	–
Hanover,	40	–	–	–	–	40	20	–	–	–	–
Hanson,	32	–	–	32	25	–	–	–	–	–	–
Hingham,	56	29	27	25½	12	29	20	1½	25	–	–
Hull,	16	8	8	–	–	14	35	2	35	–	–
Kingston,	40	32	8	27	10	10	20	3	20	–	–

* Concrete pavement, 3 miles; width, 30 feet.

† Two miles one side.

TABLE B. — Continued.

PLYMOUTH COUNTY — Concluded.

TOWNS.	Total Miles, Roads.	Intertown Roads, Miles.	Local Roads, Miles.	Dirt Roads.		Gravel Roads.		Macadam Roads.		Granite Block Pavement.	
				Miles.	Width.	Miles.	Width.	Miles.	Width.	Miles.	Width.
					Feet.		Feet.		Feet.		Feet.
Lakeville,	61	40	21	61	25	–	–	–	–	–	–
Marion,	22	7	15	12	15	8½	15	1½	12	–	–
Marshfield,	63	25	38	38	25	25	25	–	–	–	–
Mattapoisett,	33	13	20	–	–	33	–	–	–	–	–
Middleborough,	147	100	47	46.5	15	100	20	0.5	45	–	–
Norwell,	52	20	32	52	–	–	–	–	–	–	–
Pembroke,	56	most of	them.	26	25	30	–	–	–	–	–
Plymouth,	198	60	138	194	15	4	30	–	–	–	–
Plympton,	31	26	5	16	25	15	–	–	–	–	–
Rochester,	59	33	26	43	35	16	–	–	–	–	–
Rockland,	32	–	25	–	–	all.	50	–	–	–	–
Scituate,	44	30	14	44	20	–	–	–	–	–	–
Wareham,	90	65	25	80	25	10*	–	–	–	–	–
West Bridgewater,	45	38	7	45	–	–	–	–	–	–	–
Whitman,	28	16	12	–	–	26	15	2	–	–	–

SUFFOLK COUNTY.

Revere,	30	–	–	30	30	–	–	–	–	–	–
Winthrop,	23	9	14	5	33	18	–	–	–	–	–

WORCESTER COUNTY.

Ashburnham,	86	60	26	86†	–	–	16–25	–	–	–	–
Athol,	87	–	–	87	–	–	–	–	–	–	–
Auburn,	45	35	10	30	12	15	20	–	–	–	–
Barre,	119	49	70	–	–	119	25	–	–	–	–
Berlin,	39	30	3	39	12–18	–	–	–	–	–	–
Blackstone,	48	37	11	36	33	12	49	–	–	–	–
Bolton,	50	30	20	15	20	35	25	–	–	–	–
Boylston,	51	35	16	40	10	–	–	–	–	–	–
Brookfield,	60	–	–	32	22	28	–	–	–	–	–
Charlton,	118	25	93	93	4 rods.	25	4 rods.	–	–	–	–
Clinton,	34	8	26	1	–	30	20	3	30	–	–
Dana,	48	20	28	48	2 rods.	–	–	–	–	–	–
Douglas,	75	50	25	65	16–20	10	–	–	–	–	–
Dudley,	62	50	12	42	20	20	–	–	–	–	–
Fitchburg,	119	23	96	116⅛	–	–	25	4	–	1.5	33
Gardner,	69	24	45	69	15	–	–	–	–	–	–
Grafton,	68	51	17	8	15	60	25	–	–	–	–
Hardwick,	88	–	–	44	50	44	50	–	–	–	–
Harvard,	62	36	26	62	16	–	–	–	–	–	–
Holden,	85	50	35	35	18	50	25	–	–	–	–
Hopedale,	15	8	7	6	16	4	20	5	28	–	–

* Shell. † Dirt and gravel.

TABLE B. — Concluded.

WORCESTER COUNTY — Concluded.

TOWNS.	Total Miles, Roads.	Intertown Roads, Miles.	Local Roads, Miles.	Dirt Roads.		Gravel Roads.		Macadam Roads.		Granite Block Pavement.	
				Miles.	Width.	Miles.	Width.	Miles.	Width.	Miles.	Width.
					Feet.		Feet.		Feet.		Feet.
Hubbardston,	76	40	36	56	18	20	20	–	–	–	–
Lancaster,	67	50	17	67	10	–	–	–	–	–	–
Leicester,	67	33	34	67	18	–	–	–	–	–	–
Leominster,	76	30	46	56	25	20	35	–	–	–	–
Lunenburg,	72	50	22	47	12–16	25	12–16	–	–	–	–
Mendon,	45	35	10	45	14	–	–	–	–	–	–
Milford,	58	8	50	45	–	5	–	8	–	–	–
Millbury,	47	–	–	12	20	35	20	–	–	–	–
New Braintree,	52	27	25	52	2¼ rods.	–	–	–	–	–	–
Northborough,	52	15	37	52	–	–	–	–	–	–	–
Northbridge,	53	32	21	21	–	32	–	–	–	–	–
North Brookfield,	68	25	43	68	–	–	–	–	–	–	–
Oakham,	48	24	24	26	10	22	10	–	–	–	–
Oxford,	74	44	30	49	10–15	25	10–25	–	–	–	–
Paxton,	36	15	21	35	–	–	–	–	–	–	–
Petersham,	77	60	17	77	17	–	–	–	–	–	–
Phillipston,	49	*	–	49	–	–	–	–	–	–	–
Princeton,	77	47	30	77	20	–	–	–	–	–	–
Royalston,	76	72	4	76	–	–	–	–	–	–	–
Rutland,	76	36	40	76	16	–	–	–	–	–	–
Shrewsbury,	61	30	31	61	–	–	–	–	–	–	–
Southborough,	60	–	60	3	2 rods.	57	2 rods.	–	–	–	–

Southbridge,	57	35	22	57	33	–	–	–	–	–	–
Spencer,	94	75	19	72	20	20	20	2	25	–	–
Sterling,	76	51	25	56	18	20	–	–	–	–	–
Sturbridge,	84	34	50	64	12	20	17	–	–	–	–
Sutton,	92	50	42	67	20	25	–	–	–	–	–
Templeton,	84	59	25	84	18	–	–	–	–	–	–
Upton,	62	50	12	62	20	–	–	–	–	–	–
Uxbridge,	8	–	–	–	–	–	–	–	–	–	–
Warren,	67	–	–	–	–	–	–	–	–	–	–
Webster,	32	25	7	32	2¼ rods.	–	–	–	–	–	–
Westborough,	64	30	–	64	–	–	–	–	–	–	–
West Boylston,	42	*	–	42	20	–	–	–	–	–	–
West Brookfield,	51	41	10	51	10	–	–	–	–	–	–
Westminster,	86	50	36	6	3 rods.	80	–	–	–	–	–
Winchendon,	106	46	60	36	14–24	70	–	–	–	–	–
Worcester,	225	–	–	56	20	149	25	13	25	7	33

* Nearly all.

TABLE C. — *Appropriations for Highways and Bridges, together with Valuation and Rate of Taxation.*

BARNSTABLE COUNTY.

TOWNS.	AMOUNT OF MONEY EXPENDED ON HIGHWAYS.										Total Appropriation Highways and Bridges, 1891.	Value Real Estate.	Value Personal Estate.	Rate Taxation, 1891.
	Snow and Ice.	General Repairs.	Cleaning.	Sidewalks.	Gravel Roads.	Macadam Roads.	PAVED. Gutters.	PAVED. Streets.	Bridges.	New Roads.				
Barnstable,	$300 00	$10,000 00	-	-	-	-	-	-	$2,400 00	$200 00	$12,600 00	$2,249,090	$1,284,380	$10 00
Bourne,	300 00	4,700 00	-	-	-	-	-	-	-	-	5,000 00	1,066,765	239,400	11 80
Brewster,	-	1,300 00	-	-	-	-	-	-	-	-	1,300 00	350,000	175,000	12 00
Chatham,	-	-	-	-	-	-	-	-	-	-	1,700 00	644,317	223,567	14 00
Dennis,	-	3,500 00	-	-	-	-	-	-	-	-	3,500 00	-	-	10 00
Eastham,	43 65	330 00	-	-	-	-	-	-	98 00	-	490 00	189,321	62,414	12 40
Falmouth,	-	10,000 00	-	-	-	-	-	-	300 00	-	10,000 00	1,824,134	3,176,329	6 50
Harwich,	-	-	-	-	-	-	-	-	-	-	1,500 00	777,050	283,740	16 00
Mashpee,	-	883 86	-	-	-	-	-	-	100 00	303 66	1,150 00	166,940	6,410	13 46
Orleans,	-	1,855 00	-	-	-	-	-	-	-	62 00	1,800 00	385,671	113,873	11 00
Provincetown,	350 00	2,150 00	-	-	-	-	-	-	-	-	2,500 00	-	-	-
Sandwich,	500 00	600 00	$100 00	$50 00	$1,000 00	-	-	-	-	-	2,500 00	208,425	694,550	14 80
Truro,*	-	1,400 00	-	-	-	-	-	-	-	-	1,400 00	196,492	125,608	15 00
Wellfleet,	-	700 00	-	100 00	-	-	-	-	200 00	-	1,000 00	397,649	218,096	13 00
Yarmouth,	200 00	1,200 00	-	-	-	-	-	-	-	150 00	3,600 00	1,718,402	-	7 00

BERKSHIRE COUNTY.

TOWNS.	Snow and Ice.	General Repairs.	Cleaning.	Sidewalks.	Gravel Roads.	Macadam Roads.	Gutters.	Streets.	Bridges.	New Roads.	Total Appropriation Highways and Bridges, 1891.	Value Real Estate.	Value Personal Estate.	Rate Taxation, 1891.
Adams,	$300 00	-	-	$1,632 27	-	-	-	-	$509 75	$4,852 04	$6,000 00	$2,371,952	$1,134,405	$14 00
Alford,	5 00	$265 00	-	-	$100 00	-	-	-	30 00	-	400 00	135,422	73,043	10 00
Becket,	300 00	1,500 00	$10 00	-	150 00	-	-	-	250 00	-	2,000 00	232,188	152,962	15 00
Cheshire,	300 00	1,500 00	-	-	-	-	-	-	300 00	-	1,800 00	500,000	250,000	15 00
Clarksburg,	17 53	869 19	-	-	-	-	-	-	-	-	886 72	163,546	51,491	20 00
Dalton,	200 00	2,500 00	-	500 00	200 00	-	-	-	1,650 00	946 00	4,996 00	1,259,717	979,998	9 70
Egremont,	5 00	547 00	-	-	75 00	$135 00	-	-	110 00	25 00	1,000 00	357,892	76,109	10 80
Florida,	20 00	1,100 00	-	-	-	-	-	-	200 00	-	1,000 00	133,098	21,082	20 00
Great Barrington,	8 00	1,600 00	100 00	-	2,500 00	-	-	-	1,000 00	-	5,000 00	2,203,263	947,054	10 00
Hancock,	117 68	500 00	-	-	-	-	-	-	83 21	-	700 00	295,675	66,382	8 20
Hinsdale,	324 29	1,021 00	-	-	-	-	-	-	300 00	-	1,400 00	478,164	225,818	16 00
Lanesborough,	295 64	1,398 56	-	-	-	-	-	-	450 00	-	1,500 00	447,170	64,344	14 00
Lee,	2 00	3,194 61	-	-	600 00	-	-	-	1,146 47	-	4,500 00	1,227,950	527,369	20 00
Lenox,	267 28	3,115 41	-	-	-	22,060 00	-	-	1,100 00	170 04	13,000 00	1,114,850	548,803	14 50

Monterey,	25 00	600 00	-	-	-	-	-	-	75 00	-	700 00	182,508	43,043	12 00
Mount Washington,	-	254 67	-	-	-	-	-	-	-	-	280 00	71,492	8,177	10 00
New Ashford,	35 00	300 00	-	-	-	-	-	-	40 00	-	390 00	59,275	11,465	15 20
New Marlborough,	-	-	-	-	-	-	-	-	50 00	-	2,000 00	-	-	-
North Adams,	-	-	-	-	-	-	-	-	-	1,600 00	33,500 00	4,755,445	1,260,752	18 50
Otis,	-	1,000 00	-	-	-	-	-	-	-	-	1,000 00	172,883	47,150	16 00
Peru,	-	700 00	-	-	-	-	-	-	-	-	600 00	98,573	2,183	22 50
Pittsfield,	500 00	10,300 00	500 00	11,200 00	3,000 00	4,000 00	$1,000 00	-	13,000 00	2,500 00	59,000 00	8,779,130	2,406,780	16 80
Richmond,	300 00	500 00	-	-	-	300 00	-	-	200 00	-	1,450 00	450,000	110,000	13 00
Sandisfield,	15 00	-	-	-	-	-	-	-	75 00	-	2,000 00	286,121	72,869	15 60
Savoy,	50 00	1,200 00	-	-	-	-	-	-	100 00	-	1,850 00	144,000	32,000	21 00
Sheffield,	-	1,000 00	-	-	500 00	-	-	-	-	-	1,500 00	761,366	138,927	14 50
Stockbridge,	40 20	5,061 00	-	-	-	-	-	-	-	-	5,000 00	1,937,705	915,379	10 00
Tyringham,	35 00	700 00	-	-	-	-	-	-	100 00	-	800 00	187,175	42,255	12 00
Washington,	-	1,000 00	-	-	-	-	-	-	125 00	-	600 00	222,187	39,539	12 90
West Stockbridge,	-	-	-	-	-	-	-	-	-	-	-	-	-	-
Williamstown,	100 00	2,870 00	-	-	-	-	-	-	800 00	-	4,300 00	-	-	-
Windsor,	100 00	1,100 00	-	-	-	-	-	-	-	-	-	-	-	18 00

BRISTOL COUNTY.

Acushnet,	-	$1,800 00	-	-	-	-	-	-	-	-	$1,800 00	$587,830	$106,350	$9 60
Attleborough,	-	-	-	-	-	-	-	-	-	-	-	-	-	-
Berkley,	-	1,258 00	-	-	-	-	-	-	$41 80	-	1,299 80	313,182	64,443	10 50
Dartmouth,	$60 00	3,000 00	-	-	-	$12,000 00	-	-	150 00	§$4,500 00	15,000 00	1,506,400	250,450	9 40
Dighton,	25 00	545 00	$100 00	$25 00	$1,800 00	-	-	-	305 70	-	3,000 00	661,141	9,405,900	14 50
Easton,	-	4,000 00	-	-	-	-	-	-	-	2,500 00	6,500 00	1,646,281	2,658,324	6 00
Fairhaven,	-	-	-	-	-	-	-	-	-	-	-	-	-	-
Fall River,	-	-	-	-	-	-	-	$21,723 90	-	-	100,977 37	33,269,950	21,011,980	17 20
Freetown,	50 00	2,500 00	-	-	-	-	-	-	100 00	-	2,600 00	690,711	170,493	9 20
Mansfield,	75 00	2,500 00	-	-	-	1,524 00	-	-	-	-	4,000 00	1,436,268	207,844	17 00
New Bedford,	†24,000 00	-	‡10,000 00	‡15,000 00	-	‡50,000 00	-	‡25,000 00	2,500 00	-	120,000 00	20,959,300	17,559,643	‖12 00
North Attleborough,	-	-	-	-	-	-	-	-	-	-	-	-	-	-
Norton,	116 00	2,500 00	-	40 00	-	-	-	-	306 84	14 31	2,500 00	646,400	144,450	12 00
Raynham,	31 48	100 00	-	-	2,400 00	-	-	-	65 00	-	2,400 00	657,254	130,746	10 40
Rehoboth,	40 00	1,550 00	200 00	-	1,000 00	-	-	-	250 00	-	3,000 00	91,888	644,200	14 00
Seekonk,	-	3,000 00	-	-	-	-	-	-	-	-	3,000 00	637,235	230,644	10 20
Somerset,	-	-	-	-	-	-	-	-	-	-	-	-	-	-
Swansea,	19 95	611 58	-	-	2,274 30	-	-	-	177 90	-	3,083 73	605,775	173,100	12 00
Taunton,	600 00	24,600 00	1,800 00	3,000 00	-	4,000 00	$500 00	$59,000 00	300 00	-	35,000 00	12,994,625	5,075,925	17 40
Westport,	15 00	5,442 00	-*	-	-	-	-	-	-	-	5,000 00	1,339,050	189,775	12 00

* The State paid $300 for clay for road over Beach Point, and $200 for labor. † Miscellaneous. ‡ Estimation for 1893. § Special appropriation. ‖ City tax.

TABLE C. — Continued.

DUKES COUNTY.

TOWNS.	Amount of Money Expended on Highways.										Total Appropriation Highways and Bridges, 1891.	Value Real Estate.	Value Personal Estate.	Rate Taxation, 1891.
	Snow and Ice.	General Repairs.	Cleaning.	Sidewalks.	Gravel Roads.	Macadam Roads.	Paved. Gutters.	Paved. Streets.	Bridges.	New Roads				
Chilmark,	-	$270 00	-	-	-	-	-	-	-	-	$270 00	$179,671	$35,188	$10 00
Cottage City,	-	-	-	-	-	-	-	-	-	-	-	-	-	-
Edgartown,	$48 15	510 00	-	$209 00	$53 00	-	-	-	-	$410 00	500 00	528,565	206,927	15 00
Gay Head,	-	-	-	-	-	-	-	-	-	-	-	-	-	-
Gosnold,	-	-	-	-	-	-	-	-	-	-	-	-	-	-
Tisbury,	-	2,775 00	-	-	-	-	-	-	$350 00	-	3,125 00	906,442	126,267	14 00

ESSEX COUNTY.

TOWNS.	Snow and Ice.	General Repairs.	Cleaning.	Sidewalks.	Gravel Roads.	Macadam Roads.	Paved. Gutters.	Paved. Streets.	Bridges.	New Roads	Total Appropriation Highways and Bridges, 1891.	Value Real Estate.	Value Personal Estate.	Rate Taxation, 1891.
Amesbury,	-	-	-	-	-	-	-	-	-	-	-	-	-	-
Andover,	$500 00	$2,500 00	-	$488 28	$1,000 00	$4,500 00	-	-	-	-	$8,000 00	$3,290,431	$1,155,858	$13 00
Beverly,	-	-	-	-	-	-	-	-	-	-	25,000 00	9,488,650	3,698,105	14 20
Boxford,	-	1,000 00	-	-	-	-	-	-	-	-	1,000 00	581,155	122,988	9 10
Bradford,	300 00	-	-	-	-	-	-	-	$300 00	-	3,500 00	1,610,182	307,138	19 00
Danvers,	866 29	7,500 00	-	-	-	2,632 53	-	-	293 29	$100 00	7,783 65	3,006,900	893,675	15 80
Essex,	317 50	100 00	$300 00	227 50	1,800 64	-	-	-	77 00	-	2,000 00	864,240	64,800	16 60
Georgetown,	150 00	-	-	700 00	-	-	-	-	-	-	2,100 00	-	-	16 00
Gloucester,	-	-	-	-	-	2,483 83	$1,176 26	$20,352 43	453 61	10,534 39	13,750 00	10,226,530	3,986,491	15 40
Groveland,	242 00	1,500 00	-	-	-	-	-	-	383 79	-	1,800 00	707,346	192,637	16 60
Hamilton,	505 15	1,098 60	-	-	1,052 87	-	-	-	45 73	-	1,050 00	729,645	263,027	8 40
Haverhill,	-	-	-	-	-	-	-	-	-	-	-	-	-	-
Ipswich,	935 33	3,240 60	-	-	-	-	-	-	207 92	304 00	5,600 00	7,807,948	627,291	12 00
Lawrence,	-	-	-	-	-	-	-	-	-	-	-	-	-	-
Lynn,	-	-	-	-	-	-	-	-	-	-	-	-	-	-
Lynnfield,	-	-	-	-	-	-	-	-	-	-	-	-	-	-
Manchester,	150 00	4,000 00	300 00	400 00	-	-	-	-	-	650 00	6,000 00	2,599,992	4,525,998	6 10
Marblehead,	-	-	-	-	-	-	-	-	-	-	6,000 00	4,213,800	832,032	21 40
Merrimac,	304 75	2,043 00	50 00	559 95	-	-	-	-	-	-	3,000 00	936,150	280,670	17 80
Methuen,	1,400 00	5,800 00	-	500 00	-	2,500 00	-	-	-	5,000 00	15,200 00	2,331,180	901,323	15 90
Middleton,	44 80	150 20	-	-	-	-	-	-	-	-	1,600 00	473,805	90,602	13 60
Nahant,	202 87	-	-	-	-	-	-	-	-	-	5,400 00	2,216,965	2,406,573	6 50
Newbury,	-	2,300 00	-	-	-	-	-	-	700 00	-	3,000 00	769,295	180,151	10 00
Newburyport,	1,500 00	2,500 00	1,000 00	1,200 00	2,000 00	14,000 00	500 00	-	1,500 00	500 00	22,000 00	6,874,300	2,350,600	15 80

North Andover,	-	-	-	-	-	5,400 00	20 00	-	100 00	-	2,600 00	2,179,484	537,158	12 00
Peabody,	-	-	-	-	-	-	-	-	-	-	-	-	-	-
Rockport,	300 00	3,500 00	300 00	150 00	1,781 37	-	-	-	300 00	-	3,500 00	1,881,918	72,720	15 70
Rowley,	226 15	1,579 73	-	-	1,300 00	-	-	-	467 91	-	1,500 00	512,213	90,761	13 40
Salem,	3,596 50	23,750 75	4,187 91	6,631 04	-	-	-	-	4,648 50	24,325 97	70,000 00	14,778,700	12,045,000	18 00
Salisbury,	200 45	1,634 00	-	20 00	-	-	-	-	90 00	-	2,000 00	514,206	68,425	11 00
Saugus,*	-	-	-	-	-	-	-	-	-	-	-	-	-	-
Swampscott,	300 00	5,670 00	-	1,002 00	-	-	600 00	-	-	-	6,500 00	3,122,350	1,771,373	10 00
Topsfield,	325 00	1,400 00	-	-	-	-	-	-	391 00	-	2,000 00	500,000	527,822	11 00
Wenham,	225 22	1,030 57	-	-	-	-	-	-	-	-	1,000 00	467,575	120,525	11 40
West Newbury,	382 25	1,153 19	-	-	900 00	-	-	-	1,460 53	-	2,995 97	770,285	129,233	11 00
FRANKLIN COUNTY.														
Ashfield,	$320 86	$1,425 98	-	-	-	-	-	-	$700 00	†$200 00	$2,000 00	$386,350	$95,545	$17 50
Bernardston,	-	800 00	-	-	-	-	-	-	800 00	-	1,000 00	303,046	78,373	12 00
Buckland,	68 08	1,398 70	-	$128 47	-	-	-	-	263 00	418 49	2,000 00	443,275	96,221	17 50
Charlemont,	300 00	1,200 00	-	-	-	-	-	-	500 00	-	1,500 00	-	-	20 00
Colrain,	-	1,800 00	-	-	-	-	-	-	400 00	50 00	2,400 00	500	160	16 00
Conway,	-	1,200 00	-	-	-	-	-	-	1,300 00	-	2,500 00	237,740	183,298	16 20
Deerfield,	-	-	-	-	-	-	-	-	-	-	-	-	-	-
Erving,	11 00	1,022 44	-	-	-	-	-	-	-	598 75	1,598 75	286,120	84,950	17 00
Gill,	-	584 00	-	-	$100 00	-	-	-	138 00	-	822 70	384,368	95,785	10 00
Greenfield,	50 00	3,000 00	$500 00	100 00	-	$4,200 00	-	-	600 00	1,000 00	10,000 00	338,804	1,389,759	13 00
Hawley,	100 00	1,200 00	-	-	-	-	-	-	1,000 00	-	2,300 00	-	-	-
Heath,	65 00	400 00	-	-	-	-	-	-	-	-	800 00	124,275	37,049	21 00
Leverett,	10 00	704 51	-	-	-	-	-	-	-	75 52	700 00	219,670	59,359	15 00
Leyden,	-	500 00	-	-	-	-	-	-	-	-	500 00	141,041	32,909	16 00
Monroe,	-	637 03	-	-	-	-	-	-	162 97	-	800 00	89,820	52,094	22 00
Montague,	200 00	6,500 00	300 00	‡3,000 00	-	-	-	-	-	3,000 00	7,000 00	2,621,247	682,140	14 50
New Salem,	100 00	750 00	-	-	-	-	-	-	150 00	-	1,400 00	241,130	47,320	17 00
Northfield,	-	-	-	-	-	-	-	-	-	-	-	-	-	-
Orange,	-	6,789 82	-	2,643 93	-	-	-	-	-	560 00	4,000 00	1,741,045	470,580	15 40
Rowe,	200 00	775 00	-	-	-	-	-	-	500 00	-	800 00	75,022	34,622	17 15
Shelburne,	111 45	1,896 60	-	698 00	-	-	-	-	-	-	2,100 00	681,365	198,974	13 50
Shutesbury,	25 00	266 00	-	-	-	-	-	-	50 00	-	600 00	133,327	15,054	25 00
Sunderland,	60 00	637 00	-	-	-	-	-	-	-	-	900 00	351,672	55,086	11 00
Warwick,	-	1,180 00	-	-	-	-	-	-	-	-	1,600 00	232,235	46,645	14 40
Wendell,	30 00	750 00	-	-	-	-	-	-	50 00	-	1,000 00	177,642	47,971	23 00
Whately,	-	640 00	-	-	-	-	-	-	830 00	-	1,400 00	325,496	83,236	16 75

* Blank not filled out. † Ordered by county commissioners. ‡ Special appropriation.

TABLE C. — Continued.

HAMPDEN COUNTY.

TOWNS.	Amount of Money Expended on Highways.										Total Appropriation Highways and Bridges, 1891.	Value Real Estate.	Value Personal Estate.	Rate Taxation, 1891.
	Snow and Ice.	General Repairs.	Cleaning.	Sidewalks.	Gravel Roads.	Macadam Roads.	Paved. Gutters.	Paved. Streets.	Bridges.	New Roads.				
Agawam,	$50 00	$1,450 00	-	-	$350 00	-	-	-	$300 00	-	$2,000 00	$1,041,225	$185,073	$13 50
Blandford,	57 23	1,961 10	-	-	-	-	-	-	307 92	-	2,000 00	263,140	109,566	19 00
Brimfield,	150 00	1,400 00	-	-	-	-	-	-	205 00	-	1,550 00	356,000	70,000	17 00
Chester,	200 00	1,346 40	$10 00	-	-	-	-	-	1,411 56	-	3,000 00	434,802	85,572	15 00
Chicopee,	-	-	-	$2,395 46	-	-	-	-	1,600 00	-	18,000 00	4,651,050	2,123,160	12 50
Granville,	25 00	1,643 88	-	-	-	-	-	-	100 00	-	1,800 00	254,023	85,295	20 00
Hampden,	-	700 00	-	-	-	-	-	-	-	-	700 00	342,225	65,503	12 00
Holland,	-	-	-	-	-	-	-	-	-	-	-	-	-	-
Holyoke,	1,224 75	1,495 52	4,578 42	16,632 67	2,646 24	-	-	$13,825 44	897 68	$1,320 38	24,565 97	17,566,195	5,377,745	16 50
Longmeadow,	-	4,288 52	-	-	-	-	-	-	-	-	4,288 52	921,970	146,052	9 00
Ludlow,	-	2,600 00	-	-	-	-	-	-	-	-	1,500 00	658,663	231,486	11 40
Monson,	50 00	3,000 00	200 00	500 00	300 00	$300 00	-	-	-	-	3,500 00	1,169,845	591,225	15 50
Montgomery,	-	385 64	-	-	-	-	-	-	61 73	-	500 00	118,340	2,928	12 50
Palmer,	-	3,000 00	-	-	1,000 00	-	$600 00	-	600 00	-	5,800 00	1,797,943	754,090	17 40
Russell,	-	1,998 13	-	-	-	-	-	-	-	3,132 35	2,000 00	350,942	161,196	17 25
Southwick,	24 37	512 19	-	-	-	-	-	-	36 48	-	1,000 00	437,884	72,029	14 50
Springfield,	7,041 01	16,727 23	12,394 38	13,256 59	6,456 83	19,265 04	556 27	8,974 65	6,904 13	-	98,000 00	37,219,490	11,110,144	12 50
Tolland,	-	-	-	-	-	-	-	-	75 00	-	875 00	116,840	45,348	15 00
Wales,	9 35	589 51	-	-	-	-	-	-	21 80	-	700 00	212,699	66,509	11 20
Westfield,	500 00	2,650 00	500 00	2,500 00	3,000 00	-	-	-	4,368 00	2,000 00	-	5,114,011	1,855,739	16 00
West Springfield,	50 00	2,500 00	500 00	1,000 00	1,500 00	-	100 00	-	300 00	-	5,200 00	3,099,689	326,670	12 80
Wilbraham,	-	1,184 35	-	-	-	500 00	-	-	200 00	-	1,600 00	586,295	171,730	10 60

HAMPSHIRE COUNTY.

TOWNS.	Snow and Ice.	General Repairs.	Cleaning.	Sidewalks.	Gravel Roads.	Macadam Roads.	Paved. Gutters.	Paved. Streets.	Bridges.	New Roads.	Total Appropriation Highways and Bridges, 1891.	Value Real Estate.	Value Personal Estate.	Rate Taxation, 1891.
Amherst,	$25 00	-	$50 00	-	$3,500 00	-	-	-	-	-	$4,000 00	$2,396	$914,700	$15 50
Belchertown,	-	$1,400 00	-	-	-	-	-	-	-	$250 00	1,500 00	-	-	13 00
Chesterfield,	-	-	-	-	-	-	-	-	$200 00	-	1,000 00	223,244	73,715	15 00

Cummington, . .	224 00	501 07	-	-	-	-	-	-	466 95	25 00	1,000 00	232,770	71,740	17 50
Easthampton, . .	-	-	-	-	-	-	-	-	-	-	-	-	-	-
Enfield, ...	-	1,200 00	-	$1 15	-	-	-	-	156 00	-	1,200 00	378,400	342,310	7 00
Goshen, . . .	70 26	598 03	-	-	-	-	-	-	-	-	900 00	114,615	23,461	16 67
Granby, . . .	-	-	-	-	-	-	-	-	-	-	-	-	-	-
Greenwich, . . .	-	640 00	-	-	-	-	-	-	-	-	700 00	-	-	13 00
Hadley, . . .	-	1,361 00	-	-	-	-	-	-	-	-	1,500 00	875,000	125,000	15 00
Hatfield, . . .	-	67 per ct.	-	-	-	-	-	-	33 per ct.	-	3,200 00	687,142	1,230,196	9 00
Huntington, . . .	123 56	1,320 33	-	50 00	-	-	-	-	330 63	-	1,600 00	387,490	116,235	16 50
Middlefield, . . .	140 00	878 00	-	-	-	-	-	-	-	-	1,000 00	148,650	60,580	12 50
Northampton,* . .	-	-	-	-	-	-	-	-	-	-	-	-	-	-
Pelham, . . .	-	850 00	-	-	-	-	-	-	-	-	1,000 00	155,040	-	19 00
Plainfield, . . .	141 69	626 94	-	-	-	-	-	-	-	-	800 00	120,420	40,963	17 50
Prescott, . . .	22 77	528 88	-	-	-	-	-	-	36 47	-	700 00	142,980	24,015	13 00
Southampton, . .	-	1,176 69	-	-	-	-	-	-	373 92	-	1,200 00	410,190	75,157	11 80
South Hadley, . .	-	2,600 00	-	-	900 00	-	-	-	-	-	3,500 00	585,812	282,134	13 60
Ware, ...	-	5,000 00	-	1,000 00	-	-	-	-	-	-	6,000 00	2,739,640	1,032,180	15 00
Westhampton, . .	81 72	436 52	-	-	-	-	-	-	75 00	-	800 00	193,709	43,381	13 50
Williamsburg, . .	-	800 00	-	-	-	-	-	-	400 00	-	1,200 00	691,361	219,852	11 50
Worthington, . .	100 00	1,150 00	-	-	-	-	-	-	144 94	-	1,400 00	217,825	83,244	18 00

MIDDLESEX COUNTY.

Acton, ...	$50 00	-	-	-	-	-	-	-	-	-	$2,300 00	$1,203,705	$218,905	$10 20
Arlington, . . .	-	$10,000 00	-	$1,000 00	-	$6,500 00	-	-	$3,500 00	$1,000 00	22,000 00	4,861,769	800,967	16 25
Ashby, ...	-	1,200 00	-	-	-	-	-	-	-	-	1,200 00	415,000	85,000	11 50
Ashland, . . .	89 66	2,631 65	$157 03	286 98	-	-	-	-	154 98	1,228 68	4,378 68	1,063,334	178,484	17 80
Ayer, ...	50 00	200 00	100 00	800 00	$750 00	-	-	-	400 00	-	1,800 00	1,030,725	257,903	15 20
Bedford, . . .	-	2,000 00	-	-	-	-	-	-	50 00	-	2,000 00	800,567	104,663	13 00
Belmont, . . .	480 00	4,120 00	1,400 00	800 00	-	3,000 00	$300 00	-	-	9,500 00	9,000 00	2,415,805	1,092,795	12 25
Billerica, . . .	30 50	-	285 00	-	-	-	-	-	-	-	3,500 00	1,330,633	424,961	10 30
Boxborough, . .	-	600 00	-	-	-	-	-	-	-	-	600 00	199,217	39,658	10 20
Burlington, . . .	100 00	1,648 00	-	-	-	-	-	-	-	-	1,500 00	421,836	96,042	12 70
Cambridge, . . .	22,321 32	28,320 79	13,076 25	29,994 67	33,707 29	-	17,791 88	-	23,922 64	63,259 35	232,394 19	54,136,200	16,445,270	15 50
Carlisle, . . .	75 29	887 09	-	-	300 00	-	-	-	10 00	-	1,000 00	306,027	74,944	13 00
Chelmsford, . . .	-	-	-	-	-	-	-	-	-	-	4,000 00	809,035	277,140	8 50
Concord, . . .	300 00	6,000 00	1,100 00	250 00	-	840 00	-	-	225 00	-	9,000 00	total 3,	575,679	10 80

* Blank not filled out.

TABLE C. — Continued.

MIDDLESEX COUNTY — Concluded.

TOWNS.	Amount of Money Expended on Highways.										Total Appropriation Highways and Bridges, 1891.	Value Real Estate.	Value Personal Estate.	Rate Taxation, 1891.
	Snow and Ice.	General Repairs.	Cleaning.	Sidewalks.	Gravel Roads.	Macadam Roads.	Paved.		Bridges.	New Roads.				
							Gutters.	Streets.						
Dracut,	$127 81	$1,671 75	$145 00	$25 00	$1,100 00	-	-	-	$50 00	-	$3,000 00	$1,426,375	$212,515	$10 10
Dunstable,	80 85	796 97	-	-	-	-	-	-	-	-	500 00	243,036	50,672	8 50
Everett,	600 00	12,000 00	-	-	-	$7,000 00	-	-	-	$6,500 00	22,000 00	8,317,600	463,250	14 50
Framingham,	1,500 00	500 00	500 00	3,500 00	8,000 00	500 00	$500 00	-	4,500 00	12,000 00	10,000 00	6,370,560	1,564,540	16 50
Groton,	220 00	2,500 00	12 00	1,636 00	2,180 00	-	-	-	100 00	-	5,500 00	1,400,395	1,493,741	7 00
Holliston,	40 00	122 22	60 00	76 00	3,000 00	-	1,200 00	-	164 38	-	3,500 00	1,168,779	353,511	16 50
Hopkinton,	300 00	200 00	150 00	400 00	300 00	-	-	-	-	-	4,000 00	2,410,372	751,622	18 00
Hudson,	250 00	3,000 00	-	1,900 00	-	-	-	-	-	8,430 00	4,000 00	2,049,961	576,187	19 00
Lexington,	20 00	5,500 00	-	-	-	-	-	-	-	500 00	6,500 00	3,479,148	556,477	13 00
Lincoln,	150 00	3,950 00	-	-	-	-	-	-	-	1,500 00	5,000 00	682,195	1,840,582	5 70
Littleton,	-	1,250 00	-	-	800 00	-	-	-	100 00	-	1,250 00	622,550	141,495	12 50
Lowell,*	-	-	-	-	-	-	-	-	-	-	-	-	-	-
Malden,	†	-	-	10,000 00	-	-	2,000 00	-	-	‡5,000 00	43,000 00	16,541,750	2,143,100	15 00
Marlborough,	-	-	-	-	-	-	-	-	-	-	-	-	-	-
Maynard,	50 00	1,150 00	200 00	300 00	-	-	50 00	-	250 00	-	2,000 00	1,354,138	646,960	12 00
Medford,	500 00	15,000 00	-	7,000 00	1,000 00	4,000 00	1,000 00	-	1,500 00	6,900 45	16,100 00	8,525,100	1,984,165	14 60
Melrose,	231 84	4,598 21	-	3,000 00	-	4,499 25	270 00	-	6,525 65	-	17,487 28	7,372,025	405,690	14 20
Natick,	-	-	-	-	-	-	-	-	527 00	-	8,000 00	4,497,225	1,076,625	18 40
Newton,	4,511 37	60,361 74	5,363 19	16,372 21	16,568 74	-	3,511 16	-	225 00	-	65,000 00	28,013,675	9,474,485	15 00
North Reading,	75 00	120 00	-	150 00	-	-	-	-	-	-	1,500 00	446,607	56,793	15 00
Pepperell,	216 78	1,919 34	75 00	874 29	-	-	-	-	387 81	-	2,500 00	1,425,534	402,903	13 50
Reading,	43 64	4,578 79	-	1,701 24	-	-	-	-	-	1,464 23	4,500 00	2,658,204	296,245	16 00
Sherborn,	100 00	2,200 00	200 00	25 00	345 00	1,600 00	25 00	-	300 00	-	2,200 00	750,000	105,000	10 00
Shirley,	150 00	1,000 00	-	-	-	-	-	-	300 00	-	1,450 00	596,150	117,436	12 80
Somerville,	2,001 13	17,651 60	5,490 00	12,358 11	-	17,000 00	7,641 41	-	584 20	6,690 50	55,000 00	32,767,200	4,076,200	14 00
Stoneham,	-	-	-	-	-	-	-	-	-	-	-	-	-	-
Stow,	-	1,000 00	-	-	-	-	-	-	250 00	-	1,250 00	-	-	-
Sudbury,	114 00	2,882 86	-	200 00	-	-	-	-	25 00	-	3,200 00	879,970	199,510	11 00
Tewksbury,	300 00	3,000 00	-	-	-	600 00	-	-	-	-	3,900 00	1,144,350	255,733	11 50
Townsend,	-	-	-	-	-	-	-	-	-	-	-	-	-	-

Tyngsborough,	-	800 00	-	-	-	-	-	-	-	-	800 00	309,435	59,931	16 00
Wakefield,	-	-	-	-	-	-	-	-	-	-	12,000 00	4,322,550	679,945	16 50
Waltham,	3,000 00	2,100 00	7,000 00	6,000 00	7,000 00	2,500 00	2,000 00	$2,000 00	1,500 00	1,200 00	27,500 00	1,245,300	3,945,330	16 00
Watertown,	-	12,000 00	-	-	-	-	-	200 00	-	-	12,000 00	-	-	-
Wayland,	100 00	2,000 00	-	-	-	-	-	-	-	6,000 00	8,000 00	1,147,380	448,865	14 00
Westford,	-	3,000 00	-	-	-	-	-	-	-	-	3,000 00	850,000	170,000	6 20
Weston,	150 00	4,000 00	250 00	300 00	§	§	-	-	-	1,000 00	10,800 00	1,236,750	987,633	7 20
Wilmington,	250 00	2,000 00	-	-	-	-	-	-	-	-	2,300 00	658,466	76,115	12 50
Winchester,	9 25	3,600 00	500 00	300 00	1,000 00	3,600 00	300 00	-	-	-	9,700 00	3,950,580	1,087,924	15 40
Woburn,	-	-	-	-	-	-	-	-	-	-	-	-	-	-

NANTUCKET COUNTY.

Nantucket,	-	$1,500 00	-	$200 00	-	-	-	$1,000 00	-	$6,300 00	$9,000 00	$1,801,251	$1,200,976	$10 40

NORFOLK COUNTY.

Avon,	$25 00	$1,300 00	$45 00	$300 00	-	-	-	-	$6 00	-	$1,300 00	$550,630	$76,665	$20 00
Bellingham,	20 00	1,000 00	-	-	-	-	-	-	128 00	-	1,200 00	534,875	143,025	12 50
Braintree,	205 00	4,000 00	-	-	-	$3,000 00	-	-	-	-	7,500 00	2,902,750	1,005,300	14 80
Brookline,	3,306 20	26,063 48	4,445 35	14,925 84	12,163 48	13,000 00	$3,000 00	-	33,373 19	$34,532 53	157,417 31	34,472,460	16,257,100	11 60
Canton,	-	-	-	-	-	-	-	-	-	-	6,800 00	2,420,938	1,258,188	13 00
Cohasset,	420 66	8,166 61	-	-	-	-	-	-	3,916 00	10,980 41	8,060 00	2,308,866	1,589,047	5 70
Dedham,	659 44	8,808 63	221 00	13,070 00	7,506 00	-	219 84	-	126 25	345 00	14,175 00	4,600,279	1,186,849	13 90
Dover,	-	-	-	-	-	-	-	-	-	-	2,400 00	254,386	513,735	11 50
Foxborough,	-	2,500 00	-	300 00	-	-	-	-	-	-	2,500 00	1,320,767	228,581	15 80
Franklin,	300 00	1,700 00	-	2,000 00	6,000 00	-	-	-	-	-	8,000 00	2,002,715	548,635	14 50
Holbrook,	-	-	-	-	-	-	-	-	-	-	1,500 00	957,040	178,000	18 70
Hyde Park,	1,000 00	4,000 00	-	-	-	8,000 00	-	-	200 00	-	14,000 00	-	-	14 60
Medfield,	-	-	-	202 00	2,000 00	-	-	-	100 00	250 00	2,100 00	922,242	316,067	10 60
Medway,	130 00	2,051 69	-	706 46	-	-	-	-	-	-	2,000 00	1,013,670	175,815	18 00
Millis,	100 00	1,500 00	-	300 00	-	-	-	-	200 00	500 00	1,700 00	518,475	66,925	14 50
Milton,	1,300 00	10,000 00	1,000 00	1,000 00	4,758 43	12,000 00	200 00	-	3,000 00	-	33,258 43	5,426,500	8,715,422	8 00
Needham,	106 12	3,000 00	500 00	1,052 00	2,817 00	-	-	-	-	-	6,000 00	2,153,167	312,172	14 00

* Blank not filled out. † $500 to $2,000. ‡ 1892. § Extra for repairs, $5,000.

Table C. — Continued.

NORFOLK COUNTY — Concluded.

TOWNS.	Amount of Money Expended on Highways. Snow and Ice.	General Repairs.	Cleaning.	Sidewalks.	Gravel Roads.	Macadam Roads.	Paved. Gutters.	Paved. Streets.	Bridges.	New Roads.	Total Appropriation Highways and Bridges, 1891.	Value Real Estate.	Value Personal Estate.	Rate Taxation, 1891.
Norfolk,	$60 00	$1,090 00	-	-	-	-	-	-	$40 00	-	$1,000 00	$431,699	$75,092	$13 50
Norwood,	400 00	-	-	$1,000 00	$4,000 00	-	-	-	1,000 00	$2,590 91	6,000 00	2,122,750	477,902	15 80
Quincy,	1,200 00	15,000 00	-	1,000 00	-	$12,500 00	$3,000 00	-	1,500 00	2,150 00	-	11,158,125	3,268,905	13 60
Randolph,	200 00	4,000 00	-	-	-	-	500 00	-	-	-	4,000 00	1,540,700	481,980	18 00
Sharon,	75 00	2,213 66	$300 00	203 08	-	-	-	-	-	-	2,500 00	1,032,424	199,147	11 00
Stoughton,	121 00	5,090 00	-	-	-	-	-	-	-	767 00	5,700 00	1,999,395	430,495	15 00
Walpole,	289 00	2,508 00	-	-	-	-	-	-	188 00	-	3,000 00	1,520,746	441,144	11 60
Wellesley,	575 00	6,000 00	-	3,500 00	-	-	-	-	-	1,000 00	6,400 00	-	-	9 00
Weymouth,	1,095 28	11,109 02	-	-	-	-	-	-	1,684 00	3,524 66	18,214 61	4,828,760	1,705,980	17 60
Wrentham,	100 00	3,000 00	-	-	-	-	-	-	1,250 00	-	7,750 00	1,163,775	219,204	12 00

PLYMOUTH COUNTY.

TOWNS.	Snow and Ice.	General Repairs.	Cleaning.	Sidewalks.	Gravel Roads.	Macadam Roads.	Paved. Gutters.	Paved. Streets.	Bridges.	New Roads.	Total Appropriation Highways and Bridges, 1891.	Value Real Estate.	Value Personal Estate.	Rate Taxation, 1891.
Abington,	$185 30	$2,977 65	-	$630 06	-	-	-	-	$408 00	$1,904 01	$3,400 00	$1,813,010	$396,713	$19 90
Bridgewater,	30 00	446 58	$100 00	865 50	$3,407 29	-	-	-	4,864 97	610 00	5,000 00	1,857,800	505,876	11 40
Brockton,	1,889 64	-	-	-	-	-	-	$50,000 00	-	-	48,000 00	18,564,562	2,424,140	17 50
Carver,	250 00	1,200 00	-	-	-	-	-	-	-	400 00	1,600 00	517,570	154,095	8 00
Duxbury,	51 84	3,397 11	-	-	-	-	-	-	-	500 00	3,800 00	977,034	268,812	14 20
East Bridgewater,	99 40	3,606 47	-	299 10	-	-	-	-	573 02	477 03	4,975 00	1,152,492	329,642	13 50
Halifax,	-	333 80	-	-	712 13	-	-	-	-	194 04	1,000 00	239,875	27,703	12 50
Hanover,	100 90	3,341 43	-	300 00	-	-	-	-	881 00	-	3,800 00	829,462	376,022	12 50
Hanson,	100 00	1,600 00	-	300 00	-	-	-	-	200 00	2,500 00	1,800 00	479,987	126,695	17 00
Hingham,	632 31	10,185 74	-	1,000 00	-	$3,700 00	-	-	-	-	15,518 05	2,698,497	1,083,102	13 00
Hull,	81 50	5,005 05	-	384 08	3,000 00	1,300 00	-	-	572 75	-	7,300 00	2,355,316	135,859	10 10
Kingston,	175 00	1,125 00	300 00	300 00	1,000 00	1,000 00	-	-	100 00	-	4,000 00	876,430	633,835	9 20
Lakeville,	100 00	1,600 00	-	-	-	-	-	-	-	-	1,700 00	418,229	57,026	11 60
Marion,	5 00	1,000 00	-	-	500 00	700 00	-	-	-	140 00	2,650 00	585,650	322,000	10 00

Marshfield, . . .	11 70	1,384 94	-	-	3,000 00	-	-	-	260 73	917 27	4,645 67	1,031,260	144,539	15 00
Mattapoisett, . .	100 00	-	-	-	-	-	-	-	-	250 00	3,000 00	906,786	623,775	7 50
Middleborough, . .	125 00	-	-	500 00	-	-	-	-	5,475 00	300 00	14,000 00	3,015,335	612,840	14 25
Norwell, . . .	128 00	-	-	-	-	-	-	-	-	-	2,500 00	686,900	198,886	12 00
Pembroke, . . .	46 55	1,749 88	-	-	1,022 13	-	-	-	330 77	-	3,000 00	556,935	116,650	14 00
Plymouth, . . .	100 00	12,553 00	500 00	1,940 89	800 00	-	$400 00	-	-	8,385 79	22,812 14	3,843,750	2,082,850	14 00
Plympton, . . .	-	300 00	-	-	500 00	-	-	-	100 00	-	900 00	257,423	43,735	11 40
Rochester, . . .	210 00	1,400 00	-	-	-	-	-	-	100 00	-	1,500 00	426,080	70,370	10 00
Rockland, . . .	228 00	9,231 00	-	454 00	-	-	-	-	194 00	1,566 00	-	2,137,246	587,432	18 80
Scituate, . . .	200 00	3,000 00	-	500 00	-	-	-	-	-	2,500 00	3,000 00	1,974,600	144,000	13 00
Wareham, . . .	300 00	3,600 00	100 00	1,000 00	-	-	50 00	-	400 00	-	4,300 00	1,229,620	515,282	14 00
West Bridgewater, .	200 00	2,900 00	-	400 00	-	-	-	-	100 00	-	3,500 00	884,537	177,687	14 25
Whitman, . . .	207 00	650 00	100 00	2,247 00	1,750 00	3,500 00	125 00	-	-	2,450 00	12,000 00	2,603,680	658,570	18 20

SUFFOLK COUNTY.

Boston, ...	-	-	-	-	-	-	-	-	-	-	-	-	-	-
Chelsea, . . .	$2,031 76	$3,636 47	$5,238 74	$6,720 04	$3,855 54	$5,568 97	$1,216 52	$4,084 21	-	$1,864 90	$39,457 70	$18,660,300	$2,559,412	$18 00
Revere, ...	375 00	5,000 00	-	-	-	-	-	-	-	-	7,000 00	5,106,600	332,191	11 20
Winthrop, . . .	200 00	2,200 00	1,000 00	1,000 00	600 00	-	200 00	-	$7,900 00	1,800 00	15,500 00	3,676,700	99,185	12 70

WORCESTER COUNTY.

Ashburnham, . .	$645 90	$2,116 61	-	$514 12	-	-	-	-	$210 24	-	$3,700 00	$834,854	$187,885	$14 50
Athol, ...	766 79	10,135 73	-	4,115 60	-	-	-	-	-	$562 25	9,887 50	2,474,770	681,442	21 00
Auburn, . . .	80 00	900 00	-	-	$500 00	-	-	-	100 00	-	1,580 00	381,812	118,086	14 00
Barre, ...	496 00	2,700 00	-	-	2,350 00	-	-	-	1,221 70	-	4,236 34	1,053,610	1,401,466	14 00
Berlin, ...	78 00	1,000 00	-	-	-	-	-	-	10 97	-	1,000 00	441,834	62,738	9 00
Blackstone, . . .	-	5,565 80	-	-	-	-	-	-	-	-	6,500 00	1,827,900	743,950	16 20
Bolton, ...	63 00	870 00	-	-	500 00	-	-	-	120 00	-	1,200 00	425,913	69,640	10 50
Boylston, . . .	98 96	1,487 21	-	-	-	-	-	-	215 90	-	1,500 00	426,609	85,825	12 80
Brookfield, . . .	40 00	1,400 00	$30 00	30 00	800 00	-	-	-	200 00	-	2,500 00	1,045,754	248,734	11 50
Charlton, . . .	100 00	2,500 00	-	-	2,300 00	-	-	-	-	-	2,700 00	765,690	159,300	12 00
Clinton, ...	500 00	1,500 00	2,500 00	1,500 00	1,800 00	-	-	-	1,200 00	6,000 00	19,900 00	4,662,365	1,596,635	18 00

TABLE C. — Concluded.

WORCESTER COUNTY — Concluded.

TOWNS.	Amount of Money Expended on Highways.										Total Appropriation Highways and Bridges, 1891.	Value Real Estate.	Value Personal Estate.	Rate Taxation, 1891.
	Snow and Ice.	General Repairs.	Cleaning.	Sidewalks.	Gravel Roads.	Macadam Roads.	Paved. Gutters.	Paved. Streets.	Bridges.	New Roads.				
Dana,	-	$550 00	-	-	-	-	-	-	$50 00	-	$600 00	$220,473	$67,126	$17 50
Douglas,	$65 00	1,720 00	-	-	-	-	-	-	75 00	-	2,500 00	769,971	244,919	14 40
Dudley,	44 35	2,598 80	-	-	-	-	-	-	394 37	-	3,150 00	709,335	293,025	14 00
Fitchburg,	622 44	30,810 00	$3,933 20	$9,762 14	-	-	-	$761 71	9,398 33	$6,018 51	25,000 00	1,795,375	143,377	16 40
Gardner,	1,166 51	8,770 18	-	7,496 49	-	-	-	-	-	4,415 00	8,000 00	3,204,250	1,230,720	21 00
Grafton,	400 00	2,500 00	500 00	2,000 00	-	-	$200 00	-	800 00	500 00	5,900 00	1,682,925	693,560	13 00
Hardwick,	-	3,000 00	-	-	-	-	-	-	-	-	3,500 00	-	-	13 00
Harvard,	325 77	2,300 00	-	-	-	-	-	-	450 00	-	2,750 00	648,725	308,150	8 60
Holden,	255 00	681 53	100 00	-	$800 00	-	-	-	253 47	-	2,000 00	825,700	252,070	15 50
Hopedale,	57 40	2,964 3[illegible]	-	639 00	1,000 00	-	523 59	1,338 19	9,426 41	-	13,100 00	731,980	668,655	10 00
Hubbardston,	88 37	1,972 87	-	-	100 00	-	-	-	98 04	-	2,000 00	584,540	103,277	16 00
Lancaster,	100 00	-	-	-	-	-	-	-	-	-	10,500 00	-	-	8 10
Leicester,	527 50	4,500 00	-	-	-	-	-	-	-	5,563 00	10,034 00	1,329,685	808,184	11 00
Leominster,	1,385 84	6,613 62	-	1,678 00	-	-	-	-	-	1,980 63	5,000 00	3,775,128	918,413	15 00
Lunenburg,	137 00	1,461 00	-	-	-	-	-	-	180 00	-	1,800 00	664,258	73,275	15 00
Mendon,	11 64	1,539 32	-	-	-	-	-	-	10 68	-	1,500 00	465,114	76,519	11 00
Milford,	-	-	-	-	-	-	-	-	-	-	-	-	-	-
Millbury,	80 00	1,000 00	-	500 00	1,500 00	-	500 00	-	500 00	-	3,500 00	-	2,993,920	16 50
New Braintree,	-	1,200 00	-	-	-	-	-	-	-	-	1,200 00	44,300	130,000	11 00
Northborough,	175 55	1,780 24	-	-	-	-	-	-	87 50	-	1,800 00	966,210	248,598	11 00
Northbridge,	61 60	3,754 63	-	-	3,754 63	-	-	-	50 00	-	4,000 00	1,301,265	1,047,451	9 60
North Brookfield,	163 12	2,715 08	-	-	1,855 12	-	-	-	-	-	2,500 00	1,507,625	245,220	13 20
Oakham,	25 00	905 00	-	-	45 00	-	-	-	25 00	-	1,000 00	287,995	57,929	16 50
Oxford,	-	-	-	-	-	-	-	-	-	-	2,600 00	725,000	526,000	14 70
Paxton,	-	750 00	-	-	150 00	-	-	-	-	-	900 00	246,132	40,496	12 20
Petersham,	200 00	2,060 61	-	-	-	-	-	-	-	-	2,000 00	505,572	76,490	15 00
Phillipston,	-	-	-	-	-	-	-	-	-	-	800 00	283,190	36,860	16 50
Princeton,	609 70	1,659 61	-	-	-	-	-	-	305 42	-	3,200 00	687,664	129,682	10 50
Royalston,	200 00	-	-	-	-	-	-	-	-	-	2,000 00	*570,168	-	9 50
Rutland,	800 00	200 00	-	-	-	-	-	-	40 00	-	1,500 00	437,289	69,810	16 00
Shrewsbury,	-	2,500 00	-	-	-	-	-	-	-	-	2,500 00	774,995	261,244	12 80
Southborough,	20 00	50 00	50 00	25 00	1,700 00	-	55 00	-	100 00	-	2,000 00	1,500,000		10 00

Southbridge, . .	100 00	4,000 05	200 00	3,000 00	2,500 00	-	200 00	-	300 00	-	4,800 00	2,384,300	905,573	19 00
Spencer, . . .	1,615 70	5,579 00	-	2,150 11	-	$4,000 00	-	-	250 00	2,910 20	16,115 76	2,750,045	1,401,475	19 00
Sterling, . . .	529 38	2,141 58	-	-	-	-	-	-	452 17	-	2,500 00	747,890	98,675	13 50
Sturbridge, . .	-	2,667 58	-	-	-	-	-	-	-	-	3,000 00	709,435	235,945	12 50
Sutton, . . .	200 00	2,500 00	-	-	300 00	-	-	-	200 00	-	3,000 00	436,211	360,357	12 25
Templeton, . .	839 66	2,845 95	-	-	-	-	-	-	-	-	2,500 00	938,987	214,987	16 50
Upton, . . .	71 98	2,000 00	-	-	-	-	-	-	-	1,000 00	2,000 00	718,513	208,098	19 50
Uxbridge, . .	-	-	-	-	-	-	-	-	-	-	-	-	-	-
Warren, . . .	114 15	-	-	-	-	-	-	-	-	2,800 00	5,852 56	1,956,865	510,[illegible]82	15 00
Webster, . . .	400 00	500 00	600 00	600 00	2,000 00	-	-	-	300 00	-	2,800 00	1,725,836	1,051,083	11 50
Westborough, . .	-	-	-	-	-	-	-	-	-	-	3,500 00	3,707,699	731,827	16 20
West Boylston, .	112 57	1,957 22	-	-	-	-	-	-	-	190 12	2,000 00	899,842	297,693	16 80
West Brookfield, .	100 00	1,200 00	-	200 00	-	-	-	-	125 00	-	1,300 00	671,339	109,879	14 00
Westminster, . .	403 39	1,400 03	-	-	-	-	-	-	290 00	248 00	2,500 00	227,782	778,327	13 50
Winchendon, . .	663 70	3,771 98	-	-	-	-	-	-	-	401 93	3,800 00	1,548,857	586,493	15 30
Worcester, . .	9,040 33	11,961 45	12,656 27	48,841 50	-	18,302 81	-	33,364 69	1,078 70	23,811 47	-	60,942,300	16,693,608	14 00

* Total.

TABLE D. — *Road Machinery.*

BARNSTABLE COUNTY.

TOWNS.	ROLLER.					CRUSHER.										ROAD MACHINES.		WATER CARTS.	
									ELEVATOR.		SCREENS.								
	Horses.	Pattern.	Kind.	Weight.	Cost.	Size.	Cost.	No. Handlings.	Height.	Cost.	Kind.	Grades.	Bins.	Loading.	Cost Shovelling.	No.	Cost.	No.	Capacity.
Barnstable,	-	-	-	-	-	-	-	-	-	-	-	-	-	-	-	-	-	-	-
Bourne,	3 to 4	Ring	horse	1½ tons	$250[1]	-	-	-	-	-	-	-	-	-	-	1	$275	-	-
Brewster,	-	-	-	-	-	-	-	-	-	-	-	-	-	-	-	1	350	-	-
Chatham,	-	-	-	-	-	-	-	-	-	-	-	-	-	-	-	1	250	-	-
Dennis,	-	-	-	-	-	-	-	-	-	-	-	-	-	-	-	3	250[1]	-	-
Eastham,	2	Ring	horse	1,200 lbs.	45	-	-	-	-	-	-	-	-	-	-	1	150	-	-
Falmouth,	2	[2]	horse	4,500 lbs.	-	-	-	-	-	-	plain	-	-	-	-	2	500	-	-
Harwich,	-	-	-	-	-	-	-	-	-	-	-	-	-	-	-	-	-	-	-
Mashpee,	-	-	-	-	-	-	-	-	-	-	-	-	-	-	-	1	175	-	-
Orleans,	2	Ring	horse	1,000 lbs.	45	-	-	-	-	-	-	-	-	-	-	1	150	-	-
Provincetown,	-	-	-	-	-	-	-	-	-	-	-	-	-	-	-	-	-	-	-
Sandwich,	2	Ring	horse	3,800 lbs.	100	-	-	-	-	-	plain	-	-	-	-	1	250	-	-
Truro,	2	Ring	horse	-	-	-	-	-	-	-	-	-	-	-	-	-	-	-	-
Wellfleet,	-	-	-	-	-	-	-	-	-	-	-	-	-	-	-	1	125	-	-
Yarmouth,	1	-	horse	1,000 lbs.	-	-	-	-	-	-	-	-	-	-	-	-	-	-	-

BERKSHIRE COUNTY.

TOWNS.	Horses.	Pattern.	Kind.	Weight.	Cost.	Size.	Cost.	No. Handlings.	Height.	Cost.	Kind.	Grades.	Bins.	Loading.	Cost Shovelling.	No.	Cost.	No.	Capacity.
Adams,	-	-	-	-	-	-	-	-	-	-	-	-	-	-	-	1	$250	2	500
Alford,	-	-	-	-	-	-	-	-	-	-	-	-	-	-	-	1	210	-	-
Becket,	-	-	-	-	-	-	-	-	-	-	-	-	-	-	-	2	250	-	-
Cheshire,	-	-	-	-	-	-	-	-	-	-	-	-	-	-	-	-	-	-	-
Clarksburg,	-	-	-	-	-	-	-	-	-	-	-	-	-	-	-	-	-	-	-
Dalton,	-	-	-	-	-	-	-	-	-	-	-	-	-	-	-	1	225	-	-
Egremont,	-	-	-	-	-	-	-	-	-	-	-	-	-	-	-	1	200	-	-
Florida,	-	-	-	-	-	-	-	-	-	-	-	-	-	-	-	1	200	-	-
Great Barrington,	-	-	-	-	-	-	-	-	-	-	-	-	-	-	-	-	-	-	-

Hancock,	-	-	-	-	-	-	-	-	-	-	-	-	-	-	-	1	250	-	-
Hinsdale,	-	-	-	-	-	-	-	-	-	-	-	-	-	-	-	2	355	-	-
Lanesborough,	-	-	-	-	-	-	-	-	-	-	-	-	-	-	-	1	140	-	-
Lee,	-	-	-	-	-	-	-	-	-	-	-	-	-	-	-	2	400	1	1,200
Lenox,	-	-	-	-	-	-	-	Buy	broken	stone	at $2.10	per ton	-	-	-	1	225	-	-
Monterey,	-	-	-	-	-	-	-	-	-	-	-	-	-	-	-	1	275	-	-
Mt Washington,	-	-	-	-	-	-	-	-	-	-	-	-	-	-	-	1	212	-	-
New Ashford,	-	-	-	-	-	-	-	-	-	-	-	-	-	-	-	-	-	-	-
New Marlborough,	-	-	-	-	-	-	-	-	-	-	-	-	-	-	-	1	250	-	-
North Adams,	2	Ring	horse	-	-	[3]	-	1	-	-	plain	2	-	shovels	-	1	250	-	-
Otis,	-	-	-	-	-	-	-	-	-	-	-	-	-	-	-	1	250	-	-
Peru,	-	-	-	-	-	-	-	-	-	-	-	-	-	-	-	1	250	-	-
Pittsfield,	-	-	horse steam	6 tons 15 tons	$4,000	9x15	-	2	-	-	revolving.	3	-	shovels	-	4	800	-	-
Richmond,	-	-	-	-	-	-	-	-	-	-	-	-	-	-	-	1	250	-	-
Sandisfield,	-	-	-	-	-	-	-	-	-	-	-	-	-	-	-	-	-	-	-
Savoy,	-	-	-	-	-	-	-	-	-	-	-	-	-	-	-	1	225	-	-
Sheffield,	-	-	-	-	-	-	-	-	-	-	-	-	-	-	-	1	235	-	-
Stockbridge,	4	Ring	horse	6,000 lbs	[4]	-	-	-	-	-	-	-	-	-	-	-	-	1	650
Tyringham,	-	-	-	-	-	-	-	-	-	-	-	-	-	-	-	1	200	-	-
Washington,	-	-	-	-	-	-	-	-	-	-	-	-	-	-	-	1	250	-	-
West Stockbridge,	-	-	-	-	-	-	-	-	-	-	-	-	-	-	-	-	-	-	-
Williamstown,	-	-	-	-	-	-	-	-	-	-	-	-	-	-	-	2	500	-	-
Windsor,	-	-	-	-	-	-	-	-	-	-	-	-	-	-	-	1	250	-	-
BRISTOL COUNTY.																			
Acushnet,	-	-	-	-	-	-	-	-	-	-	-	-	-	-	-	1	$200	-	-
Attleborough,	-	-	-	-	-	-	-	-	-	-	-	-	-	-	-	-	-	-	-
Berkley,	-	-	-	-	-	-	-	-	-	-	-	-	-	-	-	1	150	-	-
Dartmouth,	4	Ring	horse	6 tons	$700	9x16	$800	2	-	-	-	1	-	[5]	-	1	250	1	[6]
Dighton,	-	-	-	-	-	-	-	-	-	-	-	-	-	-	-	1	150	-	-
Easton,	-	-	-	-	-	-	-	-	-	-	-	-	-	-	-	-	-	-	-
Fairhaven,	-	-	-	-	-	-	-	-	-	-	-	-	-	-	-	-	-	-	-
Fall River,	2	Ring	horse steam	3 tons 18 tons	300 4,400	10x15	600	2	-	-	plain	2	-	-	-	-	-	17	[7]
Freetown,	-	-	-	-	-	-	-	-	-	-	-	-	-	-	-	1	150	-	-
Mansfield,	4	Ring	horse	4,400	235	9x15	675	2	-	-	plain	3	2	[5]	-	2	[8]	1	600
New Bedford,	4	4 parts plain	horse steam	4½ tons 15 tons	3,000	15x9	-	1	24 ft.	-	[9]	2	1	[5]	-	1	-	1	-
No. Attleborough,	-	-	-	-	-	-	-	-	-	-	-	-	-	-	-	-	-	-	-
Norton,	-	-	-	-	-	-	-	-	-	-	-	-	-	-	-	1	250	-	-

[1] Each. [2] Not solid; made sections. [3] Size not given. [4] $352.80. [5] Without shovels.
[6] 15 barrels. [7] 300 to 750 each. [8] $250 to $300. [9] Plain, revolving.

Table D. — Continued.

BRISTOL COUNTY — Concluded.

TOWNS.	Roller.					Crusher.										Road Machines.		Water Carts.	
									Elevator.		Screens.								
	Horses.	Pattern.	Kind.	Weight.	Cost.	Size.	Cost.	No. Handlings.	Height	Cost.	Kind.	Grades.	Bins.	Loading.	Cost Shovelling.	No.	Cost.	No.	Capacity.
Raynham,	-	-	-	-	-	-	-	-	-	-	-	-	-	-	-	2	$175	-	-
Rehoboth,	-	-	-	-	-	-	-	-	-	-	-	-	-	-	-	1	250	-	-
Seekonk,	-	-	-	-	-	-	-	-	-	-	-	-	-	-	-	-	-	-	-
Somerset,	-	-	-	-	-	-	-	-	-	-	-	-	-	-	-	1	250	-	-
Swansea,	-	-	-	-	-	-	-	An	individ	ual	owns	crush	er.	-	-	1	250	-	-
Taunton,	4	hollow	horse steam	400 lbs. 7 tons	$300 5,000	9x13	$700	2	-	-	[1]	2	-	Shovels	8 cents	3	200[2]	1	-
Westport,	-	-	-	-	-	-	-	-	-	-	-	-	-	-	-	-	-	-	-

DUKES COUNTY. (No Road Machinery.)

ESSEX COUNTY.

TOWNS.	Horses.	Pattern.	Kind.	Weight.	Cost.	Size.	Cost.	No. Handlings.	Height	Cost.	Kind.	Grades.	Bins.	Loading.	Cost Shovelling.	No.	Cost.	No.	Capacity.
Amesbury,	-	-	-	-	-	-	-	-	-	-	-	-	-	-	-	-	-	-	-
Andover,	-	-	-	-	-	No. 2[3] No. 2[3]	$2,500 4,000	1	yes	-	plain	1	-	[4]	-	1	$250	1[5]	-
Beverly,	2	Ring	horse steam	4,500 lbs. 15 tons	$3,933	9x15[6]	2,900	2	15 ft.	-	[1]	4	1	[7]	-	1	-	1	600
Boxford,	-	-	-	-	-	-	-	-	-	-	-	-	-	-	-	1	250	-	-
Bradford,	-	-	-	-	-	-	-	-	-	-	-	-	-	-	-	1	250	-	-
Danvers,	-	-	-	-	-	-	-	-	-	-	-	-	-	-	-	1	135	-	-
Essex,	-	-	-	-	-	-	-	-	-	-	-	-	-	-	-	-	-	-	-
Georgetown,	-	-	-	-	-	-	-	-	-	-	-	-	-	-	-	1	200	-	-
Gloucester,	-	-	-	-	-	-	-	-	-	-	-	-	-	-	-	-	-	-	-
Groveland,	-	-	-	-	-	-	-	-	-	-	-	-	-	-	-	1	250	-	-
Hamilton,	-	-	-	-	-	-	-	-	-	-	-	-	-	-	-	-	-	-	-

Haverhill,	-	-	-	-	-	-	-	-	-	-	-	-	-	-	-	-	-	-	-
Ipswich,	2	granite	horse	2 tons	45	-	-	-	-	-	-	-	-	-	-	-	-	-	-
Lawrence,	-	-	-	-	-	-	-	-	-	-	-	-	-	-	-	-	-	-	-
Lynn,	-	-	-	-	-	-	-	-	-	-	-	-	-	-	-	-	-	-	-
Lynnfield,	-	-	-	-	-	-	-	-	-	-	-	-	-	-	-	-	-	-	-
Manchester,	4	Ring	horse	5,500 lbs.	300	9x15	2,200	1	-	-	[5]	3	3	shovels	5 cents	-	-	3	450[2]
Marblehead,	-	-	-	-	-	-	-	-	-	-	-	-	-	-	-	-	-	1	700[9]
Merrimac,	-	-	-	-	-	-	-	-	-	-	-	-	-	-	-	1	250	-	-
Methuen,	-	-	steam	10 tons	3,250	14 in.	1,750	1	-	-	plain	1	-	-	-	1	200	-	-
Middleton,	-	-	-	-	-	-	-	-	-	-	-	-	-	-	-	1	200	-	-
Nahant,	2	Ring	horse	2 tons	-	-	-	-	-	-	-	-	-	-	-	-	-	5	2,000
Newbury,	-	-	-	-	-	-	-	-	-	-	-	-	-	-	-	1	200	-	-
Newburyport,	2 or more	stone	horse steam	3,000 lbs. 12 tons	150 3,400	-	-	Buy stone teamed and shovelled for 25 cents per ton								1	225	[6]	-
North Andover,	-	-	-	-	-	-	-	-	-	-	-	-	-	-	-	-	-	2	-
Peabody,	-	-	-	-	-	-	-	-	-	-	-	-	-	-	-	-	-	-	-
Rockport,	-	-	-	-	-	-	Buy stone at $1.25 per ton				-	-	-	-	-	-	-	-	-
Rowley,	-	-	-	-	-	-	-	-	-	-	-	-	-	-	-	-	-	-	-
Salem,	4	Ring	horse steam	2 tons 15 tons	4,300	2.9x15	2,100[3]	2	-	-	[1]	3[10]	-	shovels	5 cents	1	200	1	500
Salisbury,	-	-	-	-	-	-	-	-	-	-	-	-	-	-	-	1	160	-	-
Saugus,	-	-	-	-	-	-	-	-	-	-	-	-	-	-	-	1	198	-	-
Swampscott,	-	-	-	-	-	9x15	2,500	1	-	-	[1]	4	4	shovels	10 cents	-	-	-	-
Topsfield,	-	-	-	-	-	-	-	-	-	-	-	-	-	-	-	1	260	-	-
Wenham,	-	-	-	-	-	-	-	-	-	-	-	-	-	-	-	-	-	-	-
West Newbury,	-	-	-	-	-	-	-	-	-	-	-	-	-	-	-	1	200	-	-

FRANKLIN COUNTY.

Ashfield,	-	-	-	-	-	-	-	-	-	-	-	-	-	-	-	2	[11]	-	-
Bernardston,	-	-	-	-	-	-	-	-	-	-	-	-	-	-	-	-	-	-	-
Buckland,	-	-	-	-	-	-	-	-	-	-	-	-	-	-	-	1	$250	-	-
Charlemont,	-	-	-	-	-	-	-	-	-	-	-	-	-	-	-	1	175	-	-
Colrain,	-	-	-	-	-	-	-	-	-	-	-	-	-	-	-	1	250	-	-
Conway,	-	-	-	-	-	-	-	-	-	-	-	-	-	-	-	-	-	-	-
Deerfield,	-	-	-	-	-	-	-	-	-	-	-	-	-	-	-	-	-	-	-
Erving,	-	-	-	-	-	-	-	-	-	-	-	-	-	-	-	1	250	-	-
Gill,	-	-	-	-	-	-	-	-	-	-	-	-	-	-	-	1	250	-	-
Greenfield,	6	Ring	horse	6,700	-	-	[12]	-	-	-	[1]	3	3	shovels	[13]	1	250	-	-

[1] Revolving. [2] Each. [3] Gates. [4] Without shovels. [5] Private. [6] F. & M.
[7] With and without shovels. [8] Revolving, plain. [9] Gallons. [10] And dust. [11] $150 and $225. [12] Own crusher. [13] Not much.

Table D. — Continued.

FRANKLIN COUNTY — Concluded.

TOWNS.	Roller.					Crusher.										Road Machines.		Water Carts.	
									Elevator.		Screens.								
	Horses.	Pattern.	Kind.	Weight.	Cost.	Size.	Cost.	No. Handlings.	Height.	Cost.	Kind.	Grades.	Bins.	Loading.	Cost Shovelling.	No.	Cost.	No.	Capacity.
Hawley,	-	-	-	-	-	-	-	-	-	-	-	-	-	-	-	1	$100	-	-
Heath,	-	-	-	-	-	-	-	-	-	-	-	-	-	-	-	1	250	-	-
Leverett,	-	-	-	-	-	-	-	-	-	-	-	-	-	-	-	1	200	-	-
Leyden,	-	-	-	-	-	-	-	-	-	-	-	-	-	-	-	1	250[1]	-	-
Monroe,	-	-	-	-	-	-	-	-	-	-	-	-	-	-	-	1	210	-	-
Montague,	-	-	-	-	-	-	-	-	-	-	-	-	-	-	-	1	250	-	-
New Salem,	-	-	-	-	-	-	-	-	-	-	-	-	-	-	-	1	250	-	-
Northfield,	-	-	-	-	-	-	-	-	-	-	-	-	-	-	-	-	-	-	-
Orange,	-	-	-	-	-	-	-	-	-	-	-	-	-	-	-	2	500	-	-
Rowe,	-	-	-	-	-	-	-	-	-	-	-	-	-	-	-	-	-	-	-
Shelburne,	-	-	-	-	-	-	-	-	-	-	-	-	-	-	-	-	-	-	-
Shutesbury,	-	-	-	-	-	-	-	-	-	-	-	-	-	-	-	1	250	-	-
Sunderland,	-	-	-	-	-	-	-	-	-	-	-	-	-	-	-	-	-	-	-
Warwick,	-	-	-	-	-	-	-	-	-	-	-	-	-	-	-	1	250	-	-
Wendell,	-	-	-	-	-	-	-	-	-	-	-	-	-	-	-	1	225	-	-
Whately,	-	-	-	-	-	-	-	-	-	-	-	-	-	-	-	1	240	-	-

HAMPDEN COUNTY.

TOWNS.	Horses.	Pattern.	Kind.	Weight.	Cost.	Size.	Cost.	No. Handlings.	Height.	Cost.	Kind.	Grades.	Bins.	Loading.	Cost Shovelling.	No.	Cost.	No.	Capacity.
Agawam,	-	-	-	-	-	-	-	-	-	-	-	-	-	-	-	1	$250	-	-
Blandford,	-	-	-	-	-	-	-	-	-	-	-	-	-	-	-	1	140	-	-
Brimfield,	-	-	-	-	-	-	-	-	-	-	-	-	-	-	-	1	250	-	-
Chester,	-	-	-	-	-	-	-	-	-	-	-	-	-	-	-	1	250	-	-
Chicopee,	-	-	-	-	-	-	-	-	-	-	-	-	-	-	-	-	-	-	-
Granville,	-	-	-	-	-	-	-	-	-	-	-	-	-	-	-	1	250	-	-
Hampden,	-	-	-	-	-	-	-	-	-	-	-	-	-	-	-	-	-	-	-
Holland,	-	-	-	-	-	-	-	-	-	-	-	-	-	-	-	-	-	-	-
Holyoke,	4	Ring	horse	5 tons	$400	-	$1,200	[2]	-	-	[3]	-	-	-	-	3	800	13	650[4]
Longmeadow,	-	-	-	-	-	-	-	-	-	-	-	-	-	-	-	2	[5]	-	-

Ludlow,	-	-	-	-	-	-	-	-	-	-	-	-	-	-	-	[6]	-	-	-
Monson,	-	-	-	-	-	-	-	-	-	-	-	-	-	-	-	3	600	1[6]	300
Montgomery,	-	-	-	-	-	-	-	-	-	-	-	-	-	-	-	1	250	-	-
Palmer,	-	-	-	-	-	-	-	-	-	-	-	-	-	-	-	1	250	-	-
Russell,	-	-	-	-	-	-	-	-	-	-	-	-	-	-	-	2	[7]	-	-
Southwick,	-	-	-	-	-	-	-	-	-	-	-	-	-	[8]	-	1	250	-	-
Springfield,	4	Ring	horse steam	5 tons 12 tons	600 4,500	20x10	2,000	2	-	-	[3]	3	1	shovels	8 cents	1	200	1	350
Tolland,	-	-	-	-	-	-	-	-	-	-	-	-	-	-	-	-	-	-	-
Wales,	-	-	-	-	-	-	-	-	-	-	-	-	-	-	-	1	200	-	-
Westfield,	4 to 6	Ring	horse	7 tons	450	-	-	-	-	-	-	-	-	-	-	1	250	-	-
West Springfield,	-	-	-	-	-	-	-	-	-	-	-	-	-	-	-	-	-	-	-
Wilbraham,	-	-	-	-	-	-	-	-	-	-	-	-	-	-	-	1	250	-	-

HAMPSHIRE COUNTY.

Amherst,	-	-	-	-	-	-	-	-	-	-	-	-	-	-	-	-	-	-	-
Belchertown,	-	-	-	-	-	-	-	-	-	-	-	-	-	-	-	2	$250[4]	-	-
Chesterfield,	-	-	-	-	-	-	-	-	-	-	-	-	-	-	-	1	250	-	-
Cummington,	-	-	-	-	-	-	-	-	-	-	-	-	-	-	-	1	230	-	-
Easthampton,	-	-	-	-	-	-	-	-	-	-	-	-	-	-	-	-	-	-	-
Enfield,	-	-	-	-	-	-	-	-	-	-	-	-	-	-	-	1	200	-	-
Goshen,	-	-	-	-	-	-	-	-	-	-	-	-	-	-	-	1	150	-	-
Granby,	-	-	-	-	-	-	-	-	-	-	-	-	-	-	-	1	150	-	-
Greenwich,	-	-	-	-	-	-	-	-	-	-	-	-	-	-	-	1	250	-	-
Hadley,	-	-	-	-	-	-	-	-	-	-	-	-	-	-	-	1	250	-	-
Hatfield,	-	-	-	-	-	-	-	-	-	-	-	-	-	-	-	1	260	-	-
Huntington,	-	-	-	-	-	-	-	-	-	-	-	-	-	-	-	1	255	-	-
Middlefield,	-	-	-	-	-	-	-	-	-	-	-	-	-	-	-	1	215	-	-
Northampton,	2 to 6	Ring	horse	2 tons 7 tons	$500	9x15	$2,300	2	-	-	revolving	3	-	shovels	-	3	[9]	-	-
Pelham,	-	-	-	-	-	-	-	-	-	-	-	-	-	-	-	1	250	-	-
Plainfield,	-	-	-	-	-	-	-	-	-	-	-	-	-	-	-	1	200	-	-
Prescott,	-	-	-	-	-	-	-	-	-	-	-	-	-	-	-	1	250	-	-
Southampton,	-	-	-	-	-	-	-	-	-	-	-	-	-	-	-	1	260	-	-
South Hadley,	-	-	-	-	-	-	-	-	-	-	-	-	-	-	-	1	250	-	-
Ware,	-	-	-	-	-	-	-	-	-	-	-	-	-	-	-	2	[10]	1[4]	500
Westhampton,	-	-	-	-	-	-	-	-	-	-	-	-	-	-	-	1	150	-	-
Williamsburg,	-	-	-	-	-	-	-	-	-	-	-	-	-	-	-	2	300	-	-
Worthington,	-	-	-	-	-	-	-	-	-	-	-	-	-	-	-	1	200	-	-

[1] Pays well.
[2] Crusher has not been used for twelve years.
[3] Revolving.
[4] Each.
[5] $250, $135.
[6] Private.
[7] $200, $125.
[8] With and without shovels.
[9] $200, $200, $100.
[10] $250, $200.

Table D. — Continued.

MIDDLESEX COUNTY.

TOWNS.	Roller.					Crusher.										Road Machines.		Water Carts.	
	Horses.	Pattern.	Kind.	Weight.	Cost.	Size.	Cost.	No. Handlings.	Elevator.		Screens.					No.	Cost.	No.	Capacity.
									Height.	Cost.	Kind.	Grades.	Bins.	Loading.	Cost Shovelling.				
Acton,	-	-	-	-	-	-	-	-	-	-	-	-	-	-	per ton	1	$150	-	-
Arlington,	2 to 5	[1]	2 horse	[2]	-	9x15	-	1	20 ft.	$600	plain	2	2	[3]	-	1	150	4	[4]
Ashby,	-	-	-	-	-	-	-	-	-	-	-	-	-	-	-	1	250	-	-
Ashland,	-	-	-	-	-	-	-	-	-	-	-	-	-	-	-	1	250	-	-
Ayer,	-	-	-	-	-	-	-	-	-	-	-	-	-	-	-	1	250	-	-
Bedford,	-	-	-	-	-	-	-	-	-	-	-	-	-	-	-	1	216	-	-
Belmont,	2	Ring	horse	3 tons	$300	9x15	$700	1	30 ft.	2,000	[5]	3	3	[3]	-	1	250	1	500[6]
Billerica,	-	-	-	-	-	-	-	-	-	-	-	-	-	-	-	-	-	-	-
Boxborough,	-	-	-	-	-	-	-	-	-	-	-	-	-	-	-	1	200	-	-
Burlington,	-	-	-	-	-	-	-	-	-	-	-	-	-	-	-	1	225	-	-
Cambridge,	2, 3, 4	3 Ring 1 solid	4 horse 2 steam	15 tons	8,000	9x15	4,000	1	35 ft.	2,200	[7]	4	4	[8]	10 cents	4	1,000	41	[9]
Carlisle,	-	-	-	-	-	-	-	-	-	-	-	-	-	-	-	1	250	-	-
Chelmsford,	-	-	-	-	-	-	-	-	-	-	-	-	-	-	10 cents	1	255	-	-
Concord,	4	granite	horse	3 tons	40	8x14	2,500	-	-	-	[5]	[10]	-	shovels	10-12cts.	1	250	1	600
Dracut,	-	-	-	-	-	-	-	-	-	-	-	-	-	-	-	1	285	-	-
Dunstable,	-	-	-	-	-	-	-	-	-	-	-	-	-	-	-	1	225	-	-
Everett,	2	Ring	horse	3,500 lbs.	200	9x15	3,000	2	-	-	[11]	3	3	shovels	-	1	-	3	[12]
Framingham,	4	Ring	horse	5,600 lbs.	275	7x9	2,000	1	-	-	[11]	3	-	shovels	20 cents	1	250	-	-
Groton,	-	-	-	-	-	-	-	-	-	-	-	-	-	-	-	1	250	-	-
Holliston,	-	-	-	-	-	-	-	-	-	-	-	-	-	-	-	1	150	-	-
Hopkinton,	-	-	-	-	-	-	-	-	-	-	-	-	-	-	-	1	250	-	-
Hudson,	-	-	-	-	-	-	-	-	-	-	-	-	-	-	-	1	250	-	-
Lexington,	2	Ring	horse	5,000 lbs.	280	-	-	-	-	-	-	-	-	-	-	1	150	2	-
Lincoln,	-	-	-	-	-	-	-	-	-	-	-	-	-	-	-	1	150	-	-
Littleton,	-	-	-	-	-	-	-	-	-	-	-	-	-	-	-	1	250	-	-
Lowell,	4	[1]	[13]	[14]	5,000	15x9	[15]	2	-	-	[5]	3	-	shovels	-	1	250	13	[16]
Malden,	4	plain	[13]	5-15 tons	[17]	[18]	2,300	2	-	-	[5]	3	-	shovels	-	1	244	6	600[19]
Marlborough,	-	-	-	-	-	-	-	-	-	-	-	-	-	-	-	-	-	-	-
Maynard,	-	-	-	-	-	-	-	-	-	-	-	-	-	-	-	1	200	-	-
Medford,	2	Ring	horse	4,200 lbs.	300	9x15	700	1	14	370	[11]	4	4	[3]	10 cents	2	400	6	600[19]
Melrose,	2	Ring	[13]	[20]	[21]	7x15	3,750	1	25	-	[5]	4	4	[3]	10 cents	1	250	1	600
Natick,[22]	4	Ring	horse	7,000 lbs.	-	-	-	-	-	-	[5]	3	-	shovels	-	1	250	[23]	-

Newton,	2 to 4	Ring	1 horse 2 steam	4,300 lbs. [24]	275 [25]	2-9x15	875	[26]	-	-	[5]	4	4	[27]	[28]	2	200	4	[29]
North Reading,	-	-	-	-	-	-	-	-	-	-	-	-	-	-	-	-	-	-	-
Pepperell,	-	-	-	-	-	-	-	-	-	-	-	-	-	-	-	1	250	-	-
Reading,	4	Ring	horse	5,200 lbs	200	-	-	-	-	-	-	-	-	-	-	1	165	-	-
Sherborn,	-	-	-	-	-	-	-	-	-	-	-	-	-	-	-	-	-	-	-
Shirley,	4	-	[30]	4,800 lbs.	35	-	-	-	-	-	-	-	-	-	-	1	215	-	-
Somerville,	2	Ring	horse steam	3,500 lbs. 15 tons	[31]	9x15	600	2	45	200	plain	4	4	[27]	-	2	400	17	600[19]
Stoneham,	-	-	-	-	-	-	-	-	-	-	-	-	-	-	-	-	-	-	-
Stow,	-	-	-	-	-	-	-	-	-	-	plain	-	-	-	-	1	225	-	-
Sudbury,	-	-	-	-	-	-	-	-	-	-	-	-	-	-	-	1	175	-	-
Tewksbury,	-	-	-	-	-	-	-	-	-	-	-	-	-	-	-	1	200	-	-
Townsend,	-	-	-	-	-	-	-	-	-	-	-	-	-	-	-	1	-	-	-
Tyngsborough,	-	-	-	-	-	-	-	-	-	-	-	-	-	-	-	1	[23]	-	-
Wakefield,	2	Ring	horse	-	-	[33]	-	2	-	-	[5]	-	3	shovels	-	1	-	-	-
Waltham,	2 to 4	Ring	horse	4,500 lbs.	350	9x15	3,700	1	30	-	[5]	4	3	[3]	12 cents	1	250	1	500
Watertown,	2	Ring	horse	3 tons	-	9x15[34]	-	2	-	-	plain	1	-	shovels	-	1	200	3	[35]
Wayland,	-	-	-	-	-	-	-	-	-	-	-	-	-	-	-	-	-	-	-
Westford,	-	-	-	-	-	-	-	-	-	-	plain	-	-	-	-	1	290	-	-
Weston,	-	Ring	horse	2 tons	200	-	-	-	-	-	-	-	-	-	-	1	150	-	-
Wilmington,	-	-	-	-	-	-	-	-	-	-	-	-	-	-	-	-	-	-	-
Winchester,	1 to 2	[36]	2 horse	1-2 tons	-	[37]	1,800	2	25 ft.	1,600	[11]	4	4	[3]	10 cents	1	250	2	150
Woburn,	-	-	-	-	-	-	-	-	-	-	-	-	-	-	-	-	-	-	-

NANTUCKET COUNTY. (No Road Machinery.)

NORFOLK COUNTY.

Avon,	-	-	-	-	-	-	-	-	-	-	-	-	-	-	-	-	-	-	-
Bellingham,	-	-	-	-	-	-	-	-	-	-	-	-	-	-	-	1	$250	-	-
Braintree,	3 to 4	Ring	horse	4,500 lbs.	$210	9x15	$750	1	-	-	plain	dust	-	[3]	-	1	200	-	-
Brookline,	2	Ring	steam horse stone	15 tons 4,200 lbs. 5 tons[38]	3,700 300 -	3 10x7-1 15x9-2	2,000 725 [39]	1	-	-	[40]	4[41]	-	[42]	10 cents	1	150	[43]	[44]

[1] Ring, stone. [2] 2 tons, 5 tons. [3] Without shovels. [4] 600, 500, 300, 300. [5] Revolving. [6] Gallons. [7] Steam revolving. [8] From bins. [9] 5-750, 36-625.
[10] 3-1½-1 and dust. [11] Plain, revolving. [12] 800 in all. [13] Horse, steam. [14] 3-1½-18 tons. [15] $862.50. [16] 600-750 each. [17] Steam, $4,000. [18] Not given.
[19] Each. [20] 11 tons-2,500. [21] $600, $350. [22] 8 to 10 inch stone used on road. [23] Private. [24] Fifteen tons each. [25] $6,000, $3,500. [26] 1-1, 1-2.
[27] With and without shovels. [28] 12 cents per cubic yard. [29] 2-350, 2-575. [30] Horse, stone. [31] $300, $4,500. [32] $258.58. [33] Size not given.
[34] Old fashioned. [35] 500 gallons each. [36] Solid, Ring. [37] Good size. [38] Little used. [39] $1,392.13. [40] Revolving, on 9x15; plain, 10x7. [41] Dust, 1 in., 2¼ in. and tailings.
[42] Without shovel when crusher; working otherwise, shovel. [43] Four 2-horse, one 1-horse. [44] 2,900 gallons; hire nineteen other carts, capacity 600 gallons each.

TABLE D. — Continued.

NORFOLK COUNTY — Concluded.

TOWNS.	ROLLER.					CRUSHER.										ROAD MACHINES.		WATER CARTS.	
									ELEVATOR.		SCREENS.								
	Horses.	Pattern.	Kind.	Weight.	Cost.	Size.	Cost.	No. Handlings.	Height.	Cost.	Kind.	Grades.	Bins.	Loading.	Cost Shovelling.	No.	Cost.	No.	Capacity.
Canton,	2 to 4	Ring	horse	5,100 lbs.	$235	-	-	-	-	-	-	-	-	-	-	1	$250	-	-
Cohasset,	-	-	horse[1]	-	-	-	-	-	-	-	-	-	-	-	-	1	250	-	-
Dedham,	2 to 4	Ring	horse	5,400 lbs.	225	-	-	-	-	-	-	-	-	-	-	2[2]	500	-	-
Dover,	-	-	-	-	-	-	-	-	-	-	plain	-	-	-	-	1	250	-	-
Foxborough,	2 to 4	Ring	horse	2,500 lbs.	200	-	-	-	-	-	-	-	-	-	-	1	155	-	-
Franklin,	-	-	-	-	-	-	-	-	-	-	-	-	-	-	-	1	200	-	-
Holbrook,	-	-	-	-	-	-	-	-	-	-	plain	1½ in.	-	-	-	1	200	-	-
Hyde Park,	2	Ring	horse	-	-	9x15	$2,700	-	-	-	plain	2	-	[3]	-	1	200	1	450
Medfield,	-	-	-	-	-	-	-	-	-	-	-	-	-	-	-	1	250	-	-
Medway,	-	-	-	-	-	-	-	-	-	-	-	-	-	-	-	-	-	-	-
Millis,	2	solid	horse	5 tons	-	-	-	-	-	-	-	-	-	-	-	1	250	1[4]	600
Milton,	4	Ring	horse	4,200 lbs.	300	15x9	4,500	2	-	-	-	-	2	shovels	-	1	175	2	500
Needham,	4	Ring	horse	3 tons	225	-	2,000	2	-	-	plain	-	-	shovels	6cents	1	235	-	-
Norfolk,	-	-	-	-	-	-	-	-	-	-	-	-	-	-	-	-	-	-	-
Norwood,	4	Ring	horse	-	[5]	-	-	-	-	-	-	-	-	-	-	1	275	-	-
Quincy,	2	Ring	horse steam	15 tons	6,000	15x9	-	2	-	-	plain	3	-	shovels	-	1	250	1	600
Randolph,	-	-	-	-	-	-	-	-	-	-	-	-	-	-	-	1	125	-	-
Sharon,	-	-	-	-	-	-	-	-	-	-	-	-	-	-	-	1	225	-	-
Stoughton,	-	-	-	-	-	-	-	-	-	-	-	-	-	-	-	1	260	-	-
Walpole,	-	-	-	-	-	-	-	-	-	-	plain	-	-	-	-	1	140	-	-
Wellesley,	2 to 4	Ring	horse	4,800 lbs.	-	12tons.	[6]	1	-	-	[7]	2[8]	2	shovels	10cents	1	256	hired	500[9]
Weymouth,	-	-	-	-	-	-	-	-	-	-	-	-	-	-	-	-	-	-	-
Wrentham,	-	-	-	-	-	-	-	-	-	-	-	-	-	-	-	2	[10]	-	-

PLYMOUTH COUNTY.

Abington,	-	-	-	-	-	-	-	-	-	-	-	-	-	-	-	1	$150	-	-
Bridgewater,	4	Ring	horse	5 tons	-	9 in.	[11]	-	-	-	[12]	3	-	shovels	10 cents	2	500	-	-
Brockton,	2	Ring	horse steam	2 tons 15 tons	$200 3,600	- 9x15	$750	2	-	-	[7]	3	2	shovels	10 cents	1	250	-	-
Carver,	-	-	-	-	-	-	-	-	-	-	-	-	-	-	-	-	-	-	-
Duxbury,	2	-	horse	1,600 lbs.	-	-	-	-	-	-	-	-	-	-	-	1	125	-	-
East Bridgewater,	4	Ring	horse	6,000 lbs.	240	-	-	-	-	-	-	-	-	-	-	1	250	-	-
Halifax,	-	-	-	-	-	-	-	-	-	-	-	-	-	-	-	-	-	-	-
Hanover,	-	-	-	-	-	-	-	-	-	-	plain	2	-	-	-	2	[13]	-	-
Hanson,	-	-	-	-	-	-	-	-	-	-	-	-	-	-	-	1	150	-	-
Hingham,	3	Ring	horse	2 tons	225	Buy at	one at	$1.25	per yd.	-	-	-	-	[14]	9 cents[15]	1	150	Hire	them
Hull,	-	-	-	-	-	-	-	-	-	-	-	-	-	-	-	-	-	-	-
Kingston,	-	-	-	-	-	10x7	700	2	-	-	-	-	-	shovels	5 cents	1	300	-	-
Lakeville,	-	-	-	-	-	-	-	-	-	-	plain	-	-	-	-	1	175	-	-
Marion,	2 or 3	Ring	horse	2¼ tons	[16]	9x18	1,175	2	-	-	plain	1	-	shovels	10 cents	1	215	-	-
Marshfield,	-	-	-	-	-	-	-	-	-	-	-	-	-	-	-	2	300	-	-
Mattapoisett,	-	-	steam	30,000 lbs	-	-	-	No. 2	Gates	bought	but not	yet rec	eived	-	-	1	225	-	-
Middleborough,	4	Ring	horse	-	235	9x15	2,200	1	-	-	plain	1	-	[14]	[17]	2	250[18]	1[4]	-
Norwell,	4	Ring	horse	5,000 lbs.	230	-	-	-	-	-	-	-	-	-	-	2	[19]	-	-
Pembroke,	-	-	-	-	-	-	-	-	-	-	-	-	-	-	-	1	210	-	-
Plymouth,	2	Ring	horse	1 ton	-	-	-	-	-	-	-	-	-	-	-	1	250	-	-
Plympton,	-	-	-	-	-	-	-	-	-	-	-	-	-	-	-	1	250	-	-
Rochester,	-	-	-	-	-	-	-	-	-	-	-	-	-	-	-	1	300	-	-
Rockland,	-	Ring	horse	7,800 lbs.	325	-	-	-	-	-	-	-	-	-	-	1	150	-	-
Scituate,	-	-	-	-	-	-	-	-	-	-	plain	[20]	-	-	-	1	250	-	-
Wareham,	-	Ring	horse	1,500 lbs.	300	-	-	-	-	-	-	-	-	-	-	-	-	-	-
West Bridgewater,	-	-	-	-	-	-	-	-	-	-	-	-	-	-	-	1	250	-	-
Whitman,	4	Ring	horse	7,000 lbs.	300	9x15	3,000	1	-	-	[12]	3	-	shovels	8 cents	2	[10]	1	800

SUFFOLK COUNTY.

Boston,	-	-	-	-	-	-	-	-	-	-	-	-	-	-	-	-	-	-	-
Chelsea,	2 to 4	Ring English	horse steam	4 tons 15 tons	$5,000	9x15	-	1	-	-	[12]	3	3	shovels	[21]	1	$250	-	-
Revere,	-	-	-	-	-	-	-	-	-	-	-	-	-	shovels	-	1	235	-	-
Winthrop,[23]	4	Ring	horse	4½ tons	276	[22]	-	-	-	-	-	-	-	-	-	1	250	1	600

[1] Used up. [2] Old fashioned. [3] Without shovels. [4] Private. [5] $237.50. [6] $2,000, with engine. [7] Plain, revolving. [8] Besides dust. [9] Gallons. [10] $250, $150. [11] Roller, crusher and screen cost $2,671.41. [12] Revolving. [13] $215, $160. [14] With and without shovels. [15] Per yard. [16] Borrowed. [17] Four cents a ton. [18] Each. [19] $150, $125. [20] All grades. [21] 7½ to 10 cents. [22] Buy some. [23] Hire steam roller.

TABLE D. — Concluded.

WORCESTER COUNTY.

TOWNS.	Roller.					Crusher.										Road Machines.		Water Carts.	
									Elevator.		Screens.								
	Horses.	Pattern.	Kind.	Weight.	Cost.	Size.	Cost.	No. Handlings	Height.	Cost.	Kind.	Grades.	Bins.	Loading.	Cost Shovelling.	No.	Cost.	No.	Capacity.
Ashburnham,	-	-	-	-	-	-	-	-	-	-	-	-	-	-	-	1	$250	-	-
Athol,	-	-	-	-	-	-	-	-	-	-	-	-	-	-	-	1	250	-	-
Auburn,	-	-	-	-	-	-	-	-	-	-	-	-	-	-	-	1	225	-	-
Barre,	-	-	-	-	-	-	-	-	-	-	-	-	-	-	-	-	-	-	-
Berlin,	-	-	-	-	-	-	-	-	-	-	-	-	-	-	-	1	250	-	-
Blackstone,	-	-	-	-	-	-	-	-	-	-	-	-	-	-	-	2	500	-	-
Bolton,	-	-	-	-	-	-	-	-	-	-	-	-	-	-	-	1	250	-	-
Boylston,	-	-	-	-	-	-	-	-	-	-	-	-	-	-	-	1	250	-	-
Brookfield,	-	-	-	-	-	-	-	-	-	-	-	-	-	-	-	2	700	-	-
Charlton,	-	-	-	-	-	-	-	-	-	-	-	-	-	-	-	3	300[1]	-	-
Clinton,	2 to 4	-	horse	8,300 lbs.	$450	-	-	-	-	-	-	-	-	-	-	-	-	1[3]	600
Dana,	-	-	-	-	-	-	-	-	-	-	-	-	-	-	-	1	200	-	-
Douglas,	-	-	-	-	-	-	-	-	-	-	-	-	-	-	-	2	[5]	1	-
Dudley,	-	-	-	-	-	-	-	-	-	-	-	-	-	-	-	2[4]	-	-	-
Fitchburg,	4	Ring	horse	6,840 lbs.	-	-	-	-	-	-	-	-	-	-	-	2	500	8	-
Gardner,	-	-	-	-	-	-	-	-	-	-	-	-	-	-	-	2	500	-	-
Grafton,	-	-	-	-	-	-	-	-	-	-	-	-	-	-	-	1	250	-	-
Hardwick,	-	-	-	-	-	-	-	-	-	-	-	-	-	-	-	2	500	-	-
Harvard,	-	-	-	-	-	-	-	-	-	-	-	-	-	-	-	1	250	-	-
Holden,	-	-	-	-	-	-	-	-	-	-	-	-	-	-	-	1	250	-	-
Hopedale,	-	-	-	-	-	-	$2,000	1	-	-	-	-	-	-	-	1	250	-	-
Hubbardston,	-	-	-	-	-	-	-	-	-	-	-	-	-	-	-	1	250	-	-
Lancaster,	2	Ring	horse	2,000 lbs.	-	-	-	-	-	-	-	-	-	-	-	2	-	-	-
Leicester,	-	-	-	-	-	-	-	-	-	-	-	-	-	-	-	3	225[1]	-	-
Leominster,	-	-	-	-	-	-	-	-	-	-	-	-	-	-	-	1	250	2	-
Lunenburg,	-	-	-	-	-	-	-	-	-	-	-	-	-	-	-	1	250	-	-
Mendon,	-	-	-	-	-	-	-	-	-	-	-	-	-	-	-	1	250	-	-
Milford,	2	stone	horse	6,500 lbs.	-	-	-	1	-	-	plain	2	-	shovels	-	-	-	-	-

Millbury,	-	-	-	-	-	-	-	-	-	-	-	-	-	-	-	1	300	-	-
New Braintree,	-	-	-	-	-	-	-	-	-	-	-	-	-	-	-	1	250	-	-
Northborough,	-	-	-	-	-	-	-	-	-	-	-	-	-	-	-	-	-	-	-
Northbridge,	4	Ring	horse	5,000 lbs.	320	-	-	-	-	-	-	-	-	-	-	2	250[1]	-	-
North Brookfield,	-	-	-	-	-	-	-	-	-	-	-	-	-	-	-	3	500	1	300
Oakham,	-	-	-	-	-	-	-	-	-	-	-	-	-	-	-	1	275	-	-
Oxford,	-	-	-	-	-	-	-	-	-	-	-	-	-	-	-	2	400	-	-
Paxton,	-	-	-	-	-	-	-	-	-	-	-	-	-	-	-	1	250	-	-
Petersham,	-	-	-	-	-	-	-	-	-	-	-	-	-	-	-	1	250	-	-
Phillipston,	-	-	-	-	-	-	-	-	-	-	-	-	-	-	-	1	250	-	-
Princeton,	-	-	-	-	-	-	-	-	-	-	-	-	-	-	-	1	285	-	-
Royalston,	-	-	-	-	-	-	-	-	-	-	-	-	-	-	-	1	200	-	-
Rutland,	-	-	-	-	-	-	-	-	-	-	-	-	-	-	-	1	250	-	-
Shrewsbury,	-	-	-	-	-	-	-	-	-	-	-	-	-	-	-	1	200	-	-
Southborough,	-	-	-	-	-	-	-	-	-	-	-	-	-	-	-	-	-	-	-
Southbridge,	-	-	-	-	-	-	-	-	-	-	-	-	-	-	-	1	-	1	-
Spencer,	-	-	-	-	-	[5]	5,000	1	20 feet	-	[6]	4	4	[7]	-	3	[8]	1	-
Sterling,	-	-	-	-	-	-	-	-	-	-	-	-	-	-	-	2	300	-	-
Sturbridge,	-	-	-	-	-	-	-	-	-	-	-	-	-	-	-	2	500	-	-
Sutton,	-	-	-	-	-	-	-	-	-	-	-	-	-	-	-	3	600	-	-
Templeton,	-	-	-	-	-	-	-	-	-	-	-	-	-	-	-	1	150	-	-
Upton,	-	-	-	-	-	-	-	-	-	-	-	-	-	-	-	1	250	-	-
Uxbridge,	-	-	-	-	-	-	-	-	-	-	-	-	-	-	-	-	-	-	-
Warren,	-	-	-	-	-	-	-	-	-	-	-	-	-	-	-	-	-	-	-
Webster,	-	Ring	horse	2,200 lbs.	65	-	2,200	1	-	-	[6]	3	-	-	-	1	250	-	-
Westborough,	-	-	-	-	-	-	-	-	-	-	-	-	-	-	-	-	-	-	-
West Boylston,	-	-	-	-	-	-	-	-	-	-	-	-	-	-	-	1	250	-	-
West Brookfield,	-	-	-	-	-	-	-	-	-	-	-	-	-	-	-	1	150	-	-
Westminster,	-	-	-	-	-	-	-	-	-	-	-	-	-	-	-	-	-	-	-
Winchendon,	-	-	-	-	-	-	-	-	-	-	-	-	-	-	-	2	250[1]	1[9]	800
Worcester,	4 to 6	Ring	horse steam	9,000 lbs. 15 tons	250 3,800	9x15	-	2	-	-	plain	fine	-	[7]	15 cents	1	250	2	500

[1] Each. [2] Wide tires do not track. [3] $240, $200. [4] Champion. [5] Gates No. 4. [6] Revolving. [7] Without shovels. [8] $250, $300 each. [9] Private.

TABLE E. — *Showing Replies of Selectmen and Road Commissioners on the Advisability of Assistance being rendered by the State or County, and on the Appointment of a State Highway Commission.*

BARNSTABLE COUNTY.

TOWNS.	Favor State Aid.	Favor County Aid.	Favor State Highway Commission.
Barnstable,	Yes,	No,	Yes.
Bourne,	-	-	-
Brewster,	Yes,	No,	Yes.
Chatham,	Yes,	-	Yes.
Dennis,	Yes,	Yes,	Yes.
Eastham,	Yes,	No,	Yes.
Falmouth,	No,	Yes,	No.
Harwich,	No,	No,	No.
Mashpee,	Yes,	Yes,	Yes.
Orleans,	Yes,	No,	Yes.
Provincetown,	-	-	-
Sandwich,	Yes,	No,	Yes.
Truro,	Yes,	No,	Yes.
Wellfleet,	-	Yes,	Yes.
Yarmouth,	Yes,	-	Yes.

BERKSHIRE COUNTY.

TOWNS.	Favor State Aid.	Favor County Aid.	Favor State Highway Commission.
Adams,	-	Yes,	Yes.
Alford,	No,	No,	No.
Becket,	-	Yes,	Yes.
Cheshire,	Yes,	No,	Yes.
Clarksburg,	Yes,	No,	Yes.
Dalton,	No,	No,	No.
Egremont,	-	-	-
Florida,	Yes,	No,	Yes.
Great Barrington,	No,	No,	No.
Hancock,	No,	No,	No.
Hinsdale,	Yes,	No,	Yes.
Lanesborough,	No,	No,	No.
Lee,	No,	No,	Yes.
Lenox,	Yes,	No,	Yes.
Monterey,	Yes,	No,	Yes.
Mount Washington,	-	-	Yes.
New Ashford,	Yes,	No,	Yes.
New Marlborough,	-	-	-
North Adams,	Yes,	No,	Yes.
Otis,	Yes,	-	-
Peru,	Yes,	No,	Yes.
Pittsfield,	-	-	-
Richmond,	Yes,	No,	Yes.
Sandisfield,	Yes,	No,	No.

TABLE E. — Continued.

BERKSHIRE COUNTY — Concluded.

TOWNS.	Favor State Aid.	Favor County Aid.	Favor State Highway Commission.
Savoy,	Yes,	No,	Yes.
Sheffield,	Yes,	No,	Yes.
Stockbridge,	Yes,	Yes,	Yes.
Tyringham,	Yes,	-	Yes.
Washington,	Yes,	No,	Yes.
West Stockbridge,	-	-	-
Williamstown,	-	-	-
Windsor,	Yes,	-	-

BRISTOL COUNTY.

TOWNS.	Favor State Aid.	Favor County Aid.	Favor State Highway Commission.
Acushnet,	Yes,	-	-
Attleborough,	-	-	-
Berkley,	No,	Yes,	Yes.
Dartmouth,	Yes,	-	No.
Dighton,	Yes,	-	-
Easton,	-	-	-
Fairhaven,	-	-	-
Fall River,	No,	Yes,	-
Freetown,	No,	Yes,	-
Mansfield,	Yes,	No,	Yes.
New Bedford,	Yes,	No,	Yes.
North Attleborough,	-	-	-
Norton,	-	-	-
Raynham,	Yes,	No,	Yes.
Rehoboth,	No,	Yes,	No.
Seekonk,	No,	No,	No.
Somerset,	Yes,	No,	Yes.
Swansea,	Yes,	No,	Yes.
Taunton,	-	-	-
Westport,	Yes,	No,	No.

DUKES COUNTY.

TOWNS.	Favor State Aid.	Favor County Aid.	Favor State Highway Commission.
Chilmark,	No,	No,	No.
Cottage City,	-	-	-
Edgartown,	Yes,	No,	Yes.
Gay Head,	-	-	-
Gosnold,	-	-	-
Tisbury,	Yes,	No,	Yes.

ESSEX COUNTY.

TOWNS.	Favor State Aid.	Favor County Aid.	Favor State Highway Commission.
Amesbury,	-	-	-
Andover,	Yes,	Yes,	Yes.
Beverly,	No,	No,	No.

TABLE E. — Continued.

ESSEX COUNTY — Concluded.

TOWNS.	Favor State Aid.	Favor County Aid.	Favor State Highway Commission.
Boxford,	–	–	–
Bradford,	Yes,	No,	Yes.
Danvers,	–	–	–
Essex,	–	Yes,	Yes.
Georgetown,	Yes,	–	Yes.
Gloucester,	Yes,	No,	Yes.
Groveland,	–	–	–
Hamilton,	Yes,	No,	Yes.
Haverhill,	–	–	–
Ipswich,	No,	No,	No.
Lawrence,	–	–	–
Lynn,	–	–	–
Lynnfield,	–	–	–
Manchester,	No,	No,	No.
Marblehead,	Yes,	No,	Yes.
Merrimac,	Yes,	–	Yes.
Methuen,	No,	No,	No.
Middleton,	Yes,	No,	Yes.
Nahant,	–	–	–
Newbury,	No,	No,	No.
Newburyport,	–	–	–
North Andover,	–	–	–
Peabody,	–	–	–
Rockport,	–	–	*
Rowley,	–	–	–
Salem,	Yes,	No,	Yes.
Salisbury,	No,	No,	No.
Saugus,	Yes,	–	Yes.
Swampscott,	No,	Yes,	No.
Topsfield,	No,	Yes,	Yes.
Wenham,	No,	No,	No.
West Newbury,	No,	–	–

FRANKLIN COUNTY.

TOWNS.	Favor State Aid.	Favor County Aid.	Favor State Highway Commission.
Ashfield,	Yes,	No,	Yes.
Bernardston,	Yes,	Yes,	Yes.
Buckland,	Yes,	No,	Yes.
Charlemont,	No,	No,	No.
Colrain,	Yes,	No,	Yes.
Conway,	Yes,	–	Yes.
Deerfield,	–	–	–
Erving,	Yes,	No,	Yes.
Gill,	Yes,	–	–
Greenfield,	No,	No,	No.
Hawley,	Yes,	–	–
Heath,	Yes,	No,	Yes.

* Thinks favorably.

TABLE E. — Continued.

FRANKLIN COUNTY — Concluded.

TOWNS.	Favor State Aid.	Favor County Aid.	Favor State Highway Commission.
Leverett,	-	-	-
Leyden,	Yes,	No,	Yes.
Monroe,	Yes,	No,	Yes.
Montague,	Yes,	No,	Yes.
New Salem,	Yes,	No,	Yes.
Northfield,	Yes,	No,	Yes.
Orange,	Yes,	No,	Yes.
Rowe,	No,	No,	No.
Shelburne,	Yes,	No,	Yes.
Shutesbury,	Yes,	No,	Yes.
Sunderland,	Yes,	No,	Yes.
Warwick,	Yes,	-	Yes.
Wendell,	Yes,	No,	No.
Whately,	Yes,	No,	Yes.

HAMPDEN COUNTY.

TOWNS.	Favor State Aid.	Favor County Aid.	Favor State Highway Commission.
Agawam,	Yes,	No,	Yes.
Blandford,	Yes,	No,	Yes.
Brimfield,	Yes,	No,	Yes.
Chester,	Yes,	No,	Yes.
Chicopee,	Yes,	No,	Yes.
Granville,	Yes,	No,	Yes.
Hampden,	No,	No,	No.
Holland,	Yes,	No,	Yes.
Holyoke,	Yes,	No,	No.
Longmeadow,	-	-	-
Ludlow,	Yes,	No,	Yes.
Monson,	Yes,	No,	Yes.
Montgomery,	No,	No,	No.
Palmer,	Yes,	No,	Yes.
Russell,	Yes,	No,	Yes.
Southwick,	Yes,	-	Yes.
Springfield,	Yes,	No,	Yes.
Tolland,	Yes,	-	Yes.
Wales,	Yes,	No,	Yes.
Westfield,	Yes,	Yes,	Yes.
West Springfield,	No,	No,	Yes.
Wilbraham,	-	-	-

HAMPSHIRE COUNTY.

TOWNS.	Favor State Aid.	Favor County Aid.	Favor State Highway Commission.
Amherst,	-	-	-
Belchertown,	Yes,	-	Yes
Chesterfield,	Yes,	No,	Yes
Cummington,	No,	Yes,	No.

TABLE E. — Continued.

HAMPSHIRE COUNTY — Concluded.

TOWNS.	Favor State Aid.	Favor County Aid.	Favor State Highway Commission.
Easthampton,	–	–	–
Enfield,	No,	No,	No.
Goshen,	Yes,	No,	Yes.
Granby,	–	–	–
Greenwich,	–	No,	No.
Hadley,	Yes,	No,	Yes.
Hatfield,	Yes,	No,	Yes.
Huntington,	No,	No,	No.
Middlefield,	Yes,	No,	Yes.
Northampton,	–	–	–
Pelham,	Yes,	Yes,	–
Plainfield,	Yes,	No,	Yes.
Prescott,	–	–	–
Southampton,	Yes,	No,	Yes.
South Hadley,	–	–	–
Ware,	Yes,	No,	Yes.
Westhampton,	Yes,	No,	Yes.
Williamsburg,	No,	No,	No.
Worthington,	Yes,	No,	Yes.

MIDDLESEX COUNTY.

TOWNS.	Favor State Aid.	Favor County Aid.	Favor State Highway Commission.
Acton,	Yes,	No,	–
Arlington,	No,	No,	Yes.
Ashby,	No,	Yes,	No.
Ashland,	No,	No,	No.
Ayer,	No,	No,	No.
Bedford,	–	–	–
Belmont,	*	–	*
Billerica,	No,	Yes,	Yes.
Boxborough,	Yes,	–	No.
Burlington,	–	–	–
Cambridge,	–	–	–
Carlisle,	Yes,	–	Yes.
Chelmsford,	–	–	–
Concord,	Yes,	No,	Yes.
Dracut,	No,	No,	Yes.
Dunstable,	Yes,	–	Yes.
Everett,	No,	No,	No.
Framingham,	Yes,	No,	Yes.
Groton,	Yes,	No,	Yes.
Holliston,	No,	No,	No.
Hopkinton,	Yes,	No,	Yes.
Hudson,	Yes,	No,	Yes.
Lexington,	No,	Yes,	No.
Lincoln,	–	–	–
Littleton,	–	–	–
Lowell,	Yes,	–	Yes.

* Yes and No.

TABLE E. — Continued.

MIDDLESEX COUNTY — Concluded.

TOWNS.	Favor State Aid.	Favor County Aid.	Favor State Highway Commission.
Malden,	Yes,	No,	Yes.
Marlborough,	-	-	-
Maynard,	No,	Yes,	Yes.
Medford,	Yes,	No,	Yes.
Melrose,	Yes,	No,	Yes.
Natick,	Yes,	No,	Yes.
Newton,	Yes,	Yes,	Yes.
North Reading,	-	Yes,	-
Pepperell,	Yes,	No,	-
Reading,	Yes,	No,	Yes.
Sherborn,	Yes,	No,	Yes.
Shirley,	Yes,	No,	Yes.
Somerville,	Yes,	Yes,	Yes.
Stoneham,	-	-	-
Stow,	No,	Yes,	No.
Sudbury,	Yes,	Yes,	Yes.
Tewksbury,	-	-	-
Townsend,	-	-	-
Tyngsborough,	No,	-	No.
Wakefield,	No,	Yes,	No.
Waltham,	-	-	-
Watertown,	Yes,	Yes,	Yes.
Wayland,	No,	No,	No.
Westford,	No,	No,	No.
Weston,	Yes,	-	Yes.
Wilmington,	-	-	-
Winchester,	Yes,	Yes,	Yes.
Woburn,	-	-	-

NANTUCKET COUNTY.

TOWNS.	Favor State Aid.	Favor County Aid.	Favor State Highway Commission.
Nantucket,	Yes,	-	Yes.

NORFOLK COUNTY.

TOWNS.	Favor State Aid.	Favor County Aid.	Favor State Highway Commission.
Avon,	Yes,	-	-
Bellingham,	Yes,	No,	Yes.
Braintree,	-	-	Yes.
Brookline,	Yes,	No,	Yes.
Canton,	-	-	-
Cohasset,	-	-	-
Dedham,	Yes,	No,	Yes.
Dover,	-	-	-
Foxborough,	Yes,	Yes,	Yes.
Franklin,	Yes,	No,	Yes.
Holbrook,	-	-	-

TABLE E. — Continued.

NORFOLK COUNTY — Concluded.

TOWNS.	Favor State Aid.	Favor County Aid.	Favor State Highway Commission.
Hyde Park,	Yes,	No,	-
Medfield,	Yes,	No,	No.
Medway,	Yes,	No,	Yes.
Millis,	Yes,	-	No.
Milton,	Yes,	No,	Yes.
Needham,	Yes,	-	Yes.
Norfolk,	Yes,	No,	Yes.
Norwood,	Yes,	No,	Yes.
Quincy,	Yes,	No,	Yes.
Randolph,	-	-	-
Sharon,	No,	No,	No.
Stoughton,	Yes,	-	Yes.
Walpole,	Yes,	No,	Yes.
Wellesley,	Yes,	No,	Yes.
Weymouth,	No,	No,	No.
Wrentham,	No,	No,	No.

PLYMOUTH COUNTY.

TOWNS.	Favor State Aid.	Favor County Aid.	Favor State Highway Commission.
Abington,	Yes,	No,	Yes.
Bridgewater,	Yes,	No,	Yes.
Brockton,	-	-	Yes.*
Carver,	-	-	Yes.
Duxbury,	Yes,	No,	No.
East Bridgewater,	Yes,	No,	Yes.
Halifax,	Yes,	No,	Yes.
Hanover,	No,	Yes,	Yes
Hanson,	-	-	-
Hingham,	No,	Yes,	Yes.
Hull,	Yes,	-	Yes.
Kingston,	No,	Yes,	Yes.
Lakeville,	Yes,	-	Yes.
Marion,	Yes,	Yes,	Yes.
Marshfield,	-	-	-
Mattapoisett,	Yes,	No,	Yes.
Middleborough,	-	No,	Yes.
Norwell,	-	-	-
Pembroke,	-	Yes,	Yes.
Plymouth,	Yes,	Yes,	Yes.
Plympton,	Yes,	No,	Yes.
Rochester,	Yes,	No,	Yes.
Rockland,	No,	Yes,	No.
Scituate,	Yes,	No,	No.
Wareham,	No,	No,	No.
West Bridgewater,	-	-	-
Whitman,	Yes,	No,	Yes.

* Provisionally.

TABLE E. — Continued.

SUFFOLK COUNTY.

TOWNS.	Favor State Aid.	Favor County Aid.	Favor State Highway Commission.
Boston,	-	-	-
Chelsea,	Yes,	No,	Yes.
Revere,	-	-	-
Winthrop,	Yes,	No,	Yes.

WORCESTER COUNTY.

TOWNS.	Favor State Aid.	Favor County Aid.	Favor State Highway Commission.
Ashburnham,	Yes,	No,	Yes.
Athol,	-	-	-
Auburn,	Yes,	No,	Yes.
Barre,	Yes,	-	Yes.
Berlin,	-	-	-
Blackstone,	Yes,	No,	Yes.
Bolton,	Yes,	No,	Yes.
Boylston,	No,	Yes,	No.
Brookfield,	Yes,	No,	Yes.
Charlton,	-	-	Yes.
Clinton,	-	*	†
Dana,	Yes,	No,	Yes.
Douglas,	No,	Yes,	No.
Dudley,	No,	Yes,	-
Fitchburg,	-	-	-
Gardner,	Yes,	No,	Yes.
Grafton,	Yes,	No,	Yes.
Hardwick,	Yes,	-	-
Harvard,	-	-	-
Holden,	Yes,	No,	Yes.
Hopedale,	Yes,	No,	Yes.
Hubbardston,	Yes,	No,	Yes.
Lancaster,	No,	No,	No.
Leicester,	Yes,	No,	-
Leominster,	Yes,	No,	Yes.
Lunenburg,	No,	No,	-
Mendon,	Yes,	No,	Yes.
Milford,	-	-	-
Millbury,	Yes,	No,	Yes.
New Braintree,	No,	No,	No.
Northborough,	No,	No,	Yes.
Northbridge,	-	-	Yes.
North Brookfield,	Yes,	No,	Yes.
Oakham,	Yes,	No,	Yes.
Oxford,	-	-	-
Paxton,	Yes,	No,	Yes.
Petersham,	-	-	-
Phillipston,	Yes,	-	-
Princeton,	-	-	-
Royalston,	No,	No,	No.
Rutland,	Yes,	No,	No.

* Yes with County Eng. † No and Yes.

TABLE E. — Concluded.

WORCESTER COUNTY — Concluded.

TOWNS.	Favor State Aid.	Favor County Aid.	Favor State Highway Commission.
Shrewsbury,	No,	No,	No.
Southborough,	No,	No,	No.
Southbridge,	No,	No,	*
Spencer,	Yes,	Yes,	Yes.
Sterling,	Yes,	Yes,	No.
Sturbridge,	Yes,	No,	Yes,
Sutton,	Yes,	No,	No.
Templeton,	Yes,	No,	Yes.
Upton,	No,	No,	No.
Uxbridge,	–	–	–
Warren,	Yes,	–	Yes.
Webster,	Yes,	No,	–
Westborough,	Yes,	–	Yes.
West Boylston,	–	–	–
West Brookfield,	Yes,	–	Yes.
Westminster,	Yes,	Yes,	Yes.
Winchendon,	Yes,	No,	Yes.
Worcester,	–	–	Yes.

* No objections.

SUMMARY.

	Total Number Towns and Cities.	State Aid on Main Roads.			County Aid on Main Roads.			State Highway Commission.		
		Yes.	No.	No Answer.	Yes.	No.	No Answer.	Yes.	No.	No Answer.
Barnstable,	15	10	2	3	4	7	4	11	2	2
Berkshire,	32	18	6	8	3	20	9	19	6	7
Bristol,	20	9	5	6	4	7	9	7	4	9
Dukes,	6	2	1	3	0	3	3	2	1	3
Essex,	35	11	9	15	4	13	18	13	8	14
Franklin,	26	21	3	2	1	19	6	18	4	4
Hampshire,	23	12	4	7	2	14	7	11	5	7
Hampden,	22	17	3	2	1	17	4	17	3	2
Middlesex,	54	25	15	14	12	22	20	26	12	16
Nantucket,	1	1	0	0	0	0	1	1	0	0
Norfolk,	27	18	3	6	1	16	10	15	5	7
Plymouth,	27	14	5	8	7	12	8	19	4	4
Suffolk,	4	2	0	2	0	2	2	2	0	2
Worcester,	59	32	13	14	7	33	18	32	11	16
Total,	351	192	69	90	46	185	120	193	65	93
Percentage of Total Number of Cities and Towns,	–	54¾	19¾	25½	13¼	52¾	34	55	18½	26½

TABLE G.* — *Estimated Values in Tons (2,000 Pounds) used in determining the Weights passing over the Four Roads leading into Boston on which Traffic Observations were made, August, 1892.*

KIND OF WAGON.	No. of Horses.	Weight of Horses.	Weight of Empty Wagon.	Weight of Loaded Wagon.	Weight of Load alone.	Load per Horse, exclusive of Wagon.	Total Weight of Horses, Wagon and Load.
Beer, ...	1	0.70	1.18	2.23	1.05	1.05	2.93
"	2	1.40	1.65	4.61	2.96	1.48	6.01
"	3	2.10	2.13	6.43	4.30	1.43	8.53
Caravan, ...	1	0.70	1.10	3.23	2.13	2.13	3.93
"	2	1.40	1.88	6.54	4.66	2.33	7.94
"	3	2.10	1.84	10.96	9.12	3.04	13.06
"	4	2.80	2.43	11.05	8.62	2.16	13.85
Carriage, ...	1	0.45	0.11	0.36	0.25	0.25	0.81
"	2	0.90	0.30	0.60	0.30	0.15	1.50
Coal, ...	1	0.70	0.78	2.44	1.66	1.66	3.14
"	2	1.40	1.59	4.87	3.28	1.64	6.27
"	3	2.10	2.29	8.29	6.00	2.00	10.39
Express, ...	1	0.55	0.62	1.61	1.00	1.00	2.16
"	2	1.10	1.38	3.25	1.88	0.94	4.35
Lumber, ...	1	0.70	1.00	3.00	2.00	2.00	3.70
"	2	1.40	1.30	4.37	3.07	1.54	5.77
"	3	2.10	1.58	7.09	5.50	1.83	9.19
"	4	2.80	1.90	8.90	7.00	1.75	11.70
Milk, ...	1	0.55	0.60	1.68	1.08	1.08	2.23
"	2	1.10	1.03	4.18	3.15	1.58	5.28
Stone, ...	1	0.70	0.90	2.90	2.00	2.00	3.60
"	2	1.40	1.35	5.21	3.86	1.93	6.61
"	3	2.10	1.50	11.50	10.00	3.33	13.60
"	4	2.80	2.19	12.18	10.00	2.50	14.98
Hack, ...	1	0.45	0.50	0.80	0.30	0.30	1.25
"	2	0.90	0.75	1.25	0.50	0.25	2.15
Ice, ...	2	1.40	1.98	5.25	3.28	1.64	6.65
Tip-cart, ...	1	0.70	0.87	3.40	2.53	2.53	4.10
"	2	1.40	1.25	4.41	3.16	1.58	5.81

* Table F is omitted.

TABLE G.

Traffic Observations for Seventy-two Consecutive Hours, Broadway, at Revere Street, Revere.

No. of Horses to a Wagon.	CHARACTER OF WAGON.	HORSES.				WAGONS.												Percentages of Total Number of Wagons.		PERCENTAGES OF TOTAL WEIGHT OF TRAFFIC.				TOTALS.			
		NUMBER.		Weight of one Wagon Load.	Load per Horse.	EMPTY.						LOADED.								EMPTY.		LOADED.		Horses.	Wagons.	Loads in Tons of 2,000 lbs.	Weights, Horses, Wagons and Loads.
						NUMBER.			WEIGHT (TONS).			NUMBER.			WEIGHT (TONS).												
		Out.	In.			Out.	In.	Tot.	Out.	In.	Tot.	Out.	In.	Tot.	Out.	In.	Tot.	Out.	In.	Out.	In.	Out.	In.				
1	Beer,	1	4	1.05	1.05	-	-	-	-	-	-	1	4	5	2.2	8.9	11.1	0.07	0.27	-	-	0.06	0.26	5	5	5.2	14.6
2	"	6	12	3.45	1.72	2	-	2	3.3	-	3.3	1	6	7	4.6	27.7	32.3	0.20	0.41	0.17	-	0.08	0.50	18	9	20.8	48.2
3	"	-	-	-	-	-	-	-	-	-	-	-	-	-	-	-	-	-	-	-	-	-	-	-	-	-	-
1	Caravan,	-	-	-	-	-	-	-	-	-	-	-	-	-	-	-	-	-	-	-	-	-	-	-	-	-	-
2	"	24	20	4.66	2.33	1	2	3	1.9	3.7	5.6	11	8	19	71.8	52.2	124.0	0.81	0.68	0.10	0.19	3.64	2.65	44	22	88.3	160.4
3	"	-	-	9.12	3.04	-	-	-	-	-	-	-	-	-	-	-	-	-	-	-	-	-	-	-	-	-	-
4	"	4	16	8.62	2.15	1	3	4	2.4	7.2	9.6	-	1	1	-	11.0	11.0	0.07	0.27	0.12	0.37	-	0.56	20	5	8.6	35.3
1	Carriage,	116	161	0.25	0.25	110	149	259	12.1	16.4	28.5	6	12	18	2.2	4.3	6.5	7.83	10.87	0.61	0.83	0.11	0.22	277	277	4.5	159.6
2	"	8	12	0.30	0.15	2	3	5	0.6	0.9	1.5	2	3	5	1.2	1.8	3.0	0.27	0.40	0.03	0.04	0.06	0.09	20	10	1.5	13.5
1	Coal,	2	2	1.66	1.66	-	1	1	-	0.8	0.8	2	1	3	4.8	2.4	7.2	0.14	0.13	-	0.04	0.24	0.12	4	4	4.9	10.8
2	"	8	4	3.28	1.64	-	1	1	-	1.6	1.0	4	1	5	19.6	4.9	24.5	0.27	0.14	-	0.08	1.00	0.25	12	6	16.5	34.5
3	"	-	-	-	-	-	-	-	-	-	-	-	-	-	-	-	-	-	-	-	-	-	-	-	-	-	-
1	Express,	322	346	1.00	1.00	95	108	203	57.0	64.8	121.8	227	238	465	365.5	383.2	748.7	21.74	23.35	2.92	3.29	1.84	3.77	668	668	460.4	1338.1
2	"	188	206	1.87	0.93	41	32	73	57.4	44.8	102.2	53	71	124	172.2	230.8	403.0	6.35	6.96	2.91	2.27	8.60	11 52	394	197	231.9	781.0
1	Lumber,	4	6	2.00	2.00	-	2	2	2.0	2.0	4.0	4	4	8	12.0	12.0	24.0	0.27	0.41	0.10	0.10	0.00	0.60	10	10	16.0	35.0
2	"	18	14	3.07	1.53	-	5	5	-	6.5	6.5	9	2	11	39.3	8.8	48.1	0.61	0.47	-	0.33	2.01	4.46	32	16	33.8	77.0
3	"	3	3	5.50	1.83	-	1	1	-	1.6	1.6	1	-	1	-	7.1	7.1	0.07	0.07	-	0.08	-	0.36	6	2	5.5	12.9
4	"	20	24	7.00	1.75	-	-	-	-	-	-	4	6	11	44.5	53.4	97.9	0.34	0.40	-	-	-	-	44	11	77.0	128.7
1	Milk,	3	11	1.08	1.08	-	1	1	-	0.6	0.6	3	10	13	5.1	17.0	22.1	0.20	0.74	-	0.03	0.26	0.86	14	14	14.3	32.5
2	"	2	-	3.15	1.57	-	-	-	-	-	-	1	-	1	-	4.2	4.2	0.07	-	-	-	-	0.21	2	1	3.2	5.6
1	Stone,	-	-	2.00	2.00	-	-	-	-	-	-	-	-	-	-	-	-	-	-	-	-	-	-	-	-	-	-
2	"	16	12	3.85	1.92	6	2	8	8.1	2.7	10.8	2	4	6	10.4	20.8	31.2	0.54	0.41	0.41	0.14	0.53	1.05	28	14	23.1	61.6
3	"	-	-	-	-	-	-	-	-	-	-	-	-	-	-	-	-	-	-	-	-	-	-	-	-	-	-
4	"	-	12	10.00	2.50	-	-	-	-	-	-	-	3	3	-	36.6	36.6	-	0.20	-	-	-	1.85	12	3	30.0	44.3
1	Tip cart,	35	24	2.53	2.53	14	11	25	12.2	9.6	21.8	21	13	34	71.4	44.2	115.6	2.36	1.62	0.62	0.49	3.62	2.24	59	59	86.0	178.7
2	"	44	30	3.17	1.58	10	12	22	12.5	15.0	27.5	12	3	15	52.8	13.2	66.0	1.49	1.01	0.63	0.76	2.68	0.67	74	37	47.3	145.3
	Miscellaneous,	44	69	2.28	1.34	18	14	32	34.1	22.5	56.6	26	53	79	135.1	233.9	369.0	2.97	4.52	1.73	1.14	6.86	11.85	113	111	258.4	504.7
	Totals,	868	988	1.63	1.16	300	347	647	203.6	200.7	404.3	391	443	834	1014.7	1178.4	2 93.1	46.67	53.33	10.35	10.18	32.67	46.80	1856	1481	1437.2	3822.3

Traffic Observations for Seventy-two Consecutive Hours, Broadway, at Chelsea Bridge, New England Draw.

1	Beer, . .	14	14	1.05	1.05	-	3	3	-	3.54	3.54	14	11	25	31.22	24.53	55.75	0.30	0.30	-	0.06	0.56	0.44	28	28	20.2	78.89
2	" . .	10	14	2.96	1.48	1	2	3	1.65	3.30	4.95	4	5	9	18.44	23.05	41.49	0.14	0.19	0.05	0.11	0.33	0.41	24	12	26.7	69.97
3	" . .	3	-	4.30	1.45	-	-	-	-	-	-	1	-	1	6.43	-	6.43	0.03	-	-	-	0.12	-	3	1	4.3	8.53
1	Caravan, .	26	29	2.13	2.13	11	20	31	12.10	22.00	34.10	15	9	24	48.45	20.07	77.52	0.72	0.80	0.22	0.30	0.88	0.52	55	55	51.1	150.12
2	" .	108	110	4.06	2.33	21	35	56	39.48	65.80	105.28	33	20	53	215.82	130.80	346.02	1.40	1.52	0.72	1.10	3.83	2.35	218	109	247.0	624.50
3	" .	30	27	9.13	3.04	4	3	7	7.36	5.52	12.88	6	6	12	65.76	65.76	131.52	0.28	0.25	0.13	0.10	1.10	1.19	57	19	109.4	184.50
4	" .	52	88	8.63	2.16	6	15	21	14.58	36.45	51.03	7	7	14	77.35	77.35	154.70	0.36	0.61	0.26	0.66	1.40	1.10	140	35	120.7	304.73
1	Carriage, .	288	282	0.25	0.25	270	261	531	29.70	28.71	58.41	18	21	39	6.48	7.56	14.04	7.95	7.79	0.55	0.51	0.12	0.14	570	570	9.7	328.95
2	" .	36	74	0.30	0.15	16	36	52	4.80	10.80	15.60	2	1	3	1.20	0.00	1.80	0.50	1.02	0.09	0.10	0.02	0.01	110	55	.9	66.90
1	Coal, . .	76	58	1.66	1.66	24	52	76	18.72	40.56	59.28	52	6	58	126.88	14.64	141.52	2.10	1.60	0.34	0.74	2.28	0.26	134	134	96.3	294.00
2	" . .	80	92	3.28	1.64	18	23	41	28.62	36.57	65.19	22	23	45	107.14	112.01	219.15	1.11	1.27	0.51	0.05	1.93	2.02	172	86	147.5	404.74
3	" . .	6	9	6.00	2.00	1	1	2	2.29	2.29	4.58	1	2	3	8.29	16.58	24.87	0.06	0.08	0.04	0.04	0.15	0.30	15	5	18.0	39.95
1	Express, .	804	822	1.00	1.00	410	519	929	254.20	321.78	575.98	394	303	697	634.34	487.83	1122.17	22.22	22.75	4.57	5.76	11.37	8.75	1626	1626	690.1	2836.35
2	" .	230	194	1.88	0.94	59	38	97	81.42	52.44	133.86	56	59	115	182.00	191.75	373.75	3.18	2.68	1.47	0.95	3.27	3.44	424	212	215.0	804.41
1	Lumber, .	21	32	2.00	2.00	15	4	19	15.00	4.00	19.00	6	28	34	18.00	84.00	102.00	0.58	0.89	0.27	0.07	0.32	1.52	53	53	68.0	158.10
2	" .	112	128	3.07	1.54	30	16	46	39.00	20.80	59.80	26	48	74	113.62	209.76	323.38	1.55	1.77	0.71	0.37	2.05	3.77	240	120	227.2	551.18
3	" .	3	9	5.50	1.83	1	2	3	1.58	3.16	4.74	-	1	1	-	7.09	7.09	0.03	0.08	0.03	0.06	-	0.13	12	4	5.5	20.23
4	" .	40	16	7.00	1.75	3	2	5	5.70	3.80	9.50	7	2	9	62.30	17.80	80.10	0.28	0.11	0.10	0.07	1.13	0.33	56	14	63.0	128.80
1	Milk, . .	82	78	1.08	1.08	13	37	50	7.80	22.20	30.00	69	41	110	115.92	68.88	184.80	2.27	2.16	0.14	0.40	2.00	1.24	160	100	118.8	326.80
2	" . .	12	4	3.65	1.83	1	-	1	1.03	-	1.03	5	2	7	20.90	8.36	29.26	0.17	0.06	0.02	-	0.37	0.15	16	8	22.1	41.49
1	Stone, . .	-	-	-	-	-	-	-	-	-	-	-	-	-	-	-	-	-	-	-	-	-	-	-	-	-	-
2	" . .	32	6	3.86	1.93	-	3	3	-	4.05	4.05	16	-	16	83.36	-	83.36	0.44	0.08	-	0.07	1.50	-	38	19	61.8	115.01
3	" . .	6	-	10.00	3.33	1	-	1	1.50	-	1.50	1	-	1	11.56	-	11.56	0.06	-	0.03	-	0.21	-	6	2	10.0	17.26
4	" . .	-	16	9.99	2.50	-	3	3	-	6.57	6.57	1	-	1	12.18	-	12.18	0.03	0.08	-	0.12	0.22	-	16	4	10.0	29.95
1	Tip-cart, .	4	6	2.53	2.53	3	6	9	2.61	5.22	7.83	1	-	1	3.40	-	3.40	0.11	0.17	0.05	0.04	0.06	-	10	10	2.5	18.23
2	" .	90	90	3.16	1.58	13	41	54	16.25	51.25	67.50	32	7	39	141.12	30.87	171.99	1.24	1.33	0.29	0.93	2.54	0.55	180	93	123.3	369.75
	Miscellaneous,	148	167	1.06	0.54	33	55	88	36.30	60.50	96.80	53	41	94	145.75	259.50	405.25	2.38	2.65	0.65	1.09	2.62	4.06	315	182	301.8	665.60
	Totals, .	2303	2481	1.74	1.18	954	1177	2131	621.69	811.31	1433.00	842	643	1485	2257.91	1867.79	4125.70	49.07	50.33	11.24	14.62	40.56	33.58	4084	3616	2776.9	8639.74

Table G. — Continued.

Traffic Observations for Seventy-two Consecutive Hours, Beacon Street, at Brighton Road.

No. of Horses to a Wagon.	Character of Wagon.	Horses. Number. Out.	Horses. Number. In.	Horses. Weight of one Wagon Load.	Horses. Load per Horse.	Wagons. Empty. Number. Out.	Wagons. Empty. Number. In.	Wagons. Empty. Number. Tot.	Wagons. Empty. Weight (tons). Out.	Wagons. Empty. Weight (tons). In.	Wagons. Empty. Weight (tons). Tot.	Wagons. Loaded. Number. Out.	Wagons. Loaded. Number. In.	Wagons. Loaded. Number. Tot.	Wagons. Loaded. Weight (tons). Out.	Wagons. Loaded. Weight (tons). In.	Wagons. Loaded. Weight (tons). Tot.	Percentages of Total Number of Wagons. Out.	Percentages of Total Number of Wagons. In.	Percentages of Total Weight of Traffic. Empty. Out.	Percentages of Total Weight of Traffic. Empty. In.	Percentages of Total Weight of Traffic. Loaded. Out.	Percentages of Total Weight of Traffic. Loaded. In.	Totals. Horses.	Totals. Wagons.	Totals. Loads in Tons of 2,000 lbs.	Totals. Weights, Horses, Wagons and Loads.
1	Beer, . .	1	2	1.05	1.05	–	–	–	–	–	–	1	2	3	2.23	4.46	6.89	0.02	0.03	–	–	0.04	0.08	3	3	3.2	8.80
2	" . .	4	10	2.96	1.48	1	5	6	1.65	8.25	9.90	1	–	1	4.61	–	4.61	0.03	0.08	0.03	0.14	0.08	–	14	7	3.0	24.31
3	" . .	–	3	4.30	1.45	–	–	–	–	–	–	–	1	1	–	6.43	6.43	–	0.01	–	–	–	0.11	3	1	4.3	8.50
1	Caravan, .	4	3	2.13	2.13	1	3	4	1.10	3.30	4.40	3	–	3	9.69	–	9.69	0.06	0.05	0.02	0.06	0.17	–	7	7	6.4	19.00
2	" .	106	100	4.66	2.33	14	37	51	26.32	69.56	95.88	39	13	52	255.06	84.82	339.88	0.80	0.76	0.45	1.20	4.39	1.46	206	103	242.1	579.96
3	" .	3	–	9.13	3.04	–	–	–	–	–	–	1	–	1	10.96	–	10.96	0.01	–	–	–	0.19	–	3	1	9.2	13.10
4	" .	52	44	8.63	2.16	6	7	13	14.58	17.01	31.59	7	4	11	77.35	44.20	121.55	0.20	0.17	0.25	0.29	1.33	0.76	96	24	94.8	220.34
1	Carriage, .	1541	1735	0.25	0.25	1532	1730	3262	168.52	190.30	358.82	9	5	14	3.24	1.80	5.04	23.31	26.23	2.90	3.28	0.06	0.03	3276	3276	3.5	1834.86
2	" .	304	378	0.30	0.15	152	189	341	45.60	56.70	102.30	–	–	–	–	–	–	2.30	2.86	0.79	0.98	–	–	682	341	–	409.20
1	Coal, . .	38	36	1.66	1.66	7	36	43	5.46	28.08	33.54	31	–	31	75.64	–	75.64	0.57	0.54	0.09	0.48	1.30	–	74	74	51.4	160.98
2	" . .	88	96	3.28	1.64	1	48	49	1.59	76.32	77.91	43	–	43	209.41	–	209.41	0.67	0.73	0.03	1.31	3.61	–	184	92	141.0	416.32
3	" . .	12	12	6.00	2.00	–	4	4	–	9.16	9.16	4	–	4	33.16	–	33.16	0.06	0.96	–	0.16	0.57	–	24	8	24.1	59.12
1	Express, .	839	787	1.00	1.00	408	578	986	252.96	358.36	611.32	431	209	640	693.91	336.49	1030.40	12.67	11.90	4.37	6.18	11.93	5.81	1626	1626	653.6	2535.72
2	" .	478	368	1.88	0.94	64	97	161	88.32	133.86	222.18	175	87	262	568.75	282.75	851.50	3.61	2.78	1.52	2.30	9.80	4.88	846	423	489.9	1538.98
1	Lumber, .	33	13	2.00	2.00	1	11	12	1.00	11.00	12.00	32	2	34	96.00	6.00	102.00	0.50	0.20	0.02	0.19	1.19	0.10	46	46	68.0	146.20
2	" .	66	16	3.07	1.54	2	8	10	2.60	10.40	13.00	31	–	31	135.47	–	135.47	0.50	0.12	0.05	0.18	2.33	–	82	41	95.2	205.87
3	" .	–	–	5.50	1.83	–	–	–	–	–	–	–	–	–	–	–	–	–	–	–	–	–	–	–	–	–	–
4	" .	12	4	7.00	1.75	1	1	2	1.90	1.90	3.80	2	–	2	17.80	–	17.80	0.05	0.02	0.03	0.03	0.31	–	16	4	14.0	32.80
1	Milk, . .	2	24	1.08	1.09	–	2	2	–	1.20	1.20	2	22	24	3.36	36.96	40.32	0.03	0.36	–	0.02	0.06	0.64	26	26	25.9	55.72
2	" . .	–	2	3.65	1.83	–	–	–	–	–	–	–	1	1	–	4.18	4.18	–	0.01	–	–	–	0.07	2	1	3.2	5.30
1	Stone, . .	–	–	–	–	–	–	–	–	–	–	–	–	–	–	–	–	–	–	–	–	–	–	–	–	–	–
2	" . .	58	60	3.86	1.93	4	23	27	5.40	31.05	36.45	25	7	32	130.25	36.47	166.72	3.44	0.45	0.09	0.54	2.24	0.63	118	59	123.5	285.75
3	" . .	3	–	10.00	3.33	1	–	1	1.50	–	1.50	–	–	–	–	–	–	0.02	–	0.03	–	–	–	3	1	–	3.60
4	" . .	40	20	9.99	2.50	1	3	4	2.19	6.57	8.76	9	2	11	109.62	24.36	133.98	0.15	0.09	0.04	0.11	1.89	0.42	60	15	109.8	184.74
1	Tip-cart, .	97	103	2.53	2.53	13	88	101	11.31	76.56	87.87	84	15	99	285.60	51.00	336.60	1.47	1.56	0.19	1.30	4.91	0.88	200	200	250.5	564.47
2	" .	120	124	3.16	1.58	31	36	67	38.75	45.00	83.75	29	26	55	127.89	114.66	242.55	0.91	0.94	0.67	0.78	2.20	1.97	244	122	173.8	497.10
	Miscellaneous,	94	97	3.28	2.41	53	45	98	58.30	49.50	107.80	6	7	13	16.50	19.25	35.75	0.89	0.79	1.00	0.85	0.28	0.33	191	111	21.4	238.30
	Totals, .	3995	4037	1.88	1.28	2293	2951	5244	729.05	*	1913.13	965	403	1368	2866.50	1053.83	3920.33	49.27	50.73	12.57	20.38	48.86	18.17	8032	6612	2591.8	10049.06

* 1184.08

Traffic Observations for Seventy-two Consecutive Hours, Beacon Street, at Coolidge's Corner.

1	Beer, . .	6	4	1.05	1.05	-	-	-	-	-	-	6	4	10	13.38	8.92	22.30	0.10	0.11	-	-	0.38	0.26	10	10	10.5	29.30
2	" . .	8	2	2.96	1.48	1	-	1	1.65	-	1.65	3	1	4	13.83	4.61	18.44	0.11	0.03	0.05	-	0.40	0.13	10	5	11.8	27.09
3	" . .	3	-	4.30	1.46	1	-	1	2.13	-	2.13	-	-	-	-	-	-	0.03	-	0.06	-	-	-	3	1	-	4.23
1	Caravan, .	-	-	2.13	2.13	-	-	-	-	-	-	-	-	-	-	-	-	-	-	-	-	-	-	-	-	-	-
2	" .	68	50	4.60	2.33	7	18	25	13.10	33.83	46.99	27	7	34	170.60	46.80	222.40	0.90	0.60	0.38	0.97	5.08	1.31	118	59	158.5	351.00
3	" .	-	3	9.13	3.04	-	1	1	-	1.84	1.84	-	-	-	-	-	-	-	0.02	-	0.05	-	-	3	1	-	3.94
4	" .	12	12	8.63	2.16	-	3	3	-	7.29	7.20	3	-	-	33.15	-	33.15	0.08	0.08	-	0.21	0.95	-	24	6	25.0	57.24
1	Carriage, .	950	010	0.25	0.25	910	859	1769	100.10	94.40	194.50	49	51	100	17.64	18.35	35.99	25.31	24.03	2.88	2.71	0.51	0.53	1869	1800	25.0	1070.58
2	" .	264	274	0.30	0.15	105	121	226	34.50	36.30	70.80	27	16	43	16.20	0.60	25.80	3.49	3.62	0.90	1.04	0.46	0.28	538	269	12.9	338.60
1	Coal, . .	35	28	1.66	1.66	4	28	32	3.12	21.83	24.95	31	-	31	75.60	-	75.00	0.92	0.74	0.00	0.63	2.17	-	63	63	51.4	144.65
2	" . .	54	60	3.28	1.64	4	28	32	6.36	44.50	50.86	23	2	25	112.00	0.74	121.74	0.71	0.70	0.18	1.28	3.23	0.28	114	57	82.0	252.40
3	" . .	9	6	6.00	2.00	1	2	3	2.29	4.58	6.87	2	-	2	16.58	-	16.58	0.08	0.05	0.07	0.13	0.48	-	15	5	12.0	33.95
1	Express, .	379	358	1.00	1.00	158	220	378	97.90	136.30	234.20	221	138	359	356.00	222.00	578.00	10.01	9.46	2.81	3.92	10.22	6.37	737	737	355.4	1217.70
2	" .	172	146	1.88	0.94	15	41	56	20.70	56.60	77.30	71	32	103	230.60	103.90	334.50	2.27	1.93	0.60	1.62	6.03	2.98	318	159	102.4	586.80
1	Lumber, .	20	8	2.00	2.00	-	8	8	-	8.00	8.00	26	-	20	78.00	-	78.00	0.69	0.21	-	0.23	2.24	-	34	34	52.0	109.80
2	" .	82	46	3.07	1.54	4	17	21	5.20	22.10	27.30	37	6	43	161.80	26.20	188.00	1.08	0.61	0.15	0.63	4.64	0.75	128	64	132.1	304.90
3	" .	-	-	5.00	1.83	-	-	-	-	-	-	-	-	-	-	-	-	-	-	-	-	-	-	-	-	-	-
4	" .	8	-	7.00	1.75	-	-	-	-	-	-	2	-	2	17.80	-	17.80	0.05	-	-	-	0.51	-	8	2	14.0	23.40
1	Milk, . .	34	27	1.08	1.08	14	12	26	8.40	7.20	15.00	20	15	35	33.60	25.20	58.80	0.90	0.71	0.24	0.21	0.96	0.72	61	61	37.8	107.90
2	" . .	-	-	3.65	1.83	-	-	-	-	-	-	-	-	-	-	-	-	-	-	-	-	-	-	-	-	-	-
1	Stone, . .	1	-	2.00	2.00	-	-	-	-	-	-	1	-	1	2.90	-	2.90	0.03	-	-	-	0.08	-	1	1	2.0	3.60
2	" . .	52	66	3.86	1.93	6	14	20	8.10	18.90	27.00	20	19	39	104.00	99.00	203.00	0.69	0.87	0.23	0.54	2.99	2.84	118	59	150.4	312.60
3	" . .	-	3	10.00	3.33	-	1	1	-	1.50	1.50	-	-	-	-	-	-	-	0.03	-	0.04	-	-	3	1	-	3.00
4	" . .	20	12	9.99	2.50	-	3	3	-	6.57	6.57	5	-	5	60.90	-	60.90	0.13	0.08	-	0.10	1.75	-	32	8	49.9	89.87
1	Tip-cart, .	24	30	2.53	2.53	17	16	33	14.80	13.90	28.70	7	14	21	23.80	47.60	71.40	0.63	0.79	0.43	0.40	0.68	1.37	54	54	53.1	137.90
2	" .	54	64	3.16	1.58	22	19	41	27.50	23.80	51.30	5	13	18	22.05	57.40	79.45	0.71	0.84	0.70	0.68	0.63	1.65	118	59	56.9	213.35
	Miscellaneous,	122	147	1.55	1.03	41	62	103	17.10	25.90	43.00	50	50	100	154.50	154.50	309.00	2.40	2.96	0.49	0.74	4.44	4.44	269	203	199.0	507.30
	Totals, .	2392	2256	1.64	1.19	1310	1473	2783	363.01	565.43	928.44	636	368	1004	1720.93	832 82	2553.75	51.38	48.62	10.44	16.22	49.43	23.01	4648	3787	1685.0	5932.69

TABLE G. — Continued.

Traffic Observations for Seventy-two Consecutive Hours, Western Avenue, at its Junction with Arsenal and Market Streets, Brighton.

No. of Horses to a Wagon.	CHARACTER OF WAGON.	Horses. Number. Out.	Horses. Number. In.	Horses. Weight of one Wagon Load.	Horses. Load per Horse.	Wagons. Empty. Number. Out.	Wagons. Empty. Number. In.	Wagons. Empty. Number. Tot.	Wagons. Empty. Weight (tons). Out.	Wagons. Empty. Weight (tons). In.	Wagons. Empty. Weight (tons). Tot.	Wagons. Loaded. Number. Out.	Wagons. Loaded. Number. In.	Wagons. Loaded. Number. Tot.	Wagons. Loaded. Weight (tons). Out.	Wagons. Loaded. Weight (tons). In.	Wagons. Loaded. Weight (tons). Tot.	Percentages of Total Number of Wagons. Out.	Percentages of Total Number of Wagons. In.	Percentages of Total Weight of Traffic. Empty. Out.	Percentages of Total Weight of Traffic. Empty. In.	Percentages of Total Weight of Traffic. Loaded. Out.	Percentages of Total Weight of Traffic. Loaded. In.	Totals. Horses.	Totals. Wagons.	Totals. Loads in Tons of 2,000 lbs.	Totals. Weights, Horses, Wagons and Loads.
1	Beer, . .	1	2	1.05	1.05	-	-	-	-	-	-	1	2	3	2.2	4.5	6.7	0.05	0.10	-	-	0.03	0.14	3	3	3.2	8.8
2	" . .	4	10	2.96	1.48	-	-	-	-	-	-	2	5	7	9.2	23.1	32.3	0.10	0.24	-	-	0.10	1.02	14	7	20.8	42.1
3	" . .	-	-	4.30	1.43	-	-	-	-	-	-	-	-	-	-	-	-	-	-	-	-	-	-	-	-	-	-
1	Caravan, .	-	1	2.13	2.13	-	1	1	-	1.1	1.1	-	-	-	-	-	-	-	0.05	-	0.03	-	-	1	1	-	1.8
2	" .	72	94	4.66	2.33	13	13	26	24.4	24.4	48.8	23	34	57	150.4	222.4	372.8	1.72	2.25	0.77	0.77	4.77	7.03	166	83	265.6	537.8
3	" .	24	3	9.12	3.04	1	-	1	1.8	-	1.8	7	1	8	76.7	11.0	87.7	0.38	0.05	0.06	-	2.43	0.35	27	9	73.0	108.4
4	" .	44	52	8.62	2.16	3	1	4	7.2	2.4	9.6	8	12	20	88.4	132.6	221.0	0.53	0.62	0.23	0.08	2.79	4.10	96	24	172.4	297.8
1	Carriage, .	322	353	0.25	0.25	237	258	495	26.1	28.4	54.5	85	95	180	30.6	34.2	64.8	15.38	16.85	0.83	0.90	0.97	1.08	675	675	45.0	423.0
2	" .	34	38	0.30	0.15	11	14	25	3.3	5.4	8.7	6	5	11	3.6	3.0	6.6	0.81	0.91	0.10	0.17	0.11	0.09	72	36	3.3	47.7
1	Coal, . .	13	8	1.66	1.66	1	8	9	0.8	6.2	7.0	12	-	12	29.3	-	29.3	0.62	0.38	0.02	0.20	0.93	-	21	21	19.9	51.0
2	" . .	26	28	3.28	1.64	-	14	14	-	22.3	22.3	13	-	13	-	63.3	63.3	0.62	0.67	-	0.71	-	2.00	54	27	42.6	123.4
3	" . .	-	-	6.00	2.00	-	-	-	-	-	-	-	-	-	-	-	-	-	-	-	-	-	-	-	-	-	-
1	Express, .	154	138	1.00	1.00	74	63	137	46.0	39.0	85.0	80	75	155	129.0	121.0	250.0	7.37	6.60	1.45	1.23	4.09	3.82	292	292	153.9	539.4
2	" .	74	78	1.88	0.94	5	8	13	7.0	11.2	18.2	32	31	63	104.0	101.0	205.0	1.77	1.86	0.22	0.35	3.29	3.20	152	76	118.1	329.6
1	Lumber, .	13	11	2.00	2.00	6	7	13	6.0	7.0	13.0	7	4	11	21.0	12.0	33.0	0.62	0.53	0.19	0.22	0.66	0.38	24	24	22.0	62.8
2	" .	18	20	3.07	1.54	3	2	5	3.9	2.6	6.5	6	8	14	26.2	35.0	61.2	0.44	0.48	0.12	0.08	0.83	1.11	38	19	43.0	94.3
3	" .	-	-	5.50	1.83	-	-	-	-	-	-	-	-	-	-	-	-	-	-	-	-	-	-	-	-	-	-
4	" .	-	-	7.00	1.75	-	-	-	-	-	-	-	-	-	-	-	-	-	-	-	-	-	-	-	-	-	-
1	Milk, . .	15	12	1.08	1.08	6	-	6	3.6	-	3.6	9	12	21	15.0	20.0	35.0	0.72	0.57	0.11	-	0.47	0.63	27	27	22.4	57.5
2	" . .	-	-	3.15	1.58	-	-	-	-	-	-	-	-	-	-	-	-	-	-	-	-	-	-	-	-	-	-
2	Stone, . .	38	16	3.86	1.93	17	-	17	23.0	-	23.0	2	8	10	10.0	42.0	52.0	0.91	0.38	0.73	-	0.32	1.33	54	27	38.5	112.8
3	" . .	3	3	10.00	3.33	1	-	1	1.5	-	1.5	-	1	1	11.5	-	11.5	0.05	0.05	0.05	-	0.36	-	6	2	10.0	17.2
4	" . .	4	8	10.00	2.50	1	-	1	2.2	-	2.2	-	2	2	-	24.4	24.4	0.05	0.10	0.07	-	-	0.77	12	3	20.0	35.0
1	Tip-cart, .	12	10	2.53	2.53	11	9	20	9.6	7.8	17.4	1	1	2	3.4	3.4	6.8	0.57	0.48	0.30	0.25	0.11	0.11	22	22	5.1	39.6
2	" .	278	292	3.16	1.58	138	5	143	172.5	6.2	178.7	1	141	142	4.4	621.8	626.2	6.05	6.99	5.46	0.20	0.14	1.06	570	285	448.7	1203.9
	Miscellaneous,	207	303	1.88	0.94	111	27	138	68.8	16.7	85.5	60	230	290	195.0	747.5	942.5	8.18	12.29	2.17	0.53	6.16	23.63	510	428	762.7	1385.0
	Totals, .	1356	1480	2.03	1.40	639	430	1069	407.7	18.07	588.4	355	667	1022	909.9	2222.2	3132.1	47.54	52.46	12.88	5.72	28.56	52.84	2836	2091	2290.2	5518.9

Traffic Observations for Seventy-two Consecutive Hours, Western Avenue, at Bridge over Charles River.

1	Beer,	1	2	1.05	1.05	-	-	-	-	-	-	1	2	3	2.23	4.46	6.69	0.04	0.08	-	-	0.06	0.12	3	3	8.2	8.79
2	"	8	6	2.96	1.48	2	2	4	3.30	3.30	6.60	2	1	3	9.22	4.61	13.83	0.15	0.11	0.09	0.09	0.24	0.12	14	7	8.9	30.23
3	"	-	-	4.30	1.45	-	-	-	-	-	-	-	-	-	-	-	-	-	-	-	-	-	-	-	-	-	-
1	Caravan,	1	-	2.13	2.13	1	-	1	1.10	-	1.10	-	-	-	-	-	-	0.04	-	0.03	-	-	-	1	1	-	1.80
2	"	44	38	4.66	2.33	9	3	12	16.90	5.64	22.54	13	16	29	85.00	104.60	189.60	0.84	0.73	0.44	0.15	2.22	2.73	82	41	135.1	269.54
3	"	-	9	9.13	3.04	-	-	-	-	-	-	-	3	3	-	32.88	32.88	-	0.11	-	-	-	0.86	9	3	27.4	39.18
4	"	84	72	8.63	2.16	10	3	13	24.30	7.29	31.59	11	15	26	121.60	165.80	287.40	0.80	0.69	0.63	0.19	8.17	4.33	156	89	224.2	428.19
1	Carriage,	329	324	0.25	0.25	328	324	652	36.10	35.60	71.70	1	-	1	0.36	-	0.36	12.58	12.40	0.94	0.93	0.01	-	653	653	0.3	366.10
2	"	48	30	0.30	0.15	24	15	39	7.20	4.50	11.70	-	-	-	-	-	-	0.92	0.57	0.19	0.12	-	-	78	39	-	46.80
1	Coal,	16	27	1.66	1.06	11	17	28	8.60	13.30	21.90	5	10	15	12.20	24.40	36.60	0.61	1.03	0.22	0.35	0.32	0.64	43	43	24.9	88.60
2	"	30	36	3.28	1.64	3	13	16	4.80	20.60	25.40	12	5	17	58.50	24.40	82.00	0.57	0.69	0.13	0.54	1.53	0.64	66	33	55.9	154.50
3	"	-	3	6.00	2.00	-	-	-	-	-	-	-	1	1	-	8.29	8.20	-	0.04	-	-	-	0.22	3	1	6.0	10.39
1	Express,	637	633	1.00	1.00	273	234	507	169.20	145.00	314.20	364	399	763	686.00	042.80	1228.40	24.39	24.20	4.42	3.79	15.20	16.76	1270	1270	755.3	2240.00
2	"	308	376	1.88	0.94	39	37	76	53.80	51.00	104.80	115	151	206	374.00	490.50	864.50	5.89	7.20	1.40	1.33	9.76	12.80	684	342	497.2	1345.30
3	"	12	33	2.75	0.92	2	-	2	6.00	-	6.00	2	11	13	9.80	53.80	63.00	0.15	0.42	0.16	-	0.26	1.40	45	15	24.6	94.40
4	"	-	24	3.60	0.90	-	-	-	-	-	-	-	6	6	-	39.00	39.00	-	0.23	-	-	-	1.02	24	8	21.0	52.20
1	Lumber,	9	8	2.00	2.00	1	3	4	1.00	3.00	4.00	8	5	13	24.00	15.00	39.00	0.34	0.81	0.03	0.08	0.63	0.39	17	17	26.1	84.90
2	"	12	6	3.07	1.54	-	-	-	-	-	-	6	3	9	26.20	13.10	39.30	0.23	0.11	-	-	0.68	0.84	18	9	27.6	81.90
3	"	-	-	5.50	1.83	-	-	-	-	-	-	-	-	-	-	-	-	-	-	-	-	-	-	-	-	-	-
4	"	4	-	7.00	1.75	-	-	-	-	-	-	1	-	1	8.90	-	8.90	0.04	-	-	-	0.23	-	4	1	7.0	11.70
1	Milk,	26	12	1.08	1.08	9	1	10	5.40	0.60	6.00	17	11	28	28.52	18.48	47.00	0.90	0.46	0.14	0.02	0.52	0.34	38	38	30.2	79.60
2	"	-	-	3.65	1.83	-	-	-	-	-	-	-	-	-	-	-	-	-	-	-	-	-	-	-	-	-	-
1	Tip-cart,	1	1	2.53	2.53	-	1	1	-	0.87	0.87	1	-	1	3.40	-	3.40	0.04	0.04	-	0.02	0.09	-	2	2	2.5	5.69
2	"	24	30	3.16	1.58	12	3	15	15.00	3.75	18.75	-	12	12	-	52.90	52.90	0.46	0.58	0.39	0.10	-	1.38	54	27	37.9	109.45
	Miscellaneous,	28	34	8.55	2.40	6	3	9	9.49	5.52	15.01	7	8	15	59.04	79.11	138.15	0.50	0.42	0.25	0.14	1.54	2.07	62	24	113.0	189.40
	Totals,	1622	1704	1.68	1.21	730	659	1389	362.19	299.97	662.16	506	659	1225	1408.97	1773.73	3182.70	49.58	50.42	9.46	7.85	36.53	46.16	3326	2614	2028.2	5679.26

TABLE G. — Concluded.

Traffic Observations for Seventy-two Consecutive Hours, Blue Hill Avenue, Mattapan.

No. of Horses to a Wagon.	CHARACTER OF WAGON.	Horses. Number. Out.	Horses. Number. In.	Horses. Weight of one Wagon Load.	Horses. Load per Horse.	Wagons. Empty. Number. Out.	Wagons. Empty. Number. In.	Wagons. Empty. Number. Tot.	Wagons. Empty. Weight (tons). Out.	Wagons. Empty. Weight (tons). In.	Wagons. Empty. Weight (tons). Tot.	Wagons. Loaded. Number. Out.	Wagons. Loaded. Number. In.	Wagons. Loaded. Number. Tot.	Wagons. Loaded. Weight (tons). Out.	Wagons. Loaded. Weight (tons). In.	Wagons. Loaded. Weight (tons). Tot.	Percentages of Total Number of Wagons. Out.	Percentages of Total Number of Wagons. In.	Percentages of Total Weight of Traffic. Empty. Out.	Percentages of Total Weight of Traffic. Empty. In.	Percentages of Total Weight of Traffic. Loaded. Out.	Percentages of Total Weight of Traffic. Loaded. In.	Totals. Horses.	Totals. Wagons.	Totals. Loads in Tons of 2,000 lbs.	Totals. Weights, Horses, Wagons and Loads.
1	Beer,	-	-	-	-	-	-	-	-	-	-	-	-	-	-	-	-	-	-	-	-	-	-	-	-	-	-
2	"	-	2	2.96	1.48	-	1	1	-	1.18	1.18	1	-	1	4.61	-	4.61	0.07	0.07	-	0.08	0.31	-	2	2	3.0	7.19
3	"	3	-	4.30	1.45	-	-	-	-	-	-	1	-	1	6.43	-	6.43	0.07	-	-	-	0.43	-	3	1	4.3	8.53
1	Caravan,	-	-	-	-	-	-	-	-	-	-	-	-	-	-	-	-	-	-	-	-	-	-	-	-	-	-
2	"	10	20	4.66	2.33	-	6	6	-	11.28	11.28	5	4	9	32.70	26.16	58.86	0.33	0.66	-	0.75	2.19	1.75	30	15	42.0	91.14
3	"	-	-	-	-	-	-	-	-	-	-	-	-	-	-	-	-	-	-	-	-	-	-	-	-	-	-
4	"	16	8	8.63	2.16	1	2	3	2.43	4.86	7.29	3	-	3	33.15	-	33.15	0.26	0.13	0.16	0.33	2.22	-	24	6	25.8	56.24
1	Carriage,	370	370	0.25	0.25	367	369	736	40.37	40.59	80.06	3	1	4	1.08	0.36	1.44	24.41	24.41	2.71	2.73	0.49	0.16	740	740	1.0	415.40
2	"	30	42	0.30	0.15	14	21	35	4.20	6.30	10.50	1	-	1	0.60	-	0.60	0.99	1.38	0.28	0.42	0.04	-	72	36	0.3	43.50
1	Coal,	1	-	1.66	1.66	-	-	-	-	-	-	1	-	1	2.44	-	2.44	0.07	-	-	-	0.16	-	1	1	1.6	3.14
2	"	20	8	3.28	1.64	-	4	4	-	6.36	6.36	10	-	10	48.70	-	48.70	0.66	0.26	-	0.43	3.27	-	28	14	32.8	74.66
3	"	-	-	-	-	-	-	-	-	-	-	-	-	-	-	-	-	-	-	-	-	-	-	-	-	-	-
1	Express,	202	192	1.00	1.00	112	119	231	69.44	73.78	143.22	90	73	163	144.90	117.53	262.43	13.31	12.66	4.05	4.94	9.70	7.87	394	394	161.3	681.45
2	"	92	128	1.88	0.94	22	20	42	30.36	27.60	57.96	24	44	68	78.00	143.00	221.00	3.04	4.22	2.03	1.85	5.22	9.58	220	110	127.2	432.96
1	Lumber,	7	9	2.00	2.00	2	2	4	2.00	2.00	4.00	5	7	12	15.00	21.00	36.00	0.46	0.59	0.13	0.13	1.00	1.40	16	16	24.0	51.20
2	"	16	24	3.07	1.54	4	5	9	5.20	6.50	11.70	4	7	11	17.48	30.59	48.07	0.53	0.79	0.35	0.43	1.17	2.06	40	20	33.8	87.77
3	"	3	3	5.50	1.8[illegible]	-	-	-	-	-	-	1	1	2	7.09	7.09	14.18	0.07	0.07	-	-	0.47	0.47	6	2	11.0	18.38
4	"	10	12	7.00	1.75	-	3	3	-	5.70	5.70	4	-	4	35.60	-	35.60	0.20	0.20	-	0.38	2.39	-	28	7	28.0	70.90
1	Milk,	13	21	1.08	1.08	12	6	18	7.20	3.60	10.80	1	15	16	1.68	25.20	26.88	0.86	1.38	0.48	0.24	0.11	1.68	34	34	17.3	61.48
2	"	-	-	-	-	-	-	-	-	-	-	-	-	-	-	-	-	-	-	-	-	-	-	-	-	-	-
1	Stone,	-	-	-	-	-	-	-	-	-	-	-	-	-	-	-	-	-	-	-	-	-	-	-	-	-	-
2	"	26	26	3.86	1.93	7	3	10	15.33	6.57	21.90	6	10	16	31.26	52.10	83.36	0.86	0.86	1.02	0.44	2.09	3.48	52	26	61.8	141.66
3	"	-	-	-	-	-	-	-	-	-	-	-	-	-	-	-	-	-	-	-	-	-	-	-	-	-	-
4	"	-	12	9.99	2.50	-	-	-	-	-	-	-	3	3	-	36.54	36.54	-	0.20	-	-	-	2.44	12	3	29.9	44.94
1	Tip-cart,	10	9	2.53	2.53	6	4	10	5.22	3.48	8.70	4	5	9	13.60	17.00	30.60	0.66	0.59	0.35	0.23	0.91	1.14	19	19	22.8	52.60
2	"	12	12	3.16	1.58	2	4	6	2.50	5.00	7.50	4	2	6	17.64	8.82	26.46	0.40	0.40	0.17	0.33	1.14	0.59	24	12	19.0	50.76
	Miscellaneous,	76	64	4.43	1.30	11	13	24	12.10	14.30	26.40	20	14	34	55.00	38.50	93.50	2.04	1.78	0.81	0.96	3.60	2.57	140	58	56.1	329.00
	Totals,	923	962	2.14	1.23	560	582	1142	196.35	219.10	415.45	188	186	374	546.96	523.89	1070.85	49.35	50.65	13.14	14.67	37.00	35.19	1885	1516	703.0	2722.90

Traffic Observations for Seventy-two Consecutive Hours, Blue Hill Avenue and Washington Street.

1	Beer,	4	3	1.05	1.05	-	1	1	-	1.18	1.18	4	2	6	8.92	, 4.46	13.38	0.30	0.23	-	0.09	0.66	0.38	7	7	6.3	19.46
2	"	6	8	2.96	1.48	1	-	1	·1.65	-	1.65	2	4	6	9.22	18.44	27.66	0.23	0.30	0.12	-	0.69	1.37	14	7	17.8	29.11
3	"	-	-	-	-	-	-	-	-	-	-	-	-	-	-	-	-	-	-	-	-	-	-	-	-	-	-
1	Caravan,	-	-	-	-	-	-	-	-	-	-	-	-	-	-	-	-	-	-	-	-	-	-	-	-	-	-
2	"	16	16	·4.00	2.33	1	6	7	1.88	11.28	13.16	7	2	9	45.78	13.08	58.86	0.61	0.61	0.14	0.84	3.41	0.07	32	16	42.0	94.42
3	"	-	-	-	-	-	-	-	-	-	-	-	-	-	-	-	-	-	-	-	-	-	-	-	-	-	-
4	"	20	16	8.63	2.16	-	1	1	2.43	-	2.43	5	3	8	55.25	33.15	88.40	0.38	0.30	0.18	-	4.12	2.46	36	9	69.0	116.03
1	Carriage,	204	196	0.25	0.25	158	145	303	17.38	15.95	33.33	46	51	97	16.56	18.36	34.92	15.49	14.88	1.29	1.19	1.23	1.36	400	400	24.2	248.25
2	"	104	158	0.30	0.15	41	62	103	12.30	18.60	30.90	11	17	28	6.60	10.20	16.80	3.95	6.00	0.91	1.36	0.49	0.76	262	131	8.4	165.60
1	Coal,	13	11	1.66	1.06	-	11	11	-	8.58	8.58	13	-	13	31.72	-	31.72	0.99	0.84	-	0.64	2.36	-	24	24	21.6	57.10
2	"	10	14	3.28	1.64	-	6	6	-	9.54	9.54	5	1	6	24.35	4.87	29.22	0.38	0.53	-	0.71	1.81	0.36	24	12	19.6	55.56
3	"	-	-	-	-	-	-	-	-	-	-	-	-	-	-	-	-	-	-	-	-	-	-	-	-	-	-
1	Express,	241	237	1.00	1.00	111	172	283	68.82	106.64	175.46	130	65	195	209.30	104.65	313.95	18.32	18.00	5.12	7.93	15.53	7.78	478	478	193.0	824.01
2	"	32	42	1.88	0.94	3	9	12	4.14	12.42	16.56	13	12	25	42.25	39.00	81.25	1.14	1.60	0.31	0.92	3.14	2.90	74	37	46.8	149.61
1	Lumber,	3	3	2.00	2.00	1	2	3	1.00	2.00	3.00	2	1	3	6.00	3.00	9.00	0.23	0.23	0.07	0.15	0.45	0.22	6	6	6.0	16.20
2	"	10	4	3.07	1.54	-	1	1	-	1.30	1.30	5	1	6	21.85	4.37	26.22	0.38	0.15	-	0.10	1.62	0.32	14	7	18.4	37.32
3	"	3	3	5.50	1.83	1	-	1	1.58	-	1.58	-	1	1	-	7.00	7.09	0.08	0.08	0.12	-	-	0.53	6	2	5.5	12.87
4	"	4	4	7.00	1.75	-	1	1	-	1.00	1.90	1	-	1	8.90	-	8.90	0.08	0.08	-	0.14	0.66	-	8	2	7.0	10.40
1	Milk,	22	21	1.08	1.08	7	4	11	4.20	2.40	6.60	15	17	32	25.20	28.56	53.76	1.67	1.60	0.31	0.18	1.87	2.12	43	43	34.6	90.46
2	"	-	-	3.15	1.58	-	-	-	-	-	-	-	-	-	-	-	-	-	-	-	-	-	-	-	-	-	-
1	Stone,	-	-	-	-	-	-	-	-	-	-	-	-	-	-	-	-	-	-	-	-	-	-	-	-	-	-
2	"	2	4	3.80	1.93	1	-	1	1.35	-	1.35	-	2	2	-	10.42	10.42	0.08	0.15	0.10	-	-	0.78	6	3	7.7	15.97
3	"	-	-	-	-	-	-	-	-	-	-	-	-	-	-	-	-	-	-	-	-	-	-	-	-	-	-
4	"	-	4	9.99	2.50	-	1	1	-	2.19	2.19	-	-	-	-	-	-	-	0.08	-	0.16	-	-	4	1	-	4.99
1	Tip-cart,	11	19	2.53	2.53	8	15	23	6.96	13.05	20.01	3	4	7	10.20	13.60	23.80	0.84	1.44	0.62	0.97	0.76	1.01	30	30	17.7	73.81
2	"	10	14	3.16	1.08	1	6	7	1.25	7.50	8.75	4	1	5	17.64	4.41	22.05	0.38	0.53	0.09	0.56	1.31	0.33	24	12	15.8	47.60
	Miscellaneous,	64	75	1.84	1.27	25	35	60	27.50	38.50	66.00	20	10	30	55.00	27.50	82.50	3.42	3.42	2.04	2.87	4.09	2.05	139	90	49.5	248.70
	Totals,	715	777	1.29	0.94	350	478	837	152.44	253.03	405.47	286	104	480	594.74	345.16	939.90	48.95	51.05	11.32	18.83	44.20	25.05	1402	1317	610.9	2323.47

TABLE K.* — *Statistics of Area, Roads, Valuation, Appropriation and Population, with Certain Percentages (Exclusive of Cities).*

BARNSTABLE COUNTY.

TOWNS.	Area, Square Miles.	Population, United States Census, 1890.	Total Valuation, 1890.	Tax Rate per $1,000, 1890.	Miles Roads.	Miles Roads per Square Mile.	Miles Roads per 1,000 Population.	HIGHWAY APPROPRIATIONS, EXCLUSIVE OF BRIDGES. Average Amount '89, '90, '91.	Amount per Mile of Road.	Amount per Capita.	Per Cent. of Total Tax.	Per Cent. of Total Valuation.
Barnstable,	74.0	4,023	$3,329,023	$10 00	164	2.2	40.7	$8,625	$52 60	$2 14	25.0	0.26
Bourne,	41.4	1,442	1,222,515	10 00	61	1.5	42.3	2,971	48 70	2 06	21.4	0.24
Brewster,	26.1	1,003	576,900	12 00	45	1.7	31.2	720	16 00	0 72	9.9	0.12
Chatham,	16.2	1,954	849,[illegible]51	14 00	51	3.2	26.1	1,636	32 10	0 84	12.7	0.19
Dennis,	21.8	2,899	1,283,901	11 00	76	3.5	26.2	3,082	40 50	1 06	20.5	0.24
Eastham,	16.1	602	227,593	11 20	48	3.0	79.7	376	7 80	0 62	12.2	0.17
Falmouth,	28.0	2,567	4,260,669	7 00	102	3.6	39.7	7,076	69 40	2 76	22.2	0.17
Harwich,	22.5	2,734	1,019,991	15 50	97	4.3	35.5	1,300	13 40	0 48	7.3	0.13
Mashpee,	28.0	298	163,140	10 00	46	1.6	154.3	605	13 20	2 03	29.7	0.37
Orleans,	20.8	1,219	481,176	11 00	40	1.9	32.8	1,500	37 50	1 23	24.6	0.31
Provincetown,	9.4	4,642	2,247,687	16 50	19	2.0	4.1	2,200	115 80	0 47	5.6	0.10
Sandwich,	69.8	1,819	901,375	14 80	64	0.9	35.2	2,688	42 00	1 48	19.1	0.30
Truro,	22.6	919	325,425	16 70	80	3.5	87.0	634	7 90	0 69	10.8	0.19
Wellfleet,	21.7	1,291	617,013	13 00	58	2.7	44.9	1,508	26 00	1 17	17.4	0.24
Yarmouth,	25.6	1,760	1,614,275	7 00	73	2.9	41.5	2,284	31 30	1 30	17.1	0.14
	444.0	29,172	$19,119,734	$11 98	1,024	2.3	35.2	$37,205	$36 30	$1 28	16.4	0.19

BERKSHIRE COUNTY.

TOWNS.	Area, Square Miles.	Population, United States Census, 1890.	Total Valuation, 1890.	Tax Rate per $1,000, 1890.	Miles Roads.	Miles Roads per Square Mile.	Miles Roads per 1,000 Population.	Average Amount '89, '90, '91.	Amount per Mile of Road.	Amount per Capita.	Per Cent. of Total Tax.	Per Cent. of Total Valuation.
Adams,	23.4	9,213	$3,649,919	$15 00	46	2.0	5.0	$4,468	$97 20	$0 49	7.9	0.12
Alford,	11.1	297	214,106	10 00	21	1.9	70.6	466	22 20	1 57	19.7	0.22

Becket,	51.4	946	383,858	18 00	77	1.5	81.3	2,296	29 80	2 42	33.7	0.60
Cheshire,	28.6	1,308	712,166	15 00	52	1.8	39.7	1,850	35 60	1 41	16.2	0.26
Clarksburg,	12.4	884	222,620	20 00	13	1.0	14.7	976	75 10	1 11	20.3	0.43
Dalton,	21.6	2,885	2,163,830	15 60	29	1.3	10.0	2,167	74 80	0 75	7.6	0.10
Egremont,	19.1	845	421,008	9 00	42	2.2	49.7	901	21 50	1 07	18.9	0.21
Florida,	24.1	436	163,845	20 00	36	1.5	82.5	1,380	38 40	3 16	37.0	0.84
Great Barrington,	48.7	4,612	3,178,411	10 00	82	1.7	17.8	6,157	75 10	1 33	17.4	0.19
Hancock,	37.7	506	362,990	9 60	29	0.8	57.3	752	26 00	1 49	20.6	0.21
Hinsdale,	21.4	1,739	719,799	16 00	41	1.9	23.6	1,022	25 00	0 59	9.0	0.14
Lanesborough,	29.4	1,018	513,414	14 00	47	1.6	46.2	1,430	30 20	14 05	18.4	0.28
Lee,	25.4	3,785	1,945,594	19 00	55	2.2	14.5	3,164	57 60	0 84	8.5	0.16
Lenox,	24.0	2,889	2,594,105	12 30	48	2.0	16.6	15,062	310 40	5 20	41.9	0.58
Monterey,	28.2	495	223,218	12 00	51	1.8	103.0	691	13 50	1 40	22.6	0.31
Mount Washington,	22.5	148	78,743	13 50	37	1.6	250.0	246	6 60	1 66	23.1	0.31
New Ashford,	13.0	125	70,607	12 50	12	0.9	96.0	321	26 70	2 57	29.3	0.46
New Marlborough,	48.4	1,305	557,688	15 00	100	2.1	76.7	2,316	23 20	1 77	24.9	0.42
North Adams,	–	–	–	–	–	–	–	–	–	–	–	–
Otis,	37.8	583	218,243	15 00	53	1.4	90.9	1,064	20 10	1 83	28.8	0.49
Peru,	27.1	305	118,820	19 00	45	1.7	147.3	698	15 50	2 29	29.3	0.59
Richmond,	18.4	796	476,064	11 50	39	2.1	49.0	883	22 60	1 11	13.0	0.19
Sandisfield,	53.1	807	367,771	17 63	85	1.6	105.0	1,177	13 80	1 46	18.2	0.32
Savoy,	39.3	569	176,823	21 00	59	1.5	103.6	945	16 00	1 66	23.8	0.54
Sheffield,	50.7	1,954	888,245	16 20	94	1.9	48.1	1,747	18 60	0 89	12.0	0.20
Stockbridge,	22.1	2,132	2,765,255	10 10	43	1.9	20.2	4,395	102 10	2 06	15.1	0.16
Tyringham,	18.9	412	226,385	12 00	25	1.3	60.6	730	29 20	1 77	25.2	0.32
Washington,	39.5	434	201,889	12 30	50	1.3	115.0	500	10 00	1 15	17.2	0.25
West Stockbridge,	18.2	1,492	639,816	13 40	33	1.8	22.1	897	27 20	0 60	8.8	0.15
Williamstown,	49.0	4,221	2,211,455	13 00	65	1.3	15.4	2,995	47 10	0 71	10.0	0.13
Windsor,	33.5	612	216,681	13 50	66	2.0	107.7	992	15 10	1 68	27.6	0.49
	898.0	47,753	$26,679,368	$14 35	1,475	1.6	30.9	$62,688	$42 50	$1 31	16.4	0.24

* For Tables H, I, J, see Appendix J.

TABLE K. — Continued.

BRISTOL COUNTY.

TOWNS.	Area, Square Miles.	Population, United States Census, 1890.	Total Valuation, 1890.	Tax Rate per $1,000, 1890.	Miles Roads.	Miles Roads per Square Mile.	Miles Roads per 1,000 Population.	Highway Appropriations, exclusive of Bridges.				
								Average Amount '89, '90, '91.	Amount per Mile of Road.	Amount per Capita.	Per Cent. of Total Tax.	Per Cent. of Total Valuation.
Acushnet,	17.4	1,027	$602,560	$11 30	32	1.8	31.1	$1,954	$61 10	$1 90	29.9	0.32
Attleborough,	27.6	7,577	4,026,335	15 00	65	2.4	8.6	6,070	93 50	0 80	9.0	0.15
Berkley,	17.1	894	367,087	9 00	49	2.9	54.8	984	20 10	1 10	24.4	0.27
Dartmouth,	75.6	3,122	1,898,300	12 80	77	1.0	24.6	9,087	179 00	2 80	40.3	0.48
Dighton,	22.8	1,889	748,814	14 50	49	2.1	25.9	1,800	36 80	0 95	15.2	0.24
Easton,	29.3	4,493	4,204,280	6 00	67	2.3	14.9	9,848	213 00	2 29	35.4	0.24
Fairhaven,	13.2	2,919	1,605,333	15 00	38	2.9	13.0	7,060	186 00	2 15	29.4	0.44
Freetown,	36.2	1,417	861,279	9 20	55	1.5	38.8	2,148	39 10	1 52	24.8	0.25
Mansfield,	20.4	3,432	1,573,969	17 00	50	2.4	14.6	1,289	25 80	0 38	4.6	0.08
North Attleborough,	19.4	6,727	3,708,528	13 80	66	3.4	9.8	6,343	96 10	0 95	10.3	0.17
Norton,	29.3	1,785	792,000	12 00	57	1.9	31.9	2,090	36 70	1 17	21.9	0.26
Raynham,	19.9	1,340	851,576	12 90	51	2.6	38.0	2,699	52 90	2 02	25.9	0.32
Rehoboth,	45.1	1,786	739,585	14 00	107	2.4	60.0	2,961	27 60	1 66	25.0	0.40
Seekonk,	17.9	1,317	822,540	9 50	52	2.9	39.5	2,883	55 50	2 19	32.1	0.35
Somerset,	10.4	2,106	1,022,882	15 00	26	2.5	12.3	2,216	85 10	1 05	14.0	0.22
Swanzey,	24.0	1,456	769,600	13 60	44	1.8	30.2	2,935	66 70	2 01	27.5	0.38
Westport,	55.1	2,599	1,292,875	16 00	78	1.4	30.0	5,073	64 50	1 94	25.3	0.39
	480.7	45,886	$25,887,543	$12 74	963	2.0	21.0	$67,440	$70 00	$1 47	18.3	0.26

COUNTY OF DUKES COUNTY.

Chilmark, ...	19.4	353	$211,607	$12 00	29	1.5	82.1	$344	$11 90	$0 97	12.9	0.16
Cottage City, ...	7.9	1,080	1,510,800	15 20	27	3.4	125.0	1,966	72 80	1 82	8.1	0.13
Edgartown, ...	29.7	1,156	707,522	15 30	50	1.7	43.2	419	8 40	0 36	3.7	0.06
Gay Head, ...	5.2	139	23,002	13 50	3	0.6	21.6	–	–	–	–	–
Gosnold, ...	13.2	135	206,082	3 95	18	1.4	133.3	–	–	–	–	–
Tisbury, ...	37.6	1,506	862,101	15 30	69	1.8	45.8	3,238	46 90	2 14	22.9	0.38
	113.0	4,369	$3,521,114	$12 54	196	1.7	44.8	$5,967	$30 50	$1 36	11.1	0.17

ESSEX COUNTY.

Amesbury, ...	12.9	9,798	$4,449,721	$16 40	40	3.1	4.1	$10,192	$255 00	$1 04	12.6	0.23
Andover, ...	32.4	6,142	4,166,933	17 00	88	2.7	14.3	7,333	83 60	1 20	11.6	0.18
Beverly, ...	16.8	10,821	13,156,375	13 60	62	3.7	5.6	28,947	467 00	2 86	15.1	0.22
Boxford, ...	25.4	865	686,271	9 00	55	2.2	63.6	1,133	20 60	1 31	17.1	0.17
Bradford, ...	7.9	3,720	1,901,336	20 00	23	2.9	6.2	4,400	191 30	1 18	11.8	0.23
Danvers, ...	13.8	7,454	3,900,575	15 40	55	4.0	7.4	7,716	140 50	1 03	11.8	0.20
Essex, ...	15.3	1,713	866,462	16 50	28	1.8	16.3	1,800	64 40	1 05	12.4	0.21
Georgetown, ...	14.0	2,117	1,031,200	15 00	33	2.4	15.6	1,537	46 60	0 73	9.1	0.15
Groveland, ...	8.7	2,191	914,201	16 80	28	3.2	12.8	1,338	47 80	0 61	9.4	0.15
Hamilton, ...	14.9	961	837,430	8 20	30	2.0	31.2	1,400	46 70	1 46	19.0	0.17
Ipswich, ...	35.5	4,439	2,350,810	12 00	60	1.7	13.5	3,760	62 70	0 85	12.4	0.16
Lynnfield, ...	10.0	787	601,362	9 25	16	1.6	20.3	1,233	77 10	1 57	20.3	0.21
Manchester, ...	6.8	1,789	7,471,964	5 16	22	3.2	12.3	4,327	196 70	2 42	10.6	0.06
Marblehead, ...	4.1	8,202	4,741,200	16 80	30	7.3	3.6	4,500	150 00	0 55	4.9	0.09
Merrimac, ...	8.4	2,633	1,356,750	17 00	25	3.0	9.5	3,819	152 70	1 45	13.7	0,28
Methuen, ...	22.6	4,814	3,131,251	15 00	63	2.8	13.1	9,957	158 00	2 07	20.6	0.32

TABLE K. — Continued.

ESSEX COUNTY — Concluded.

TOWNS.	Area, Square Miles.	Population, United States Census, 1890.	Total Valuation, 1890.	Tax Rate per $1,000, 1890.	Miles Roads.	Miles Roads per Square Mile.	Miles Roads per 1,000 Population.	Highway Appropriations, exclusive of Bridges. Average Amount '89, '90, '91.	Amount per Mile of Road.	Amount per Capita.	Per Cent. of Total Tax.	Per Cent. of Total Valuation.
Middleton,	14.9	924	$564,407	$13 60	29	1.9	31.4	$1,333	$46 00	$1 44	16.4	0.24
Nahant,	1.0	880	4,598,611	6 50	12	12.0	13.6	4,400	366 30	5 00	14.5	0.10
Newbury,	24.4	1,427	963,120	9 00	43	1.8	30.1	2,300	53 50	1 61	24.4	0.24
No. Andover,	27.5	3,742	2,499,847	12 00	78	2.8	20.8	5,353	68 60	1 43	15.6	0.21
Peabody,	17.0	10,158	7,293,450	15 60	37	2.2	3.6	13,383	362 00	1 32	11.4	0.18
Rockport,	7.0	4,087	2,139,874	15 80	25	3.6	6.1	5,037	201 50	1 23	14.2	0.24
Rowley,	18.2	1,248	592,545	12 70	37	2.0	29.6	1,238	33 50	0 99	14.6	0.21
Salisbury,	20.3	1,316	569,200	11 00	31	1.5	23.6	1,500	48 40	1 14	21.8	0.27
Saugus,	11.2	3,673	2,492,868	18 00	24	2.1	6.5	4,688	195 30	1 28	9.8	0.19
Swampscott,	3.1	3,198	4,859,327	10 00	18	5.8	5.6	4,333	240 50	1 40	9.6	0.09
Topsfield,	12.9	1,022	1,066,590	11 00	38	2.9	37.2	2,133	56 10	2 08	17.5	0.20
Wenham,	8.0	886	550,000	10 00	18	2.3	20.3	833	46 30	0 94	13.1	0.15
W. Newbury,	14.3	1,796	910,431	11 00	42	2.9	23.4	1,098	26 20	0 61	10.1	0.12
	429.3	102,803	$80,664,111	$13 08	1,090	2.5	10.6	$141,021	$129 40	$1 37	12.5	0.17

FRANKLIN COUNTY.

TOWNS.	Area, Square Miles.	Population, United States Census, 1890.	Total Valuation, 1890.	Tax Rate per $1,000, 1890.	Miles Roads.	Miles Roads per Square Mile.	Miles Roads per 1,000 Population.	Average Amount '89, '90, '91.	Amount per Mile of Road.	Amount per Capita.	Per Cent. of Total Tax.	Per Cent. of Total Valuation.
Ashfield,	39.7	1,025	$479,562	$17 50	81	2.0	78.9	$1,733	$21 40	$1 69	19.0	0.36
Bernardston,	22.1	770	388,438	11 00	43	1.9	55.8	500	11 60	0 65	10.0	0.13
Buckland,	20.1	1,570	537,054	12 50	48	2.4	30.6	1,947	40 60	1 24	22.8	0.36

Charlemont,	26.4	972	349,488	17 00	52	2.0	53.4	1,300	25 00	1 34	18.6	0.37
Colrain,	32.0	1,671	562,748	18 00	66	2.1	39.5	1,576	23 90	0 94	14.4	0.28
Conway,	37.7	1,451	732,665	16 70	86	2.3	59.2	2,100	24 40	1 45	14.5	0.29
Deerfield,	35.2	2,910	1,331,551	14 50	81	2.3	27.8	2,461	30 40	0 85	12.4	0.18
Erving,	14.4	972	345,494	19 00	23	1.6	23.6	877	38 20	0 90	11.9	0.25
Gill,	14.6	960	459,239	10 00	32	2.2	33.4	667	20 90	0 70	12.9	0.15
Greenfield,	20.0	5,252	4,786,758	12 50	55	2.8	10.5	9,667	176 00	1 84	12.5	0.17
Hawley,	30.8	515	149,268	22 00	51	1.7	99.0	1,067	20 90	2 07	28.3	0.72
Heath,	25.0	503	165,623	17 70	57	2.3	113.2	953	16 70	1 90	28.9	0.58
Leverett,	23.8	702	279,505	15 50	43	1.8	61.2	367	8 50	0 52	7.8	0.13
Leyden,	28.5	407	176,823	11 50	56	2.0	137.2	700	12 50	1 72	21.1	0.40
Monroe,	11.1	282	140,162	19 00	19	1.7	67.4	700	36 80	2 48	27.8	0.50
Montague,	30.4	6,296	3,305,327	13 50	90	3.0	14.3	7,718	86 90	1 23	15.4	0.23
New Salem,	30.1	856	292,460	18 00	78	2.6	91.3	1,133	14 50	1 32	20.4	0.39
Northfield,	35.6	1,869	798,983	13 00	65	1.8	34.8	1,698	26 20	0 91	15.6	0.21
Orange,	36.6	4,568	2,068,885	15 50	83	2.3	18.2	5,372	64 80	1 18	15.2	0.26
Rowe,	24.1	541	303,601	10 00	40	1.7	73.9	700	17 50	1 29	21.4	0.23
Shelburne,	23.6	1,553	924,715	12 00	51	2.2	32.8	1,500	29 40	0 97	13.0	0.16
Shutesbury,	26.6	453	149,528	25 50	48	1.8	106.0	800	16 70	1 77	20.8	0.53
Sunderland,	13.9	663	396,807	11 00	32	2.3	48.3	500	15 60	0 75	10.1	0.13
Warwick,	37.4	565	273,770	16 70	67	1.8	118.5	1,270	19 00	2 25	27.6	0.46
Wendell,	32.3	505	220,030	20 00	64	2.0	126.8	767	12 00	1 52	15.5	0.35
Whately,	19.0	779	403,161	10 00	48	2.5	61.6	667	13 90	0 86	12.0	0.17
	691.0	38,610	$20,021,645	$15 37	1,459	2.1	37.8	$48,740	$33 40	$1 26	15.8	0.24

HAMPDEN COUNTY.

Agawam,	24.9	2,352	$1,223,219	$13 20	55	2.2	23.4	$2,123	$38 70	$0 90	12.2	0.17
Blandford,	52.9	871	372,706	19 00	93	1.8	107.0	2,100	22 60	2 41	28.6	0.56
Brimfield,	35.2	1,096	425,800	17 00	68	1.9	62.0	1,333	19 60	1 22	17.1	0.31

TABLE K. — Continued.

HAMPDEN COUNTY — Concluded.

TOWNS.	Area, Square Miles.	Population, United States Census, 1890.	Total Valuation, 1890.	Tax Rate per $1,000, 1890.	Miles Roads.	Miles Roads per Square Mile.	Miles Roads per 1,000 Population.	Highway Appropriations, exclusive of Bridges. Average Amount '89, '90, '91.	Amount per Mile of Road.	Amount per Capita.	Per Cent. of Total Tax.	Per Cent. of Total Valuation.
Chester,	35.9	1,295	$520,480	$20 00	70	1.9	54.0	$1,500	$21 40	$1 16	15.9	0.29
Granville,	45.3	1,061	351,334	21 00	76	1.7	71.5	1,921	25 30	1 81	25.3	0.55
Hampden,	18.9	831	415,120	10 00	32	1.7	38.5	633	19 80	0 76	13.4	0.15
Holland,	13.5	2·1	98,371	16 50	34	2.5	169.0	426	12 50	2 12	27.9	0.43
Longmeadow,	24.6	2,183	1,071,860	15 00	60	2.4	27.4	4,100	68 30	1 88	29.5	0.38
Ludlow,	28.2	1,939	880,408	11 20	58	2.1	29.9	1,067	18 40	0 55	9.9	0.12
Monson,	47.8	3,650	1,757,753	15 80	114	2.4	31.2	4,100	35 90	1 12	14.2	0.23
Montgomery,	15.0	266	147,462	14 50	29	1.9	109.0	433	14 90	1 63	14.0	0.29
Palmer,	32.5	6,520	2,559,456	15 00	94	2.9	14.4	3,667	39 00	0 56	7.8	0.14
Russell,	18.9	879	492,032	13 50	28	1.5	31.8	700	25 00	0 80	8.7	0.14
Southwick,	23.1	914	508,680	14 25	61	2.6	66.7	800	13 10	0 87	10.2	0.16
Tolland,	31.3	393	162,938	18 00	40	1.3	102.0	600	15 00	1 53	21.2	0.37
Wales,	16.6	700	283,228	10 90	26	1.6	37.2	700	26 90	1 00	17.7	0.25
Westfield,	48.5	9,805	6,798,908	15 50	110	2.3	11.2	5,167	47 00	0 53	4.6	0.08
West Springfield,	18.3	5,077	3,362,767	12 50	50	2.7	9.8	4,399	87 90	0 87	9.1	0.13
Wilbraham,	22.9	1,814	751,727	11 60	45	2.0	34.8	1,067	23 70	0 59	11.8	0.14
	554.3	41,847	$22,184,249	$14 97	1,143	2.1	27.4	$36,836	$32 20	$0 88	10.5	0.17

HAMPSHIRE COUNTY.

TOWNS.	Area, Square Miles.	Population, United States Census, 1890.	Total Valuation, 1890.	Tax Rate per $1,000, 1890.	Miles Roads.	Miles Roads per Square Mile.	Miles Roads per 1,000 Population.	Average Amount '89, '90, '91.	Amount per Mile of Road.	Amount per Capita.	Per Cent. of Total Tax.	Per Cent. of Total Valuation.
Amherst,	26.9	4,512	$3,290,128	$15 75	69	2.6	15.3	$4,667	$67 70	$1 03	8.8	0.14
Belchertown,	55.1	2,120	819,365	15 20	127	2.3	60.0	1,809	14 20	0 85	13.3	0.22

Chesterfield,	32.4	608	293,594	16 00	59	1.8	97.0	900	15 20	1 48	18.2	0.31
Cummington,	22.8	787	307,015	17 70	55	2.4	69.8	833	15 10	1 06	15.2	0.27
Easthampton,	14.3	4,395	2,307,947	16 00	42	2.9	9.6	3,143	74 90	0 72	8.3	0.14
Enfield,	17.5	952	634,680	5 00	40	2.3	42.0	1,233	30 80	1 29	25.0	0.20
Goshen,	17.1	297	134,047	16 67	31	1.8	104.2	582	18 80	1 96	23.8	0.43
Granby,	27.5	765	438,523	13 50	54	2.0	70.6	775	14 40	1 01	12.7	0.18
Greenwich,	20.0	526	272,330	10 00	41	2.1	78.0	713	17 40	1 36	21.1	0.26
Hadley,	24.8	1,669	1,000,873	17 00	54	2.2	32.4	2,229	41 30	1 34	12.8	0.22
Hatfield,	17.3	1,246	924,503	8 10	37	2.1	29.7	960	26 00	0 77	11.7	0.10
Huntington,	27.2	1,385	501,950	16 00	50	1.8	36.1	1,167	23 40	0 84	13.4	0.23
Middlefield,	24.2	455	237,685	10 00	39	1.6	85.7	767	19 70	1 69	25.0	0.32
Pelham,	25.4	486	165,165	18 00	49	1.9	100.8	800	16 30	1.65	23.8	0.48
Plainfield,	21.8	435	152,405	16 00	47	2.2	108.0	800	17 00	1 84	28.0	0.52
Prescott,	18.3	376	167,152	13 00	42	2.3	111.6	400	9 50	1 06	16.1	0.24
Southampton,	27.3	1,017	498,936	10 00	71	2.6	69.8	967	11 40	0 80	16.9	0.16
South Hadley,	18.5	4,261	1,770,816	19 00	38	2.1	8.9	6,500	171 00	1 52	20.7	0.37
Ware,	29.3	7,329	3,736,071	16 80	84	2.9	11.4	3,667	43 60	0 50	5.8	0.10
Westhampton,	27.8	477	238,212	13 50	46	1.7	96.2	1,000	21 80	2 10	28.1	0.42
Williamsburg,	25.5	2,057	899,807	11 50	47	1.8	22.8	1,000	21 30	0 49	8.5	0.11
Worthington,	32.5	714	301,021	17 00	64	2.0	89.6	1,000	15 60	1 40	17.8	0.33
	553.5	36,869	$19,092,225	$14 17	1,186	2.1	32.2	$35,912	$30 30	$0 97	12.0	0.19

MIDDLESEX COUNTY.

Acton,	20.0	1,897	$1,449,415	$8 50	60	3.0	31.6	$1,667	$27 80	$0 88	11.7	0.11
Arlington,	5.2	5,629	5,564,662	15 20	37	7.1	6.6	15,167	410 00	2 70	16.4	0.27
Ashby,	23.3	825	493,026	8 00	63	2.7	76.4	1,667	26 40	2 02	25.7	0.34
Ashland,	12.5	2,532	1,271,394	18 20	38	3.0	15.0	2,900	76 30	1 18	12.0	0.23
Ayer,	9.4	2,148	1,324,141	15 20	25	2.7	11.6	1,067	42 60	0 50	5.1	0.08
Bedford,	14.1	1,092	878,236	13 00	34	2.4	31.1	1,233	36 30	1 13	10.2	0.14

TABLE K. — Continued.

MIDDLESEX COUNTY — Concluded.

TOWNS.	Area, Square Miles.	Population, United States Census, 1890.	Total Valuation, 1890.	Tax Rate per $1,000, 1890.	Miles Roads.	Miles Roads per Square Mile.	Miles Roads per 1,000 Population.	Highway Appropriations, exclusive of Bridges. Average Amount '89, '90, '91.	Amount per Mile of Road.	Amount per Capita.	Per Cent. of Total Tax.	Per Cent. of Total Valuation.
Belmont,	4.6	2,098	$3,183,235	$11 50	25	5.4	11.9	$6,000	$240 00	$2 86	15.1	0.19
Billerica,	26.0	2,380	1,795,395	10 40	57	2.2	23.9	3,000	52 60	1 26	13.5	0.17
Boxborough,	11.8	325	238,875	11 35	28	2.4	86.1	643	23 00	1 98	22.5	0.27
Burlington,	12.4	617	510,094	11 90	34	2.7	55.0	1,333	39 20	2 16	21.4	0.26
Carlisle,	16.1	481	380,971	13 00	37	2.3	76.9	1,000	27 10	2 08	19.6	0.26
Chelmsford,	23.3	2,695	1,772,035	8 50	77	3.3	28.6	3,833	49 80	1 42	22.6	0.22
Concord,	25.2	4,427	3,605,306	10 80	56	2.2	12.6	9,700	173 00	2 19	24.6	0.27
Dracut,	21.3	1,996	1,591,607	11 20	50	2.3	25.0	2,833	56 60	1 42	15.8	0.18
Dunstable,	16.8	416	293,558	13 00	36	2.1	86.5	467	13 00	1 12	14.1	0.16
Framingham,	25.4	9,239	7,861,630	16 00	86	3.4	9.3	22,500	262 00	2 75	18.3	0.32
Groton,	33.7	2,057	2,896,917	5 00	74	2.2	36.0	5,333	72 00	2 59	30.4	0.18
Holliston,	19.4	2,619	1,522,290	17 00	46	2.4	17.6	2,133	46 40	0 81	7.9	0.14
Hopkinton,	27.2	4,088	2,222,199	19 75	66	2.4	16.1	3,000	45 50	0 73	6.9	0.13
Hudson,	12.2	4,670	2,490,115	20 00	48	3.9	10.3	3,000	62 50	0 64	6.2	0.12
Lexington,	16.0	3,197	3,378,189	12 10	50	3.1	15.6	7,300	146 00	2 29	16.5	0.22
Lincoln,	14.8	987	1,539,688	8 40	38	2.6	38.5	3,500	92 10	3 54	22.9	0.23
Littleton,	17.4	1,025	770,095	12 50	44	2.5	42.9	1,300	29 60	1 27	12.8	0.17
Maynard,	5.7	2,700	1,960,586	11 00	19	3.3	7.0	1,467	77 20	0 54	6.7	0.07
Melrose,	5.1	8,519	6,724,705	13 70	36	7.1	4.2	14,967	415 00	1 75	14.8	0.22
Natick,	16.1	9,118	5,439,375	16 40	62	3.9	6.8	5,067	81 90	0 55	5.1	0.09
No. Reading,	13.5	874	529,725	13 50	27	2.0	30.9	1,000	37 10	1 15	13.0	0.19
Pepperell,	22.6	3,127	1,772,722	11 50	70	3.1	22.4	1,833	26 20	0 59	7.3	0.10
Reading,	10.1	4,088	2,837,130	14 00	45	4.5	11.0	6,500	144 20	1 59	14.1	0.23
Sherborn,	17.6	1,381	826,290	11 00	39	2.2	28.2	2,600	66 70	1 88	25.8	0.31

Shirley, ...	15.8	1,191	681,136	12 80	43	2.7	36.1	1,000	23 30	0 84	10.8	0.15
Stoneham, ...	6.6	6,155	3,406,871	17 20	36	5.5	5.8	12,900	359 50	2 10	21.2	0.38
Stow, ...	18.0	903	827,624	6 60	44	2.4	48.7	1,067	24 20	1 18	14.4	0.13
Sudbury, ...	25.4	1,197	1,063,245	11 00	66	2.6	55.1	2,100	35 90	1 75	17.0	0.20
Tewksbury, . . .	22.2	2,515	1,465,495	11 00	59	2.7	23.4	3,700	62 80	1 48	24.1	0.25
Townsend, ...	32.2	1,750	1,125,471	10 00	76	2.4	43.4	2,800	35 00	1 59	22.0	0.30
Tyngsborough, . . .	17.9	662	370,621	10 00	36	2.0	54.2	1,200	31 20	1 82	24.6	0.32
Wakefield, ...	7.6	6,982	4,603,565	16 00	42	5.5	6.0	9,800	232 90	1 40	12.7	0.16
Watertown, . . .	4.1	7,073	7,287,622	14 50	32	7.8	4.5	14,333	448 00	2 02	13.2	0.20
Wayland, ...	16.3	2,060	1,565,119	11 80	42	2.6	20.4	2,100	50 20	1 05	9.6	0.13
Westford, ...	31.4	2,250	1,079,853	11 20	81	2.6	36.0	2,000	24 70	0 89	16.7	0.19
Weston, ...	16.6	1,664	2,224,383	7 20	40	2.4	24.0	8,700	218 00	5 25	51.6	0.40
Wilmington, . . .	17.8	1,213	740,167	14 00	44	2.5	36.3	1,267	28 80	1 04	12.0	0.17
Winchester, . . .	6.0	4,861	4,667,055	17 70	25	4.2	5.1	7,250	290 00	1 49	8.9	0.16
	736.7	127,723	$98,231,633	$12 56	2,073	2.8	16.2	$204,227	$98 50	$1 60	14.3	0.21

NORFOLK COUNTY.

Avon, ...	4.5	1,384	$618,085	$21 00	13	2.9	9.4	$1,000	$77 00	$0 73	8.0	0.16
Bellingham, . . .	17.8	1,334	622,410	11 00	44	2.5	33.0	1,067	34 30	0 80	12.2	0.17
Braintree, ...	13.3	4,848	3,449,650	12 80	46	3.5	9.5	7,800	169 20	1 61	15.2	0.22
Brookline, ...	6.8	12,103	46,437,100	9 00	54	8.0	4.5	53,800	997 00	14 45	11.7	0.11
Canton, ...	19.2	4,538	3,738,412	19 00	42	2.2	9.3	9,400	224 00	2 07	14.7	0.25
Cohasset, ...	9.6	2,448	3,760,338	7 10	23	2.4	9.4	8,000	348 00	3 26	35.6	0.21
Dedham, ...	21.6	7,123	5,474,629	14 80	76	3.5	10.6	10,667	140 40	1 50	11.8	0.19
Dover, ...	14.5	727	737,535	7 80	31	2.1	42.5	2,100	67 75	2 89	33.4	0.28
Foxborough, . . .	19.9	2,933	1,513,440	20 30	52	2.6	17.7	4,700	90 49	1 6[illegible]	18.0	0.31
Franklin, ...	27.3	4,831	2,392,425	13 00	66	2.4	13.6	7,500	113 50	1 52	19.5	0.31
Holbrook, ...	7.6	2,474	1,107,230	21 00	19	2.5	7.7	4,000	210 50	1 62	17.4	0.36
Hyde Park, ...	4.6	10,193	7,470,115	15 60	40	8.7	3.9	9,600	240 00	0 96	8.1	0.13

TABLE K. — Continued.

NORFOLK COUNTY — Concluded.

TOWNS.	Area, Square Miles.	Population, United States Census, 1890.	Total Valuation, 1890.	Tax Rate per $1,000, 1890.	Miles Roads.	Miles Roads per Square Mile.	Miles Roads per 1,000 Population.	HIGHWAY APPROPRIATIONS, EXCLUSIVE OF BRIDGES.				
								Average Amount '89, '90, '91.	Amount per Mile of Road.	Amount per Capita.	Per Cent. of Total Tax.	Per Cent. of Total Valuation.
Medfield,	19.1	1,493	$1,191,438	$11 00	39	2.0	26.1	$1,433	$36 80	$0 96	10.2	0.12
Medway,	13.8	2,985	1,211,890	17 50	37	2.7	12.4	1,767	47 80	0 59	7.9	0.15
Millis,	12.7	786	501,490	12 00	37	2.9	47.1	2,000	54 10	2 54	27.3	0.40
Milton,	12.9	4,278	14,411,350	8 00	47	3.6	11.0	22,000	468 00	5 14	20.1	0.15
Needham,	12.7	3,035	2,271,729	12 20	45	3.5	14.8	2,667	59 30	0 88	8.2	0.12
Norfolk,	14.8	913	501,156	12 50	39	2.6	42.7	1,000	25 70	1 10	13.7	0.20
Norwood,	10.0	3,733	2,564,558	16 60	30	3.0	8.0	6,800	226 40	1 84	16.0	0.27
Randolph,	10.0	3,946	2,044,710	17 60	31	3.1	7.8	3,333	107 40	0 84	8.7	0.16
Sharon,	24.2	1,634	1,170,470	11 00	54	2.2	33.0	1,933	35 80	1 18	14.5	0.17
Stoughton,	16.4	4,852	2,366,365	14 00	50	3.0	10.3	3,333	66 60	0 69	9.2	0.14
Walpole,	21.6	2,604	1,945,210	14 20	58	2.7	22.2	3,167	54 60	1 22	12.2	0.16
Wellesley,	10.4	3,600	6,231,584	8 00	32	3.0	8.9	4,667	145 90	1 30	9.0	0.08
Weymouth,	19.0	10,866	6,441,845	16 40	63	3.3	5.8	14,333	227 50	1 32	12.8	0.22
Wrentham,	32.2	2,566	1,354,008	13 00	85	2.6	33.1	4,700	55 30	1 86	25.2	0.34
	396.5	102,227	$121,529,172	$13 71	1,153	2.9	11.3	$192,767	$167 00	$1 88	12.9	0.16

PLYMOUTH COUNTY.

TOWNS.	Area, Square Miles.	Population, United States Census, 1890.	Total Valuation, 1890.	Tax Rate per $1,000, 1890.	Miles Roads.	Miles Roads per Square Mile.	Miles Roads per 1,000 Population.	Average Amount '89, '90, '91.	Amount per Mile of Road.	Amount per Capita.	Per Cent. of Total Tax.	Per Cent. of Total Valuation.
Abington,	10.2	4,260	$2,184,645	$19 40	39	3.8	9.1	$4,200	$107 70	$0 99	9.6	0.19
Bridgewater,	28.1	4,249	2,244,551	10 40	65	2.3	15.3	3,667	56 40	0 86	13.6	0.16
Carver,	41.5	994	641,700	8 60	65	1.6	65.4	1,126	17 30	1 13	19.3	0.18
Duxbury,	25.5	1,908	1,200,484	14 50	70	2.7	36.7	3,900	55 70	2 04	21.0	0.32

East Bridgewater,	17.5	2,911	1,483,091	12 80	46	2.6	15.8	3,000	65 30	1 03	14.4	0.20
Halifax,	17.1	562	264,375	12 40	31	1.8	55.1	567	18 30	1 01	15.7	0.21
Hanover,	13.4	2,093	1,178,160	11 00	40	3.0	19.1	5,000	125 00	2 39	32.2	0.42
Hanson,	16.1	1,267	606,680	15 50	32	2.0	25.2	1,167	36 50	0 92	11.3	0.19
Hingham,	24.8	4,564	3,724,662	12 00	56	2.3	12.2	12,000	214 30	2 63	24.9	0.37
Hull,	2.2	989	2,442,212	11 70	16	7.3	16.2	4,500	281 00	4 55	16.3	0.18
Kingston,	19.3	1,659	1,648,830	9 20	40	2.1	24.1	4,000	100 00	2 41	22.9	0.24
Lakeville,	36.1	935	487,284	11 00	61	1.7	65.3	1,600	26 10	1 71	28.9	0.33
Marion,	14.6	871	792,520	10 00	22	1.5	25.2	2,100	95 50	2 41	24.7	0.27
Marshfield,	30.1	1,713	1,115,299	14 50	63	2.1	36.8	3,333	52 90	1 94	18.1	0.30
Mattapoisett,	17.5	1,148	1,552,600	7 50	33	1.9	28.7	2,000	60 60	1 74	16.1	0.13
Middleborough,	72.1	6,065	3,365,716	13 75	147	2.0	24.2	10,667	72 50	1 76	19.8	0.32
Norwell,	21.0	1,635	884,197	12 50	52	2.5	31.8	5,400	103 90	3 29	46.7	0.62
Pembroke,	24.8	1,320	647,925	14 00	56	2.3	42.4	2,600	46 40	1 98	26.0	0.40
Plymouth,	109.3	7,314	5,755,400	13 20	198	1.8	27.0	12,700	64 10	1 73	15.7	0.22
Plympton,	15.0	597	306,399	11 80	31	2.1	51.9	833	26 90	1 39	21.0	0.27
Rochester,	35.8	1,012	479,435	10 00	59	1.6	58.3	1,300	22 00	1 27	23.6	0.27
Rockland,	10.1	5,213	2,694,735	17 60	32	3.2	6.1	4,400	137 50	0 84	8.6	0.16
Scituate,	17.8	2,318	1,867,845	11 00	44	2.5	19.0	3,600	81 80	1 55	15.3	0.13
Wareham,	40.2	3,451	1,645,132	13 00	90	2.2	26.1	3,433	38 10	0 99	14.5	0.11
West Bridgewater,	16.8	1,917	1,032,038	13 75	45	2.7	23.5	2,000	44 50	1 04	13.0	0.19
Whitman,	6.9	4,441	3,104,640	15 50	25	3.6	5.7	5,000	200 00	1 12	9.1	0.16
	683.8	65,406	$43,350,555	$12 56	1,458	2.1	22.3	$104,093	$71 50	$1 59	16.8	0.24

SUFFOLK COUNTY.

Revere,	5.9	5,668	$4,968,835	$12 00	30	5.1	5.3	$5,667	$188 90	$1 00	9.8	0.11
Winthrop,	1.6	2,726	3,521,361	12 40	23	14.4	8.4	3,333	144 80	1 22	7.2	0.09
	7.5	8,394	$8,490,196	$12 20	53	7.1	6.3	$9,000	$170 00	$1 07	8.9	0.11

Table K. — Concluded.

WORCESTER COUNTY.

TOWNS.	Area, Square Miles.	Population, United States Census, 1890.	Total Valuation, 1890.	Tax Rate per $1,000, 1890.	Miles Roads.	Miles Roads per Square Mile.	Miles Roads per 1,000 Population.	Highway Appropriations, exclusive of Bridges.				
								Average Amount '89, '90, '91.	Amount per Mile of Road.	Amount per Capita.	Per Cent. of Total Tax.	Per Cent. of Total Valuation.
Ashburnham,	41.6	2,074	$1,008,058	$17 80	86	2.1	41.5	$2,800	$32 60	$1 03	16.0	0.28
Athol,	34.4	6,319	3,005,374	19 00	87	2.5	13.8	5,200	59 80	0 82	8.6	0.17
Auburn,	16.5	1,532	499,898	13 00	45	2.7	29.4	1,500	33 40	0 98	21.2	0.30
Barre,	45.7	2,239	1,449,226	14 00	119	2.0	53.2	2,667	22 50	1 18	12.2	0.18
Berlin,	13.6	884	495,996	8 50	39	2.9	44.1	1,067	27 30	1 21	22.6	0.22
Blackstone,	16.8	6,138	2,555,435	17 20	48	2.9	7.8	4,400	91 60	0 72	9.7	0.17
Bolton,	19.8	827	495,562	10 00	50	2.5	60.5	1,000	20 00	1 21	18.0	0.20
Boylston,	18.9	770	530,389	12 50	51	2.7	66.2	1,400	27 50	1 82	18.1	0.26
Brookfield,	27.7	3,352	1,271,653	18 90	60	2.2	17.9	3,000	50 00	0 90	13.8	0.24
Charlton,	43.8	1,847	939,260	11 00	118	2.7	64.0	2,800	23 70	1 51	22.8	0.30
Clinton,	7.5	10,424	6,044,017	15 80	34	4.5	3.3	14,000	412 00	1 34	13.2	0.23
Dana,	19.6	700	286,863	16 00	48	2.4	68.5	433	9 00	0 62	8.4	0.15
Douglas,	37.7	1,908	1,023,616	14 00	75	2.0	39.3	1,967	26 20	1 03	12.7	0.19
Dudley,	22.3	2,944	1,002,360	14 00	62	2.8	21.0	2,600	42 00	0 88	16.8	0.26
Gardner,	23.1	8,424	4,136,802	21 00	69	3.0	8.2	10,167	147 00	1 21	11.4	0.25
Grafton,	22.7	5,002	2,203,150	18 00	68	3.0	13.6	2,000	29 40	0 40	5.3	0.09
Hardwick,	39.9	2,922	1,402,815	11 50	88	1.8	30.1	2,133	24 20	0 73	11.8	0.15
Harvard,	25.8	1,095	962,187	7 00	62	2.4	56.5	1,333	21 50	1 22	17.0	0.14
Holden,	37.1	2,623	1,068,240	15 50	85	2.3	32.4	2,067	24 40	0 79	11.3	0.19
Hopedale,	5.7	1,176	1,371,970	12 00	15	2.6	12.7	8,600	573 00	7 30	55.6	0.63
Hubbardston,	42.2	1,346	700,750	15 00	76	1.8	56.5	1,900	25 00	1 41	16.2	0.27
Lancaster,	28.3	2,201	2,990,048	9 70	67	2.4	30.4	8,300	124 00	3 77	29.3	0.28
Leicester,	24.9	3,120	1,955,413	12 00	67	2.7	21.4	533	8 00	0 17	2.2	0.03
Leominster,	29.4	7,269	4,511,349	17 00	76	2.6	10.4	4,000	52 60	0 55	4.8	0.09
Lunenburg,	29.1	1,146	725,849	14 00	72	2.5	62.8	1,400	19 40	1 22	13.5	0.19

Mendon,	18.1	919	549,807	13 00	45	2.5	49.0	1,500	33 40	1 63	21.1	0.27
Milford,	15.0	8,780	4,871,754	17 00	58	3.9	6.6	11,400	197 00	1 30	13.4	0.23
Millbury,	16.8	4,428	2,026,180	15 00	47	2.8	10.6	2,333	49 70	0 53	6.9	0.11
New Braintree,	21.4	573	449,080	9 75	52	2.4	90.7	1,300	25 00	2 27	26.0	0.29
Northborough,	18.6	1,952	1,254,092	12 70	52	2.8	26.6	1,900	36 50	0 97	11.6	0.15
Northbridge,	19.0	4,603	2,314,327	9 30	53	2.8	11.5	5,100	96 20	1 11	21.0	0.22
North Brookfield,	22.2	3,871	1,711,214	13 20	68	3.1	17.6	3,333	49 00	0 86	13.7	0.19
Oakham,	21.5	738	344,744	16 80	48	2.2	65.0	667	13 90	0 91	11.2	0.19
Oxford,	27.6	2,616	1,335,918	14 00	74	2.7	28.3	1,667	22 50	0 64	8.0	0.12
Paxton,	15.8	445	285,457	11 00	36	2.3	80.9	717	19 90	1 61	18.1	0.25
Petersham,	38 2	1,050	592,270	13 00	77	2.0	73.3	2,100	27 30	2 00	24.2	0.35
Phillipston,	24.1	502	269,465	14 20	49	2.1	97.5	733	14 90	1 46	16.9	0.27
Princeton,	36.5	982	817,346	11 00	77	2.1	78.4	2,300	29 90	2 34	23.7	0.28
Royalston,	43.7	1,030	590,163	9 00	76	1.7	73.7	1,333	17 60	1 29	21.8	0.23
Rutland,	33.3	980	494,185	15 00	76	2.3	77.5	2,100	27 60	2 14	24.8	0.42
Shrewsbury,	21.6	1,449	1,168,670	11 60	61	2.8	42.0	2,700	44 30	1 86	21.0	0.23
Southborough,	15.4	2,114	1,371,738	14 50	60	3.9	28.4	2,000	33 30	0 95	10.8	0.15
Southbridge,	20.8	7,655	3,260,540	18 30	57	2.7	7.5	5,000	87 70	0 65	7.5	0.15
Spencer,	34.1	8,747	4,085,554	17 00	94	2.8	10.8	11,400	121 20	1 30	13.5	0.28
Sterling,	31.3	1,244	848,333	11 70	77	2.5	61.8	1,333	17 30	1 07	11.5	0.16
Sturbridge,	39.8	2,074	965,233	12 75	84	2.1	40.5	3,333	39 70	1 61	25.3	0.35
Sutton,	34.3	3,180	1,289,702	12 50	92	2.7	29.0	2,633	28 60	0 83	15.1	0.20
Templeton,	32.5	2,999	1,153,206	17 70	84	2.6	28.0	2,333	27 80	0 78	11.4	0.20
Upton,	20.8	1,878	927,417	15 70	62	3.0	33.0	2,667	43 00	1 42	14.9	0.29
Uxbridge,	30.2	3,408	2,085,190	17 20	84	2.8	24.6	5,260	62 00	1 52	17.0	0.25
Warren,	28.5	4,681	2,389,038	15 00	67	2.3	14.3	3,500	52 20	0 75	8.8	0.15
Webster,	14.5	7,031	2,773,118	10 00	32	2.2	4.6	2,000	62 50	0 28	6.0	0.07
Westborough,	22.7	5,195	2,783,504	15 70	64	2.8	12.3	2,233	34 90	0 43	4.9	0.08
West Boylston,	13.2	3,019	1,197,535	16 80	42	3.2	13.9	1,800	42 90	0 60	8.5	0.15
West Brookfield,	21.1	1,592	784,674	12 00	51	2.4	32.0	1,300	25 50	0 82	11.6	0.17
Westminster,	37.3	1,688	761,617	17 00	86	2.3	51.0	2,333	27 10	1 38	18.9	0.31
Winchendon,	45.5	4,390	2,030,849	16 00	106	2.3	24.2	6,333	59 60	1 44	18.6	0.31
	1509.5	174,095	$90,421,200	$14 03	3,758	2.5	21.6	$183,848	$48 90	$1 05	12.7	0.20

TABLE L. — *Statistics of Area, Roads, Valuation, Appropriations and Population, with Certain Percentages.* (*State, Exclusive of Cities.*)

STATE AND COUNTIES.	Area, Square Miles.	Population, United States Census, 1890.	Total Valuation, 1890.	Tax Rate per $1,000, 1890.	Miles Roads.	Miles Roads per Square Mile.	Miles Roads per 1,000 Population.	Highway Appropriations, exclusive of Bridges.				
								Average Amount '89, '90, '91.	Amount per Mile of Road.	Amount per Capita.	Per Cent. of Total Tax.	Per Cent. of Total Valuation.
Barnstable,	444.0	29,172	$19,119,734	$11 98	1,024	2.3	35.2	$37,205	$36 30	$1 28	16.4	0.19
Berkshire,	898.0	47,753	26,679,368	14 35	1,475	1.6	30.9	62,688	42 50	1 31	16.4	0.24
Bristol,	480.7	45,886	25,887,543	12 74	963	2.0	21.0	67,440	70 00	1 47	18.3	0.26
Dukes,	113.0	4,369	3,521,114	12 54	196	1.7	44.8	5,967	30 50	1 36	11.1	0.17
Essex,	429.3	102,803	80,664,111	13 08	1,090	2.6	10.6	141,021	129 40	1 37	12.5	0.17
Franklin,	691.0	38,610	20,021,645	15 37	1,459	2.1	37.8	48,740	33 40	1 26	15.8	0.24
Hampden,	554.3	41,847	22,184,249	14 97	1,143	2.1	27.6	36,836	32 20	0 88	10.5	0.17
Hampshire,	553.5	36,869	19,092,225	14 17	1,186	2.1	32.2	35,912	30 30	0 97	12.0	0.19
Middlesex,	736.7	127,723	98,231,633	12 56	2,073	2.8	16.2	204,227	98 50	1 60	14.3	0.21
Nantucket,	52.0	3,268	2,996,610	11 50	114	2.2	34.8	7,200	63 10	2 20	20.2	0.24
Norfolk,	396.5	102,227	121,529,172	13 71	1,153	2.9	11.3	192,767	167 00	1 88	12.9	0.16
Plymouth,	683.8	65,406	43,450,555	12 56	1,458	2.1	22.3	104,093	71 50	1 59	16.8	0.24
Suffolk,	7.5	8,394	8,490,196	12 20	53	7.1	6.3	9,000	170 00	1 07	8.9	0.11
Worcester,	1,509.5	174,095	90,421,200	14 03	3,758	2.5	21.6	183,848	48 90	1 05	12.7	0.20
State,	7,549.8	828,422	$582,189,355	$13 27	17,145	2.3	20.7	$11,36944	$66 30	$1 37	13.7	0.20

TABLE M.—*Statistics of Area, Roads, Valuation, Appropriations and Population, with Certain Percentages, of Cities.*

CITIES.	Area, Square Miles.	Population, United States Census, 1890.	Total Valuation, 1890.	Tax Rate per $1,000, 1890.	Miles Roads.	Miles Roads per Square Mile.	Miles Roads per 1,000 Population.	Highway Appropriations, exclusive of Bridges.				
								Average Amount, '89-'91.	Amount per Mile of Road.	Amount per Capita.	Per Cent. of Total Tax.	Per Cent. of Total Valuation.
Boston,	38.2	448,477	$822,041,800	$13 30	435	11.4	1.0	$1,307,119	$3,003 00	$2 91	12.0	0.16
Brockton,	20.2	27,294	17,477,847	15 20	98	4.9	3.6	44,667	456 00	1 64	15.1	0.26
Cambridge,	6.4	70,028	67,471,925	15 60	97	15.1	1.4	117,789	1,214 00	1 68	10.7	0.17
Chelsea,	2.3	27,909	20,798,339	17 60	45	19.6	1.6	28,500	634 00	1 02	7.6	0.14
Chicopee,	25.7	14,050	6,377,070	12 60	81	3.1	5.8	9,000	111 00	0 64	10.5	0.14
Everett,	3.4	11,068	7,889,650	14 50	40	11.8	3.6	16,333	408 00	1 48	13.3	0.21
Fall River,	37.8	74,398	53,474,458	16 40	108	2.9	1.5	81,359	753 00	1 09	8.7	0.15
Fitchburg,	28.5	22,037	15,476,206	16 40	119	4.2	5.4	23,333	196 00	1 06	8.7	0.15
Gloucester,	27.1	24,651	13,945,439	15 50	91	3.4	3.7	10,000	110 00	0 41	4.5	0.07
Haverhill,	26.3	27,412	17,870,772	17 00	101	3.8	3.7	32,500	322 00	1 18	10.3	0.18
Holyoke,	16.8	35,637	22,073,825	16 00	80	4.8	2.2	18,000	225 00	0 50	4.8	0.08
Lawrence,	7.2	44,654	30,476,223	14 80	66	9.2	1.5	32,117	486 00	0 72	6.7	0.11
Lowell,	12.3	77,696	62,046,799	17 00	109	8.9	1.4	71,667	657 00	0 92	6.9	0.12
Lynn,	11.4	55,727	40,721,028	15 00	125	11.0	2.2	37,667	302 00	0 68	5.8	0.09
Malden,	4.9	23,031	17,257,475	15 10	70	14.3	3.0	20,000	286 00	0 87	7.2	0.12
Marlborough,	21.6	13,805	6,284,638	16 20	81	3.7	5.9	15,300	189 00	1 11	12.8	0.24
Medford,	7.1	11,079	9,932,225	17 60	70	9.9	6.3	30,000	429 00	2 71	18.2	0.30
New Bedford,	20.1	40,733	36,869,754	16 30	113	5.6	2.8	110,400	978 00	2 71	18.0	0.30
Newburyport,	8.5	13,947	9,646,770	14 80	68	8.0	4.9	11,833	174 00	0 85	8.0	0.12
Newton,	27.5	24,379	36,159,025	14 60	169	6.1	6.9	67,500	399 00	2 77	12.3	0.19

TABLE M. — Concluded.

CITIES.	Area, Square Miles.	Population, United States Census, 1890.	Total Valuation, 1890.	Tax Rate per $1,000, 1890.	Miles Roads.	Miles Roads per Square Mile.	Miles Roads per 1,000 Population.	Highway Appropriations, exclusive of Bridges.				
								Average Amount, '89, '91.	Amount per Mile of Road.	Amount per Capita.	Per Cent. of Total Tax.	Per Cent. of Total Valuation.
Northampton,	40.5	14,990	$9,194,091	$15 50	108	2.7	7.2	$17,667	$163 50	$1 18	11.2	0.19
Pittsfield,	42.1	17,281	10,292,696	14 60	135	3.2	7.8	16,100	119 00	0 93	10.1	0.16
Quincy,	16.5	16,723	13,677,410	13 60	78	4.7	4.7	50,400	646 00	3 01	27.9	0.37
Salem,	8.2	30,801	26,178,190	17 00	70	8.5	2.3	50,800	726 00	1 65	10.7	0.19
Somerville,	5.5	40,152	32,557,500	14 00	80	14.5	2.0	43,500	544 00	1 08	9.0	0.13
Springfield,	32.2	44,179	44,493,633	12 40	125	3.9	2.8	91,000	727 00	2 06	15.4	0.20
Taunton,	46.4	25,448	17,823,032	17 60	160	3.4	6.3	36,667	229 00	1 44	11.5	0.21
Waltham,	14.0	18,707	15,210,714	14 00	85	6.1	4.5	25,167	296 00	1 34	11.2	0.17
Woburn,	12.6	13,499	8,918,306	16 50	67	5.3	5.0	15,051	225 00	1 11	9.8	0.17
Worcester,	39.0	84,655	73,417,460	15 60	225	5.8	2.7	151,900	675 00	1 79	12.9	0.21
North Adams, town of,	18.9	16,074	5,890,971	2,000	87	4.7	5.5	13,612	156 50	0 85	11.0	0.23
Total,	629.2	1,410,521	$1,571,945,271	$15 56	3,386	5.4	2.4	$2,596,948	$765 00	$1 84	11.2	0.17

TABLE N. — *Statistics of Area, Roads, Valuation, Appropriations and Population, with Certain Percentages, of State.*

STATE AND COUNTIES.	Area, Square Miles.	Population, 1890.	Total Valuation, 1890.	Tax Rate per 1,000.	Miles Roads.	Miles Roads per Square Mile.	Miles Roads per 1,000 Population.	HIGHWAY APPROPRIATIONS, EXCLUSIVE OF BRIDGES. Average Amount, '89, '90, '91.	Amount per Mile of Road.	Amount per Capita.	Per Cent. of Total Tax.	Per Cent. of Total Valuation.
Barnstable, ...	444	29,172	$19,119,734	$11 98	1,024	2.3	35.2	$37,205	$36 30	$1 28	16.4	0.19
Berkshire, ...	959	81,108	42,863,035	14 54	1,697	1.8	20.9	92,400	54 50	1 14	13.8	0.22
Bristol, ...	585	186,465	134,054,787	13 35	1,344	2.3	7.2	295,866	220 00	1 58	13.2	0.22
Dukes, ...	113	4,369	3,521,114	12 54	196	1.7	44.8	5,967	32 50	1 36	11.1	0.17
Essex, ...	518	299,995	219,502,533	13 53	1,611	3.2	5.4	315,938	196 00	1 05	9.2	0.14
Franklin, ...	691	38,610	20,021,645	15 37	1,459	2.1	37.8	48,740	33 40	1 26	15.8	0.24
Hampden, ...	629	135,713	95,128,777	14 79	1,429	2.3	10.5	154,836	108 00	1 14	11.0	0.16
Hampshire, ...	594	51,859	28,286,316	14 23	1,294	2.2	25.0	53,579	40 60	1 01	11.5	0.19
Middlesex, ...	852	431,167	361,959,890	13 11	2,941	3.5	6.8	626,534	213 00	1 45	11.1	0.17
Nantucket, ...	52	3,268	2,996,610	11 50	114	2.2	34.8	7,200	63 10	2 20	20.2	0.24
Norfolk, ...	413	118,950	135,206,582	13 70	1,231	3.0	10.4	243,167	198 00	2 04	14.5	0.18
Plymouth, ...	704	92,700	60,828,402	12 66	1,556	2.2	16.8	148,760	95 50	1 60	16.3	0.24
Suffolk, ...	48	484,780	851,330,335	13 83	533	10.9	1.1	1,344,619	2562 00	2 78	11.8	0.16
Worcester, ...	1,577	280,787	179,314,866	14 09	4,102	3.0	17.0	359,081	75 00	1 28	12.5	0.20
State, ...	8,179	2,238,943	$2,154,134,626	$13 52	20,531	2.5	9.2	$3,733,892	$182 00	$1 67	11.9	0.17

TABLE O. — *Statistics showing Expenditures on Highways, exclusive of Cities.*

STATE AND COUNTIES.	TOWNS EXPENDING — $1,000 or less.	Total.	$1,000 to $2,000.	Total.	$2,000 to $3,000.	Total.	$3,000 to $4,000.	Total.	$4,000 to $5,000.	Total.	$5,000 to $6,000.	Total.	$6,000 to $7,000	Total.
Barnstable,	4	$2,335	4	$5,944	4	$10,143	1	$3,082	–	–	–	–	–	–
Berkshire,	14	9,998	7	9,670	4	9,774	1	3,164	2	$8,863	–	–	1	$6,157
Bristol,	1	984	3	5,043	7	17,932	–	–	–	–	1	$5,073	2	12,413
Dukes,	4	763	1	1,966	–	–	1	3,238	–	–	–	–	–	–
Essex,	1	833	10	13,610	2	4,433	2	7,579	6	26,648	2	10,390	–	–
Franklin,	12	8,198	9	13,224	2	4,561	–	–	–	–	1	5,372	–	–
Hampden,	7	4,292	5	6,888	2	4,223	1	3,667	3	12,599	1	5,167	–	–
Hampshire,	11	8,497	6	7,209	1	2,229	2	6,810	1	4,667	–	–	1	6,500
Middlesex,	2	1,110	14	18,101	8	19,466	6	20,033	–	–	2	10,400	2	12,500
Norfolk,	–	–	6	8,200	3	6,767	3	9,833	4	18,067	–	–	1	6,800
Plymouth,	2	1,400	4	5,193	4	8,700	6	20,933	4	17,100	3	15,400	–	–
Suffolk,	–	–	–	–	–	–	1	3,333	–	–	1	5,667	–	–
Worcester,	5	3,083	16	23,700	19	44,799	4	13,166	2	8,400	4	20,500	1	6,333
State,	63	$41,493	85	$118,748	56	$133,027	28	$94,838	22	$96,344	15	$77,969	8	$50,703

TABLE O. — Concluded.

STATE AND COUNTIES.	Towns Expending — $7,000 to $8,000.	Total.	$8,000 to $9,000.	Total.	$9,000 to $10,000.	Total.	$10,000 to $15,000.	Total.	$15,000 to $20,000.	Total.	$25,000 to $30,000.	Total.	$30,000 and over.	Total.
Barnstable,	1	$7,076	1	$8,625	–	–	–	–	–	–	–	–	–	–
Berkshire,	–	–	–	–	–	–	–	–	1	$15,062	–	–	–	–
Bristol,	1	7,060	–	–	2	$18,935	–	–	–	–	–	–	–	–
Dukes,	–	–	–	–	–	–	–	–	–	–	–	–	–	–
Essex,	2	15,049	–	–	1	9,957	2	$23,575	–	–	1	$28,947	–	–
Franklin,	1	7,718	–	–	1	9,667	–	–	–	–	–	–	–	–
Hampden,	–	–	–	–	–	–	–	–	–	–	–	–	–	–
Hampshire,	–	–	–	–	–	–	–	–	–	–	–	–	–	–
Middlesex,	2	14,550	1	8,700	2	19,500	3	42,200	1	15,167	1	22,500	–	–
Nantucket,	1	7,200	–	–	–	–	–	–	–	–	–	–	–	–
Norfolk,	2	15,300	1	8,000	2	19,000	2	25,000	1	22,000	–	–	1	$53,800
Plymouth,	–	–	–	–	–	–	3	35,367	–	–	–	–	–	–
Suffolk,	–	–	–	–	–	–	–	–	–	–	–	–	–	–
Worcester,	–	–	2	16,900	–	–	4	46,967	–	–	–	–	–	–
State,	10	$73,953	5	$42,225	8	$77,059	14	$173,109	3	$52,229	2	$51,447	1	$53,800

TABLE P. — *Statistics of Towns, arranged by Counties, showing the Varying Amounts expended on their Highways, and the Percentage of the Number of Towns in the Different Groups to the Total Number of Towns in the State.*

STATE AND COUNTIES.	PERCENTAGE OF TOWNS SPENDING —													
	$1,000 or less.	$1,000 to $2,000.	$2,000 to $3,000.	$3,000 to $4,000	$4,000 to $5,000.	$5,000 to $6,000.	$6,000 to $7,000.	$7,000 to $8.000.	$8,000 to $9,000.	$9,000 to $10,000.	$10,000 to $15,000.	$15,000 to $20,000.	$20,000 to $30,000.	$30,000 or over.
Barnstable,	26.7	26.7	26.6	6.7	–	–	–	6.7	6.6	–	–	–	–	–
Berkshire,	46.7	23.3	13.4	3.3	6.7	–	3.3	–	–	–	–	3.3	–	–
Bristol,	5.9	17.6	41.1	–	–	5.9	11.8	5.9	–	11.8	–	–	–	–
Dukes,	66.7	16.7	–	16.6	–	–	–	–	–	–	–	–	–	–
Essex,	3.5	34.5	6.9	6.9	20.7	6.9	–	6.9	–	3.4	6.9	–	3.4	–
Franklin,	46.2	34.6	7.7	–	–	3.9	–	3.8	–	3.8	–	–	–	–
Hampden,	36.8	26.3	10.5	5.3	15.8	5.3	–	–	–	–	–	–	–	–
Hampshire,	50.0	27.3	4.6	9.1	4.5	–	4.5	–	–	–	–	–	–	–
Middlesex,	4.5	31.8	18.2	13.7	–	4.5	4.5	4.5	2.3	4.6	6.8	2.3	2.3	–
Nantucket,	–	–	–	–	–	–	–	100.0	–	–	–	–	–	–
Norfolk,	–	23.1	11.5	11.5	15.4	–	3.9	7.7	3.9	7.7	7.7	3.8	–	3.8
Plymouth,	7.7	15.4	15.4	23.1	15.4	11.5	–	–	–	–	11.5	–	–	–
Suffolk,	–	–	–	50.0	–	50.0	–	–	–	–	–	–	–	–
Worcester,	8.8	28.1	33.3	7.0	3.5	7.0	1.8	–	3.5	–	7.0	–	–	–
State,	19.7	26.6	17.5	8.7	6.9	4.7	2.5	3.1	1.6	2.5	4.4	0.9	0.6	0.3

www.ingramcontent.com/pod-product-compliance
Lightning Source LLC
Chambersburg PA
CBHW020806230426
43666CB00007B/882